REFLECTION-IN-MOTION

Reflection-in-Motion

Reimagining Reflection in the Writing Classroom

JACLYN FISCUS-CANNADAY

UTAH STATE UNIVERSITY PRESS
Logan

© 2025 by University Press of Colorado

Published by Utah State University Press
An imprint of University Press of Colorado
1580 North Logan Street, Suite 660
PMB 39883
Denver, Colorado 80203-1942

All rights reserved

 The University Press of Colorado is a proud member of Association of University Presses.

The University Press of Colorado is a cooperative publishing enterprise supported, in part, by Adams State University, Colorado School of Mines, Colorado State University, Fort Lewis College, Metropolitan State University of Denver, University of Alaska Fairbanks, University of Colorado, University of Denver, University of Northern Colorado, University of Wyoming, Utah State University, and Western Colorado University.

∞ This paper meets the requirements of the ANSI/NISO Z39.48-1992 (Permanence of Paper).

ISBN: 978-1-64642-692-8 (hardcover)
ISBN: 978-1-64642-693-5 (paperback)
ISBN: 978-1-64642-694-2 (ebook)
https://doi.org/10.7330/9781646426942

Library of Congress Cataloging-in-Publication Data

Names: Fiscus-Cannaday, Jaclyn, author.
Title: Reflection-in-motion : reimagining reflection in the writing classroom / Jaclyn Fiscus-Cannaday.
Description: Logan : Utah State University Press, [2024] | Includes bibliographical references and index.
Identifiers: LCCN 2024058228 (print) | LCCN 2024058229 (ebook) | ISBN 9781646426928 (hardcover) | ISBN 9781646426935 (paperback) | ISBN 9781646426942 (ebook)
Subjects: LCSH: English language—Rhetoric—Study and teaching (Higher) | Reflective learning. | Critical thinking. | Self-knowledge, Theory of. | College students' writings. | Feminism and rhetoric.
Classification: LCC PE1404 .F56 2024 (print) | LCC PE1404 (ebook) | DDC 808.0420711—dc23/eng/20250113
LC record available at https://lccn.loc.gov/2024058228
LC ebook record available at https://lccn.loc.gov/2024058229

Cover photograph by Jacky Pun / Unsplash.

For Parker and Quinn. I love you more than you could ever imagine—and even more than that. There's nothing you could ever do that would change my love for you. I love you forever and always. You're always enough.

Contents

List of Tables ix

Prologue xi

1. Reflecting Back to Move Reflection Forward 3

2. Feminist Methodologies for Researching Reflection-in-Motion in Writing Classrooms 28

3. Reflection-in-Motion—Emerging Rhetorics of Reflection Within the Writing Classroom 69

4. Practicing Reflection in the Everyday Moments of the Composition Classroom 122

5. Reflection Research, Reflective Pedagogy—Where Do We Go from Here? 167

Epilogue 204

Acknowledgments 209

Works Cited 213

Index 223

About the Author 235

Tables

1.1. Data collection overview   23
2.1. Focal participant overview   52
3.1. Teacher definitions of reflection   79
4.1. Definitions, foundational experiences, and exemplary moments for reflection   140
4.2. Patterns of potential reflective activity   155
4.3. Identified moments of potential reflective activity   162

Prologue

November 2020—Tallahassee, FL

Flour, butter, ice water. My hands move methodically—scooping, measuring, and dumping into bowls. Scanning Grandma's handwritten recipes quickly to confirm what my body already knows, using the embodied memories of baking pies for the last 30 years as my guide. Cutting together flour and butter first to make a crumbly mixture, I relax into the familiar rhythm of the pastry cutter. Push, twist, rock. Push, twist, rock. Running my hands through and satisfied with the texture, I start to add small splashes of water. "We can always add water, but we can't take water out," my grandmother's voice says soothingly in my memories. Push, twist, rock. Push, twist, rock. I allow the repetitiveness of the movement to calm me, to quiet my busy brain. I run my thumb over the unevenness of the pasty cutter's chipped wooden handle; my mind wanders, entering a reflective state—projecting forward. I subconsciously add a splash more water, and then go back to my rhythm. Push, twist, rock. Push, twist, rock. My mind is remembering baking with Grandma for my parents' all-are-invited Thanksgiving dinners. Grandma always flew in to help in the kitchen, being sous chef for my mom. For the desserts, though, Grandma took the lead, taking me under her wing as a baker-in-training. My mom stepping in to help too, if we had gotten all the other prep done. Three generations of love in the kitchen.

I consider whether my 6-month-old daughter, Parker (who is asleep in her carrier strapped to my chest), will enjoy helping bake as much as I enjoyed helping Mom and Grandma. Push, twist—pause. I smile with my eyes as I imagine a future, toddler version of Parker clumsily pouring ingredients into bowls next year, wondering if she will hate the feeling of flour on her hands

https://doi.org/10.7330/9781646426942.c000

like I do. On autopilot, I check the dough and decide it's ready to form into a ball and roll out. As I sprinkle water on the counter, I let out a stifled laugh (remembering last minute to hold in the big belly laugh that was about to emerge so I don't wake Parker). I can imagine my mom laughing loudly along with me, as I reflect upon the first time we tried my great aunt's "plastic wrap method" for rolling the dough—a method Grandma suggested we try so I didn't have to flour the counter and thus my hands (a method I now use by sprinkling a touch of water on my countertop, laying plastic wrap on the barely glistening countertop, setting my round ball of dough down atop the plastic wrap, layering another piece of plastic wrap on top of the dough, and then rolling the dough out while it's sandwiched between the two layers.) We put so much water on the countertop that first time that the pie crust went flying off the counter and landed on the floor with a splat—only to be met with our laughter and Grandma's lighthearted suggestion to "try again." We did not get it right the second or the third time, but after years of "trying again," I move through the steps without a conscious thought: just enough wrap for the plastic to cover the rolled-out dough, just enough water for the wrap to stick to the counter, just enough pressure and patience for the wrap to stay as the top layer while I roll.

The peacefulness of this moment contrasts with my overall affect. It's November 2020, and we're in the first 6 months of the Covid-19 pandemic (a timing that I'm constantly reminded of, as I celebrate each milestone of my daughter, Parker, who was born 2 weeks after the World Health Organization named Covid-19 a global pandemic). I have gotten through quarantine with more joy than most because of Parker's birth and my consequent parental leave. However, tomorrow is Thanksgiving, and while our family knew we would feel some lingering loneliness as we remained separated for the holiday (the whole country was still waiting for vaccines, so we weren't alone in that), our family did not know that we would be consumed with grief.

Grandma—though as careful as she could be, only leaving her house masked to get groceries—was diagnosed with Covid-19. She was in the hospital. And we were terrified. It was so hard to move through the fear on the day we should have been welcoming Parker to our family tradition—four generations of love should have been laughing in my kitchen. Doing the tradition anyway, though, without Grandma or my mom's physical presence but with the warmth of Parker on my chest, inspires a glimmer of reflective activity that gives me brief respite from my grief.

    As I bake, using Grandma's recipes, imagining Grandma's voice and Mom's laugh, feeling the rhythm of the pastry cutter, combining ingredients, rolling the dough, reliving memories, feeling Parker's body against mine as she rests in her carrier—all of it works to make me reflectively project forward, think back, gain perspective, and then project forward once more. My reflection makes me realize that no matter what happens with Grandma's health, her love will live on through this tradition. I can share this tradition of baking with my daughter and have her too experience a bit of Grandma's kind of love, the kind of love that is pure and joyful, full of unabashed forgiveness and unrelenting gratitude. Regardless of what happens next, my mom, Parker, and I will carry this tradition on together. Parker will feel Grandma's love no matter what.

*****

This book shares stories about reflection, and I want to begin by acknowledging that sharing of these stories is intimate, raw. Reflection is deeply personal; it emerges from the sedimented rhetorical hauntings of our pasts. I hope that in starting this book with sharing my own experiences of reflection, I honor the risk that it has been for my participants to teach me so much about reflection. In the opening example above, I share a story about a time that I reflected during my data-collection period for this book. The materiality, affect, and embodiment within this moment worked together to produce something I defined, identified, and practiced as reflection; I found reflection in the weight of my daughter on my chest, the rhythmic cutting in of water to my butter/flour mixture, and the melancholy of the moment. Reflection meant a sort of deep introspection, a self-excavation that resulted in some sort of realization. In this case, reflection brought me comfort, but it certainly was not something I saw as necessary for reflection to take place.

My ideas about reflection were shaped, largely, by my past as an athlete. As a child and young adult, I spent upward of 20 hours a week figure skating. I often found reflection in the monotony of doing a figure skating routine over and over. Even now when I no longer skate, if I can get into a mindless rhythm of movement (e.g., walking, folding laundry, rowing, baking, etc.), I am more likely to have rhetorical factors work in synergy to make room for reflective thought. Based on my past experiences of reflection, I often find reflection as introspective. I was a synchronized figure skater, which involves 16–20 people working in coordinated movement choreographed to music, and my reflective practice in that athletic environment shaped my reflective activity inside the ice-skating arena. Together as a team, we often practiced what I came to identify as "reflection" by watching tapes of our practices and competitions to critically analyze and project what we would do differently the next time. To me, then, reflection could be a kind of deep consideration about the way I viewed the world—or it could be a way of learning from the past to improve the future. My version of reflection was perhaps something closer to what researchers specify as "reflexivity" at times but closer to "metacognition" or "transfer" at others. I locate reflection and name it as such in the above example, then, because it made me rethink a familial tradition, which in turn inspired me to reconsider how I would be passing that tradition down.

That rhetorical action of reflection, the agency of my baking-turned-reflection, was distributed across many factors—the time, the current events, the place, the embodied sensations, the materials, the emotions, the relationships, the memories, the people, and so on. For my reflection to work, they all had to be there, working together in concert to lay the conditions necessary for that reflective activity to emerge. Though my reflection was done in seeming isolation because I did not have to communicate it to another person for the reflection to happen, my reflection was interactive all the same, entangled with the contextual factors within my rhetorical situation. The reflection had rhetorical effect—I made pies—but it also brought self-actualization and spiritual growth. I found solace in realizing that my daughter would get to know Grandma and how she showed love through baking with me in the kitchen. But, even now writing this book about reflection, I wonder, would another reflection researcher in writing studies consider this moment to be reflection?

I started researching reflection because my own definition of it did not map onto rhetoric and composition's traditional notions of reflection. When I was a 1st-year MA student 10 years ago, sitting in the second row of my TA orientation, I avidly took notes, hoping to commit each word of our writing program administrator (WPA) to memory. This was in part because of the kind of student I was—an overeager 20-something who brought my own lunch to eat in our orientation classroom during the hour break—but it was also because I had never taken a composition theory course. My student aptitude combined with my inexperience left me consumed with anxiety, not knowing how I could possibly be prepared to teach first-year writing (FYW) the next week. (It probably did not help that I was neurodivergent but did not know it yet; it took years of wondering why my brain worked differently in graduate school before I finally sought help and learned I had clinical depression, anxiety, and ADHD.)

All I remembered about my own FYW course was that my teacher complimented my evidence incorporation and analysis—but (as reviewers like to remind me even now) I should be more careful about my grammar. (Thank goodness for my copy editors, or you, my reader, might notice my inability to remember and execute prescriptive grammar rules. ADHD is not a friend to details, in my case.) Perhaps my FYW teacher did not feel like she needed to give me much instruction on her expectations of "good writing" because I grew up with privilege; I was upper-class, white, and steeped in the discourse conventions of academic writing in my home and schools.

According to my WPA (Anis Bawarshi), who began our orientation with a lecture situating our FYW program in the larger context of composition history, part of my job as a FYW instructor was to disambiguate the academic discourse conventions that had come so naturally to me, that seemed to be part of my bones. Throughout the lecture, I realized that much of what we were teaching—genre awareness, rhetorical awareness, argument, revision—all seemed to map onto my ways of knowing and doing writing. As a feminist and antiracist pedagogue who hoped to welcome students' literacies and honor the goals they had for this class, I was happy to learn that our WPA encouraged an inclusive pedagogy: to teach genre awareness but also encourage students to break conventions for rhetorical purpose, to teach academic argumentation style but also encourage communication as a form of rhetorical listening, and to acknowledge the word count requirements dictated by the university, but also to encourage all modes of communication in our pedagogy. I am grateful that my first introduction to the field was a relatively progressive view of what FYW pedagogy can be.

Yet, as I went through orientation and reviewed the sample course materials to get ideas for developing my own, something seemed odd to me: All the samples of prompting for reflection that we reviewed happened through writing. There were sample prompts for reflection that included written free-writes to brainstorm for projects, written explanations of multimodal assignments, written letters that documented learning throughout the course, and so on. Though I agreed that reflection was important to the writing process, and these writing activities could be useful catalysts for reflection for some students, I struggled with the idea of only incorporating formalized written reflection in my course—and only reflection about writing itself—because I knew that it was not all-encompassing of what students named, identified, and practiced as reflection. Even me, a white woman steeped in privilege, could not consistently practice reflection in these genres; they often felt flat and performative to me in my undergraduate experience.

The exception to that overwhelming distrust of "reflective" assignments happened in my third year as an undergraduate student at the University of Michigan. Professor Anne Curzan used reflection to powerfully reshape my view of language in her course Introduction to the English Language—an innocuous title for a course that shaped my worldview and the trajectory of my future. Curzan's course served as a requirement for secondary education teachers, providing foundational linguistic knowledge so students understood language variation, acquisition, and change. I started the course as a dual English and history major, while getting a certificate in secondary education. I started the course with a worldview that I was an eloquent academic writer and speaker because I was an avid reader; I thought that was why academic communication came naturally to me. Finally, I started the course believing that it was up to the writer or speaker to accommodate to the listener or reader. I left the course as an English and linguistics major who wanted to pursue an honors thesis and attend graduate school to learn more about linguistic variation and antiracist writing pedagogy. I left the course with a reality check that the language that I used was Standard American English (or what April Baker-Bell recently coined "White Mainstream English," to showcase standard language's relationship to systemic racism—a term I will adopt throughout the remainder of this book). I had access to White Mainstream English because of my privilege: the languages that my parents spoke and their parents spoke, the languages in the books that I read, and the languages that most closely resembled my home languages. I left the course realizing that communication is a relationship between interlocutors—and that breaking with genre and audience expectations can and should be done for rhetorical effect.

My core ideologies about language and how it worked were transformed. Sure, that was because of an exposure to the course content that opened my eyes to both linguistic diversity and linguistic discrimination—we engaged with smart and important work from scholars like Rusty Barrett, Deborah Cameron, Penelope Eckert, Kira Hall, Don Kulick, William Labov, Robin Lakoff, Rosina Lippi-Green, Sally McConnel-Ginet, John Rickford, Geneva Smitherman, Deborah Tannen, Peter Trudgill, and so many more[1]—but it was

---

1. Note that this course took place in 2010, so contemporary work from scholars like Jamila Lysicott, April Baker-Bell, Carmen Kynard, H. Samy Alim, Adrienne Lo, Angela Reyes, and others were not as popularized at the time. I am truly indebted to their scholarship about antiracist pedagogy and raciolinguistics in my current understandings of race and language, and I will be using contemporary work throughout this book as well.

also because of the reflective nature of the pedagogy. We started each day with teaching Curzan one new slang word, we wrote personal narratives about our language ideologies, created hypothetical letters to the editor about current events related to sociolinguistic topics of our course, imagined how we would interact with school administrators' language policies, and so on. We were tasked to think deeply about how we used language, reflect upon our deep-rooted ideologies about language correctness, reflect on how what we "knew" about language might be more complicated than we originally thought, reflect on how what we were learning was related to current events, and hypothesize how we might apply what we were learning to our future careers.

As I recount this foundational experience about my understanding of reflection, it may seem like the static, written assignments that I was describing as the samples that I saw in my FYW orientation. However, for me at least, the reflection I did in that course was so much more robust than the isolated reflective writing assignments: Reflection was integrated into our everyday movements, the daily fabric of the course. They mapped onto my experiences of reflection; I was a synchronized figure skater who viewed reflection as a way to both learn from mistakes and capitalize on strengths by creating a mindful awareness of embodied actions. For me, reflection was something that happened continuously, a series of small moments linking together to help achieve a larger goal. We used reflection constantly at practice, dissecting our movements after program run-throughs before doing another—and then using mindfulness to help perform the desired changes. This practice was interactive and dynamic, a verbal communication with the team and the coach—while also being internal in that we each had to use our reflection to share with the group our perspectives, try to apply what we learned in the next practiced program, and report back what worked in our body and what didn't.

I was able to map that definition of reflection onto my experience in Curzan's course. In her lectures, Curzan always engaged us with interactive moments where we paused to consider questions she posed, talked with those around us about our ideas, and then offered her our own perspectives on class topics. I reflected within our "discussion" sections; our graduate student instructors (GSIs) facilitated engagement with our peers in small-group activities where we imagined applications of our learning, peer-reviewed each other's assignments during class workshops, and considered opposing viewpoints within class debates. I reflected in the collaborative conversations in office hours; Curzan's thoughtful questions and suggestions for outside reading always left me buzzing with excitement. I reflected on my own; I mentally outlined our papers on walks to class, chatted with loved ones about our latest lecture, reconsidered my ideologies about language during any of our monotonous drills during a skating practice, and so on. In other words, the course material, the assignments, and just the overall pedagogy of the course did certainly set me up for reflective thinking—but it was also the synergy of those factors with Curzan's teaching persona, my burgeoning friendships with students in the class, the inclusive and accessible class dynamic of feeling like my thoughts were welcomed and valued, the technologies working with my learning preferences, the past experiences I had with reflection, and the fact that my most pressing physical needs were met, so I had time and energy to do reflective work.

My lived experiences taught me that reflection was integrated in my own daily practice, as well as the course design. My inspiration for teaching, bell hooks, wrote, "Critical reflection on my experience as a student in unexciting classrooms enabled me not only to imagine how the classroom could be exciting but that this excitement could co-exist with and even stimulate serious intellectual and/or academic engagement" (hooks, 2009, p. 150). I knew that I was a white woman walking through the academy with an immense amount of privilege, and I thought that I could and should think back to what worked (and what did not work) for me as a student, so I could try to make my pedagogy capacious and welcoming to the variety of students that I would serve. My hope was to make my classroom an "exciting place, never boring" (hooks, 1994, p. 7), and I knew that I could start with what I knew to be true about reflection, and then learn from my students how to adjust my pedagogy to better include what they knew about reflection.

As I sat in my FYW GSI orientation nearly 5 years later, overwhelmed and anxious about designing my own FYW course, I decided that I wanted to design pedagogy that honored reflective activities students already did throughout their writing process. Maybe my pedagogy could make space for students who tend to reflect while moving (like I did at skating practice) by accounting for that labor in a low-stakes comic. Maybe my pedagogy could make space for students who tend to reflect through interaction (like I did in class discussions) by requiring students to submit recordings of student-peer brainstorming meetings. Maybe my pedagogy could make space for the students who reflected through self-prompted reflection (like I did with attending office hours) by asking them to turn in the drafting materials they generated to prepare for the time we spent together or because of our time together.

My burgeoning ideas about reflection, built from my embodied knowledge of how reflection worked in my own life—about how reflection could take different mediums, could integrate different modalities, could take place throughout the writing process, or could emerge from different rhetorical contexts for varying rhetorical effect—were not revolutionary. As I would come to learn in the coming years through my research about reflection, reflection has the potential to facilitate learning; it has the potential to create new knowledge. However, I am careful here to hedge—to repeat *it has the potential to*—because I think it is imperative that we recognize that reflection does not always have to result in learning in the Western, mainstream sense of mastery or growth (Li, 2012). As my research participants have taught me, reflection can, and often does, just involve *sitting with*—a time to be present, to notice, and to acknowledge. I can't wait to tell you all about it.

REFLECTION-IN-MOTION

1
Reflecting Back to Move Reflection Forward

Autumn, a first year-student at an Asian American, Native American, Pacific Islander–serving institution in the Pacific Northwest, sits across from me in my office. Our rapport is familiar now. It's our second interview together, but I also see her daily in her first-year-writing class with Grace, a PhD student who is the graduate student instructor (GSI) of Autumn's first-year writing (FYW) course. Autumn is sharing self-prompted reflective contexts that she used to do reflection outside of class. Autumn talks quickly, smiling.

"Each week," Autumn says, "I meet up with my 'big,' Gray." I nod, she mentioned Gray in our first interview. "Big" refers to the mentor in her coed band fraternity. The two got to know each other earlier in the year, and by the end of the spring quarter, Autumn saw Gray as one of her closest confidants and mentors. As she explained, Gray is "that one person to go to and talk to and think okay am I overthinking this or not" whenever she is "unsure" about anything.

Autumn continues, eyes on me and noting my nod as a sign to continue onward: "We always meet up at the [union] after our physics class—the class we share. It's always quiet there because it's right before the food court closes. Sometimes cleaners are even working. I really like this time. Not many people are around, but if they are, most people are chilling with headphones and working. Or maybe eating and gossiping, talking about everything from relationships to weekend plans. For us, it's more than that. It's really important. It's where we had our first heavy talk."

I nod, asking, "What do you mean by heavy?" I encourage her to continue as I busily take notes.

"Time, place, history?!" I write. It seems like these are all important parts to the story.

"Heavy like deeply personal. We really got into it."

"Gotcha," I say with a nod.

She continues, "We kind of have a booth there. We almost always chose seats just over by the trash can. It's quieter there—I guess people don't like being by the trash. But it works for us. It gives us a bit more privacy. When we go there, it's not like the whole thing is one big reflection. We use the space to vent about everything going on. But I find that I do some reflecting too. It's like the memories [that the space held] is more important than the space itself."

"I hear that," I say.

Autumn had told me in the first interview that reflection is "taking the time to be honest with yourself." As she explained, "a lot of the times you get caught up in whatever you're doing . . . you don't take the time to sit back and say, 'Wait why am I doing this?'" Her definition of reflection was shaped by Autumn's past experiences of journaling, which she habitually engaged in during high school to put things in perspective and still writes in now, although biweekly instead of daily. Though I know her definition of reflection, Autumn's discussion of this particular example has not given me enough to understand how and why she connects conversations with Gray at the union to her practice of reflection.

"Tell me more about the space and why reflection works in it," I encouraged.

"So, here's the thing. I really need trust for reflection to happen, regardless of the space. We have that. But the space does help. It's like a neutral ground for reflection. It's no one's space. It doesn't belong to either of us. Our booth gives us just enough privacy for me to feel like I'm not talking with an audience. There are other places we hang that might have these same qualities—my dorm room, the bus, Gray's house—but it just wouldn't feel right. We don't talk like that in those places. This is where we go to talk like this."

"Thank you for trusting me to know about your spot," I say, meaning it. I know that the kinds of reflection that Autumn does with Gray are deeply personal. They're sometimes about her upcoming writing assignments, which falls under the purview of my research project, but more often than not, it's more about her life trajectory: Autumn is no longer sure about her intended major, and she's struggling with finding her footing at such a large school. A lot of her reflection with Gray helps her work through that.

"Alright, I think that's it for today," I say. "Want to set up some time for us to do some writing tutoring work? It's the least I can do for all the time you spent with me today."

"Nah," she says. "I'm feeling good about the next assignment, but thanks. I might hit you up when I'm working on the portfolio."

"Please do!" I say with enthusiasm. "See you next time!"

After we meet, I head to the bus, and once there, I get out my ethnographic notebook to add a summarizing note about today's interview. In it, I make connections: Autumn told me in her first interview that the transition to college life had been challenging for her. Her nearly constant state of uncertainty seems to be a catalyst for Autumn's reflection—and so does this relationship with Gray and their special place. It seems like her positionality, combined with Gray's role as Autumn's mentor, Gray's upper-level-student status, the trust that Autumn has in Gray, and the memories within the space, made Autumn prone to what she identifies as reflective activity.

*****

The story I share above comes from a research project investigating reflection-in-motion—or reflection as it is identified, defined, and practiced in everyday moments—at three Minority Serving Institutions (MSIs) in the United States. MSIs, or "institutions of higher learning that serve minority populations" (U.S. Department of Education, n.d.), are an important site of inquiry because they are built with the intent of explicitly designing their education practices for students of the global majority. MSIs are an incredibly important support system for minoritized students because they "operate as explicitly race-conscious (as well as class-conscious) higher education spaces that are managing to thrive, despite the many pressures they face within our contemporary higher education culture" (Lamos, 2012, p. 6). As of this writing, MSIs include Asian American and Native American Pacific Islander Serving Institutions (AANAPISIs), or schools with at least 10% of enrolled students being Asian American and Native American Pacific Islander; Historically Black Colleges and Universities (HBCUs), or schools formed before 1964 for the purpose of schooling Black Americans; Hispanic Serving Institutions (HSIs), or postsecondary institutions that have 25% or more of enrolled full-time students being Hispanic; and Tribal Colleges and Universities (TCUs), or schools in Native areas that exist to support Native students in areas otherwise geographically isolated from postsecondary institutions. I had the privilege of working with three MSIs during the research project I report on in this book: a large, urban AANAPISI in the American Pacific Northwest (henceforth referred to as "Urban State U"); a rural community college and HSI in a rural location in the Western United States (henceforth called "Rural CC"); and a mid-size HBCU in the American South (henceforth called "Southern HBCU").

In this book, I explore how students and teachers at these three MSIs define, identify, and practice as "reflection" in their writing classroom. By centering teachers' and students' explanations of reflection and self-reported instances of reflection at three MSIs, I present alternative viewpoints to what reflection is and how it is practiced, according to those who teach and attend "institutions of higher learning that serve minority populations" (U.S. Department of Education, n.d.).

All too often, we have taken white, Western theories of reflection to preselect what reflection means to our students. And yet, as we know, our students have a much broader range of lived experiences, identities, and epistemologies. To provide the field with a more capacious understanding of reflection, I hope to lean in and listen with "feminist ears" (Ahmed, 2021) to the students and teachers at these three MSIs. To do that work, I adopted what Venus Evans-Winters calls a "mosaic," a Black feminist mixed-method approach of collecting both traditional and nontraditional data to create a full view of a complex research problem (2019, p. 24). In my case, my mosaic is made up of focal student and teacher interviews, daily observations of courses, and whole-class surveys from six classes at three different MSIs. Privileging MSIs as the sites of reflection research, while also adopting feminist methods that privileged participant experience, allowed me to reimagine what reflection could be, according to underrepresented voices in our field.

Upon gathering my data, I then interpreted it using a feminist storytelling methodology.

Feminist storytelling is an established feminist research methodology in rhetoric and composition in which researchers use narratives to illuminate alternative perspectives (Royster and Kirsch, 2012, p. 50). In their discussion of this research methodology, they cite Carmen Kynard and Robert Eddy's work, which incorporates storytelling as a way of providing an intersectional theoretical lens for their research project located at two HBCUs (2009, pp. 30–32). Feminist researchers who engage in storytelling as methodology often take up an intersectional theoretical lens so that they can see unconscious bias or weaknesses and connect the story to overarching, institutional patterns (Ilmonen, 2020, p. 349). As such, I see storytelling as a methodology particularly well-suited for research done at MSIs, particularly when the researcher is white and walks through the world with so much privilege that their standpoint can be clouded to misrepresent the stories of their research participants—as is the case with me.

I am a white woman that is overwhelmingly privileged. I am a straight-passing, upper-class, able-bodied American. I have access to White Mainstream English. My body moves through white spaces unmarked, but that doesn't mean it is unmarked; it is marked so thoroughly with privilege. In the *Introduction to Intersectional Qualitative Research* (2022), Jennifer Esposito and Venus E. Evans-Winters address this ethical conundrum for researchers hoping to take up intersectional feminist approaches (like I do in this project). They explained that a feminist perspective requires "a conscientious effort on the part of the researcher to examine their personal biases, motives, beliefs, and thought processes in relationship to the research study" (2022, p. 17). As a feminist researcher, who tries to adopt a self-reflexive approach about my identity as a white woman of privilege, I purposefully resisted being a white researcher talking to predominantly white students about their experiences. Selecting sites with no thought about the racial diversity of the campuses would inevitably produce research and pedagogical implications that serve an imagined white, upper-class, and monolingual student familiar with college norms, which is of course not representative of all college students. All too often, research is done by white researchers at PWIs with no attention to the ways intersectional identities may play a role in research findings. Of the 1,500,000 faculty at postsecondary institutions in 2020, about 75% of full-time professors are white (National Center for Education Statistics, n.d.). This is not a new problem. It is an old problem that is getting worse: "It appears that in the last twenty years rhetoric and composition has become less—not more—diverse" (Ribero and Arellano, 2022). To solve this problem, we of course need to hire and retain graduate students and faculty of color (something that I feel strongly about and work toward at my institution), but we also need to celebrate the amazing work being done at MSIs and learn about how to best serve students of color too. Therefore, I chose to design a research project that prioritizes gaining perspectives from BIPOC students and teachers, as well as their white contemporaries teaching and learning in MSIs. In doing so, I hoped to reimagine what reflection might be, according to the research participants.

In the story that begins this chapter, for example, we can see how Autumn's definition of reflection was based upon past experiences. Autumn was one of the eight focal students that I had the privilege of interviewing at Urban State U. Her past experiences of journaling haunted perceptions of what reflection could entail for Autumn, along with where she practiced it. For reflection to move from identification to practice, the contextual factors had to work in harmony. In Autumn's case, her definition of reflection was built from her past journaling practice. She was then able to transfer this practice to a more interactive, conversational practice because she was in a constant state of uncertainty and had built trust with Gray to navigate these feelings. As Autumn explained in her first interview, her reflective practice is often dependent upon "trusting people with information or not trusting people with information." And, since the two have built trust with this weekly practice, Autumn could use this new modality to reflect via conversation—but only in this safe space with Gray on "neutral ground," like she discussed in the interview I account for above. It was not entirely surprising, then, that I learned in the third interview that Autumn's favorite activity for reflection in Grace's class was her student-teacher conferences with Grace.

Grace prioritized student-teacher conferences with her students so much that she offered weekly conferences with students in lieu of her fourth day of class. Students elected a time to meet with Grace in her solo office, about a 10-minute walk from their classroom, and Grace used the time in whatever ways that students preferred: brainstorming, reviewing works in progress, giving feedback on completed drafts, answering questions about class, and planning students' end-of-term writing portfolios. Autumn saw these conferences with Grace as times of intended reflection, but Autumn admitted that reflection was something that came once she had trust in Grace. Even then, reflection did not happen every time—and even when it did, the reflective activity emerged intermittently throughout their conversations. As Autumn explains, "It was more like later in the semester when Grace would have her door open, soft music playing, a bit more of a rapport between us and I was more planning the assignment, not getting any feedback that day. There were some moments where it all worked together to happen." At first, Autumn admitted to me that some of the conferences felt a bit performative because of the power relationships between her and Grace. Autumn was sensitive to relationship, timing, affect, materials, and space in her ability to practice reflection. She knew, cognitively, that these conference times "can be reflective." Yet, as she told me, "They're not always, though. It really just depends on how I'm feeling, what we're talking about." It seems to me that this is why reflection is rhetorical: It is embedded within specific contexts—and then subjected to the distributed agency amid all the contextual factors in the rhetorical situation.

Autumn drew me maps of her two places of habituated reflection throughout her FYW class: the booth she sat in to chat with Gray, as well as Grace's office. In her drawing of the booth, she located where she sat and where Gray sat. Likewise, she located where Grace sat and where she sat. Autumn's reflection was situated within contexts that have real and perceived boundaries. The patterns of embodiment were distinct enough for her to represent it in a still image; she never imagined that they'd switch sides or places. Despite the situation feeling more fixed to Autumn, the kinds of reflection she did in these spaces felt different. Autumn was insistent that reflective rhetorical activity can happen at various times in the writing process: before, during, or after an event and at various stages of writing—brainstorming, composing, revising, or somewhere in between those moments. The agency of her reflection was entangled within the dynamic configurations and interactions among various material, emotional, and human actants present within a space. For Autumn, main forces included the habitual nature of these meetings, the arrangement of the spaces themselves, the people and relationships within them, Autumn's experience with reflection and consequent definitions, her ongoing journaling as reflective practice, and her comfort in the settings. The agency of how her reflection occurred was distributed among both the human and nonhuman agents to produce reflective activity. I hope, in sharing the opening story, I have started to illuminate the robust and diverse ways that students and teachers in this study theorize and practice reflection. In the next section, then, I describe how reflection research has been done—and how this book offers new perspectives of what reflection means, according to these focal students and teachers—and thus offer a more capacious understanding of what reflection can be.

Reflection Research

In *A Rhetoric of Reflection* (2016), Yancey argues that there are three generations of reflection research: the first generation in the 1970s and 1980s, which "identif[ied] and describ[ed] internal cognitive processes assumed to be part of composing" (p. 9); the second generation in the 1980s and 1990s, which "developed mechanisms for externalizing reflection, making it visible and thus explicitly available to writers" (p. 9); and the third (ongoing) generation as revising the earlier generations' work by acknowledging reflection's rhetorical power beyond a means for assessment. Scholarship documenting and theorizing reflection began in earnest when cognitivist research scholars noticed reflection being part of the writing process (e.g., Flower & Hayes, 1981; Perl, 1980). Once researchers established how integral reflection was in the writing process, scholars then researched how a written articulation of reflection might give even more power to reflection as a pedagogical tool (e.g., Sommers, 1988) through documents like writer's memos or portfolio cover letters. In 1998, Kathleen Yancey offered the first book-length investigation of reflection with *Reflection in the Writing Classroom*, offering the finding that "reflection is rhetorical" (p. 12), which inspired the third wave of reflection scholarship.

Though there was limited scholarship about how to teach reflection in FYW, and even less data about best practices for teaching new teachers how to introduce reflection in their classrooms (Penrose, 2012), contemporary reflection has focused on best practices for incorporating reflective pedagogy: "Our collective scholarship about reflection tells us that reflective writing is a powerful tool for learning if it is done purposefully and reiteratively" (Jankens & Latawiec, 2021). Reflection scholars have prioritized investigating what kinds of rhetorical effects reflective activity can result in—especially when scaffolded to ensure alignment between the prompt and reflection's goal (Driscoll & Powell, 2016; Jankens & Lataweic, 2021). Reflection can be used to help students engage in purposeful question/answer dyads that lead to rhetorical genre awareness (Jankens, 2019) and more rhetorically aware revision (Lindenman et al., 2018); though, students can still produce reflective texts that detail much more rhetorically aware revisions than produced in the actual revised draft (Lindenman et al., 2018), the disconnect is often a result of the extreme stakes of the revised material. Students use the written reflective document outlining their revisions to "schmooze" (Yancey, 1996) rather than reflect authentically. Rhetorical reflection, when done in a safe space, is deeply connected with revision processes because reflection can help students articulate prior learning experience, moving from a description of what happened to an articulation of what they learned (Leaker & Ostman, 2010)—and all while attending to emotions that surface during the revision process (Ballenger & Meyers, 2019). Reflection is evenly distributed among rhetorical awareness of student writing, interpretation of feedback, their own writer identity, and emotions (Miller et al., 2023). It can also, especially when paired with personal writing, help students engage in alternative rhetorics (Hsu, 2018), even helping students investigate their own ideologies and perhaps reframe them (Flower, 2021).

In nearly every example of reflection research, researchers—when deciding what to gather as samples of reflective activity—often place bounds around what counts as reflection and limiting it to writing: selecting things like portfolio cover letters or writer memos as data to explore their research questions about reflections. Researchers decide what counts for reflective activity and then investigate it. As a result, researchers can inadvertently preordain reflection as rational, argumentative, and written work produced for another. A Western perspective of reflection is one way of doing reflective work; it employs a thought process where students "[stand] back from the situation in order to analyze it and [propose] solutions to be subsequently tested" (Raelin, 2001, p. 12). Yet, it certainly is not the only way that reflection is employed cross-culturally.

A few researchers have broken the trend—locating researching reflection in other genres. For example, Pamela Flash (2016) explored reflection in conversations within faculty meetings, and Kevin Roozen (2016) argued that the interviews with focal students are examples of reflective activity. Irvin spends the entirety of *Reflection Between the Drafts* (2020) to investigate moments of constructive reflection and reflection-in-action to better serve our students. Some scholars have incorporated an attention to the body, developing pedagogies that require students to take up a yoga or martial arts practice. For example, Barry Kroll (2008) wrote about his integration of aikido in his writing classes, showing how students' exposure to another way of engaging with an "opponent" can result in alternative perspectives on academic "argument." Likewise, Christy Wenger incorporated a case study of requiring class yoga in her FYW class to showcase how mindfulness is "best seen as a skill that can be developed with practice" (2015). In both examples, the scholars lean into Eastern traditions to help students re-see a Westernized approach to writing. As Becky Thompson so thoughtfully pointed out, "the increasing interest in contemplative practice—including mindfulness, meditation, and yoga—in the last twenty years reflects an awareness of the classroom as a living, breathing space" (2018, p. 7). In practicing embodied reflection, we can see how reflection can be used to develop habits of mind, invite an exploration of identities into the classroom, and work through complicated emotions about writing. Reflection has been used to model skills we find important for writers to practice, like mindfulness or open-mindedness (Jackson, 2020).

There is evidence that connects reflection's embodied traditions to anti-oppression pedagogical practices. We can see theoretical contributions taken up by feminist and antiracist composition pedagogues, who are influenced by Paulo Freire's and bell hooks's work, and consider how reflection can be used to unpack and destabilize deep-rooted ideologies and critically engage in difference. Teaching open-mindedness is an incredibly important mindset to develop as we work toward what Kathleen Yancey calls "the cause," or the way we teach students to "articulate ideas, speak to others, and create movements through composing" (Yancey, 2018, p. 163). This is especially true when teaching white students to acknowledge and understand the depths of their privilege and how some of their ideologies are imbued with white supremacist values (McIntyre, 2016).

Critical pedagogues use reflection often to get students to rethink ideologies and work across difference. Compositionists have discussed why developing open-mindedness is so important. It can be essential as we work toward Yancey's "cause" or the way we teach students to "articulate ideas, speak to others, and create movements through composing" (Yancey, 2018, p. 163). Educators have found that this is especially true when teaching white students to acknowledge and understand the depths of their privilege and how some of their ideologies are imbued with white supremacist values (McIntyre, 2016). Beth Berila, for example, posited in *Integrating Mindfulness Into Anti-Oppression Pedagogy* that social justice–oriented pedagogies are essential—and that critical reflection should be a key component of that pedagogy. Berila writes: "The stakes for learning how to navigate [social justice-]related conversations are high, because the students in our classrooms will be shaping our societies for years to come. If they do not learn the skills in our courses, I am not sure where they will learn them" (2015, p. 2).

Feminist pedagogues, in particular, take up reflection in their classrooms. In *Composing Feminism(s): How Feminists Have Shaped Composition Theories and Practices*, Kay Siebler insisted that feminist compositionists were largely inspired by feminist theories and thus could not be bound to a singular definition. Instead, she identified 16 themes that had emerged in publications about feminist composition theories—loosely organizing these themes into three categories: Themes of teacher critical reflection, goals for the classroom and classroom strategies, and student concerns and classroom strategies. Feminist compositionists were especially concerned with issues of advocating for teacher reflexivity, encouraging critical thinking, reshaping traditional power dynamics, attending to students' mental and physical needs with inclusive pedagogy, encouraging dissent and dissonance, welcoming personal experience in writing, inviting discussions about oppression into the classroom, incorporating active learning techniques, listening to students and encouraging input into classroom pedagogies, and facilitating a joy for learning. Some of these practices are common in the field writ large because "feminism is not a 'special' category in composition, but [it is] infused in mainstream composition theory and practice, although not recognized as such" (2008, p. 4). In their own overview of feminist pedagogies in the first and second editions of Gary Tate et al.'s *A Guide to Composition Pedagogies*, Susan Jarrat (2001) and Laura Micciche (2012) echo the foci that Siebler lists but emphasize that what distinguishes feminist pedagogues from mainstream compositionists who may adopt feminist practices (without attribution) is feminist pedagogues' "shared goal of actualizing social justice through teaching and learning methods" (Micciche, 2012, p. 128).

Outside of the classroom, reflection is essential for social justice aims, especially representation. Reflection can be practiced as a way of connecting the personal to the political, a key component of feminist theory (Nash, 2019). In fact, reflection was often practiced within the feminist movement itself through consciousness-raising groups, which were groups created for feminists to engage in cross-cultural communication and self-reflexivity (Randolph & Ross-Valliere, 1979). Academics often engage in narrative writing in their scholarship, a kind of public-facing reflection, to "create visibility for the underrepresented" (Nash & Viray, 2013, p. 35). Many compositionists practice "autoethnographic and memoiristic" (Brown, 2020, p. 608) reflective writing to cope with the field's overwhelming privileging of whiteness. We see this within work that Jacqueline Jones Royster called "reflective story-telling," Mary Louise Pratt (1991) called "testimonio," Victor Villanueva called "memoria," and Aja Martinez called "counterstory." These ways of doing reflective writing illuminate lived experiences in places where people of color are traditionally ignored or undervalued, like they have been in the academy. And yet, we so infrequently ask our students to engage in this kind of reflective work—or, at least, have yet to research reflection in which we locate this kind of reflection activity as emblematic of the reflection happening in our writing classrooms.

Instead, in nearly every example of reflection research, researchers—when deciding what to gather as samples of reflective activity—often place bounds around what counts as reflection and limiting it to writing: selecting things like portfolio cover letters or writer memos as data to explore their research questions about reflections. Researchers decide what counts for reflective activity and then investigate it. Kara Taczak and Liane Robertson (2017), for instance, investigated reflective practices of nine students, four in a literature-themed class and five in a teaching-for-transfer class, in which key words and theoretical concepts of transfer were introduced and multigenre writing and reflective practice were required. They qualitatively coded students' reflective essays, interviewed students and teachers about their essays, and conducted a survey about the students' experiences. Taczak and Robertson concluded that reflection was integral to transfer activity. Likewise, in *Writing Across Contexts* (2014), Kathleen Yancey et al. advocated for a "teaching for transfer" (TFT) curriculum that utilizes reflective writing to help students transfer knowledge across contexts. As a result, researchers can overemphasize reflection as rational, argumentative thought produced for another.

Jessica Thomsen discussed this phenomenon at length in her dissertation, "Alternative Cartographies: Reflection(s) for the Complexities of Writing and Sustainability" (2021). Thomsen posited that our field's overemphasis of rational reflection is a result of composition's reliance on rhetorical understandings from Aristotle, Plato, and Descartes, and consequent commitment to logic and argument in writing instruction. Given how much we rely on Toulmin's understanding of argument (Lunsford, 2002), Thomsen writes, it makes sense that we see expectations of argumentation style imbue reflection assignments (e.g., reflective assignments requiring students to use evidence from their writing and/or course experience to indicate that they have met the course outcomes), and consequently result in reflective writing becoming a narrative of success (Emmons, 2003). As Tony Scott warned us nearly two decades ago, "reflection *can be* a particularly invasive means of reinforcing institutional authority" (2005, p. 27, emphasis original).

Asao Inoue and Tyler Richmond (2016) illuminated the negative consequences of this clearly when researching Hmong students' reflective practices. Upon demonstrating how their Hmong student research participants internalize racist white discourse in their reflections, Inoue and Richmond concluded their research with this tough question: "When teachers consciously or unconsciously expect students to reproduce a dominant, white, middle-class set of dispositions in reflective texts . . . are they unknowingly creating hostile and unfair conditions for some students of color?" (p. 143). In the conclusion of *A Rhetoric of Reflection*, the edited collection in which their work appears, Kathleen Yancey (2016) claims, "The version [of reflection that] faculty know best is simply one construction, located in the values of the dominant culture" (p. 318). Reflection is not always about writing, even in the writing classroom. It is often a way of theorizing lived experiences, reimagining ideologies, and becoming more attuned and present.

One way that reflection upon experience occurs is through storytelling. Storytelling is central to all cultures, but its traditions take different genres and modalities (Bishop & Ostrom, 2003). Sometimes researchers take up these practices as methodologies for their own work. Storytelling is central to Black literacy practices (Smitherman, 2006). Black feminist theory (BFT), for example, adopts reflective storytelling to show how personal experience illuminates institutionalized, intersectional, and systemic oppression (Collins, 2000). It's an "urgent voicing of something to which one bears witness" (Reyes & Rodríguez, 2012, p. 525). This is certainly something we see historically (see, for example, canonical texts like *This Bridge Called My Back*, *But Some of Us Are Brave*, and *Words of Fire*) and continues today. Black feminists and *New York Times* best sellers like Brittany Cooper, Angela Davis, Roxane Gay, bell hooks, and Audre Lorde use their personal experience to theorize intersectional identities, pay witness to their systemic oppression, and inspire social change.

Likewise, "testimonio," or the Latinx practice of telling stories to "expose brutality, disrupt silencing, and build community" (Delgado et al., 2012, p. 363), is an important genre of reflection that contributes to theoretical understandings of Latinx feminism and does social activism work. Testimonio "has the unique characteristic of being a political and conscienticized reflection that is often spoken" (Reyes & Rodriguez, 2012, p. 524), with perhaps the most canonical example taken up by Gloria Anzaldúa, for instance. Again, scholars have taken up this storytelling practice as methodology; the edited collection *Latina Leadership: Language and Literacy Education across Communities (Writing, Culture, and Community Practices)* includes testimonios as interludes between its chapters.

Despite these rich histories of storytelling that our students come from—and the respect we hold of storytelling in rhetoric and composition research—reflection research has not broadened to include storytelling as a site for reflection research. Instead, contemporary reflection scholarship has been most preoccupied with how various written, academic genres help practice metacognition and thus can facilitate transfer of writing knowledge to other contexts (see, for example, Beaufort, 2007; Nowacek, 2011). Portfolios and accompanying cover letters have been used to gain insight into students' learning throughout writing courses (e.g., Anson, 1994), for example. Reflective writing shared with instructors has been used to understand students' rhetorical choices—especially as a tool for assessment for multimodal writing (e.g., Shipka, 2009)—or to document labor of drafting and/or revision (e.g., Sommers, 1988); and freewrites have been used to help students brainstorm (e.g., Elbow, 1993).

Inoue spent his 2019 chair address for Conference on College Composition and Communication offering a poignant critique of how *The Framework for Success in Postsecondary Writing: Scholarship and Applications* (Behm et al., 2017) hypervalues certain literacies—namely Westernized ways of knowing and being. Amid Inoue's critique, he asks the audience, rhetorically, "Is the Framework being used as method to get students to write White, but not used to attend to an ever-widening universe of reflective discourses?" (2019, p. 14). The ways of knowing and doing in our field are so steeped in Westernized views of success, meritocracy, and capitalism that how we have defined and asked students to practice reflection has narrowed to become nearly synonymous with metacognition. In doing so, we have flattened the multiplicity of what reflection can mean, where it can live, and what it can do. We've made reflection, quite simply, white. A way of defending our rhetorical choices—and perhaps explaining how what we have done might lead to future success.

Yancey (2016) theorized that what sets apart our current scholarship about reflection from earlier research is "our increasing appreciation of the epistemological value of reflection, of its ability to help us make new meanings, of its rhetorical power" (p. 10). To me, this is what makes reflection research so exciting: reflection does rhetorical work for students. That work might include a Westernized sense of learning, or mastery, but it could also involve a self-awareness and self-reflexivity that is valued in global traditions of reflection (Li, 2012). There are rich histories of embodied reflection—histories of mindfulness, yoga, martial arts, and meditation—that have influenced some of the thinking in composition theory about the role of reflection in the writing classroom. If we look a bit further than the more canonical storytelling of where reflection lives and how it is practiced, there is evidence that connects reflection's embodied traditions to anti-oppression practices. We can see theoretical contributions taken up by feminist and antiracist composition pedagogues, who are influenced by Paulo Freire's and bell hooks's work, and consider how reflection can be used to unpack and destabilize deep-rooted ideologies and critically engage in difference. The literature demonstrates that the way we define reflection, as a field, influences how practitioners have taken it up pedagogically—and these pedagogical choices have the potential to unintentionally encourage students to enact ideologies that are not representative of their cultural identities and ways of knowing. It is important, then, that we pause to define what I mean by "reflection" to better understand the subject of inquiry for this book.

Definitions of Reflection

Like many terms in writing studies, "reflection" is a word trying to capture an abstract process, a process that means different things to different people based on their lived experiences of what it might entail. As a field, we've tried to tackle what reflection means exactly. In their article, "Reflection as Relationality: Rhetorical Alliances and Teaching Alternative Rhetorics," V. Jo Hsu wrote, "As a discipline, we have struggled to reach any functional consensus about the definition of reflection—despite its pervasive usage" (2018, p. 149). After surveying the students in the story, Hsu noticed the same: "Students used the term reflection as an ambiguous catchall, which stood for a wide variety of specific rhetorical moves that connect individual stories with social exigencies" (p. 150). I found the same in my research, which I detail in the next section. Participants generally saw reflection as a way of doing awareness, introspection, perspective, learning, and mindfulness.

DEFINITIONS OF REFLECTION: ACCORDING TO REFLECTIVE PRACTITIONERS

There is not, according to my focal participants (five focal teachers and twenty focal students) and surveyed students (63 usable surveys), an agreed-upon definition of reflection. This is not necessarily surprising, as "reflection" is a word describing an abstract, cognitive process. Therefore, in each interview (an excerpt of which we saw in the opening of this chapter), I asked my focal participants what reflection meant to them. I hoped that these questions could help me understand the ways that my focal participants' understandings of reflection echoed, complicated, or disrupted the ways that the field has taken up theories of reflection. Upon completing the interviews, I turned to grounded theory, a coding system that identifies emergent patterns from data (Glaser & Strauss, 1967). I adopted this approach because it allowed me to do rhetorical listening of my participants' answers. Feminist researchers have used grounded theory since the 1990s because it centers research participants' knowledge as valuable data (Plummer & Young, 2010). Grounded theory prioritizes listening to research participants; qualitative researchers use it to find common themes in participants' qualitative responses so that they can offer general findings that emerge from participant experience/expertise (rather than from the scholarly literature).

Throughout my coding, I found that participants generally agreed that reflection was a cognitive process that could take place within a variety of modalities (e.g., conversations with others, internal processing, writing, drawing, meditating, etc.) and result in various rhetorical effects (e.g., mindfulness, introspection, learning, perspective, and awareness). Some folks, for example, saw reflection as a kind of awareness (similar to metacognition) that analyzed decisions or choices. They might mention doing that often through conversations with loved ones on a weekly basis. Others saw it as a kind of internal rumination, a form of introspection that tended to focus on feelings, emotions, identities, and personhood. They might mention doing that while baking. Some saw it as a practice that could alter perspective, perhaps of a deep-rooted ideology, a relationship, or life trajectory. They might mention doing that work in journal-writing. A few mandated that reflection needed to transfer knowledge across contexts and/or time. They might mention articulating that in assigned reflections for class. One even presented reflection as a practice of mindfulness. They mentioned doing that internally during a class.

I therefore identified the following potential rhetorical effects of reflection: reflection-for-awareness, reflection-for-introspection, reflection-for-learning, reflection-for-mindfulness, and reflection-for-perspective. Each of their definitions and consequent practices of reflection was deeply rooted in their lived experience and past experiences of reflection. Despite all the differences between participants, I found that they generally agreed on a few points: (a) Reflection results in rhetorical action (that does real work in the world), (b) reflection emerges from rhetorical contexts (that are haunted by past rhetorical contexts), and (c) reflection is subject to definitions of reflection (that are based on past experiences). My findings both productively build from and push against scholarly work on reflection, which I discuss in the next section.

DEFINITIONS OF REFLECTION ACCORDING TO REFLECTION RESEARCHERS

Perhaps the most canonical definitions of reflection were inspired by Kathleen Yancey's *Reflection in the Writing Classroom* (1998). Yancey offered three types of reflection: reflection-in-action, "means of *writing* with text-in process" (1998, p. 13, emphasis added); reflection-in-presentation, or "formal reflective text *written* for an 'other' often in a rhetorical situation invoking assessment" (1998, p. 13, emphasis added); and constructive reflection, or the "generalizing and identity-formation processes that accumulate over time, with specific reference to *writing* and learning" (1998, p. 13, emphasis added). As Lennie Irvin discusses in *Writing Across the Drafts*, the field has looked to these definitions as inspiration for where we look for reflection—but we most often focus on what Yancey called "reflection-in-presentation." Irvin, then, encourages the field to return to the capaciousness of Yancey's established definitions of reflection, paying special attention to how we might research constructive reflection and reflection-in-action to better serve our students.

Yancey's three theoretical understandings of reflection were groundbreaking for the field's understanding of reflection: Reflection was integral to the writing process and helpful in understanding the writing process. Reflection could be preemptive, ongoing, or retroactive. Reflection could be done with a variety of intentions: as a learning tool, as a way of moving through difficult emotion, as a way of explaining rhetorical choices, and so on. Yet, reflection had new parameters: It was about writing—and typically expressed through writing. Yancey's choice to limit reflection to and about writing are not entirely unsurprising. Compositionists are researchers of writing after all, so looking for reflection in writing and/or about writing makes sense. But it leaves us with questions: Can constructive reflection exist in a whole-class discussion about the challenges of transitioning to college? Might participating in student-teacher conferences function as a kind of reflection-in-action? Can moments like a verbal framing of a draft to a peer review be reflection in presentation?

Yancey's definitions of reflection relied mainly on Dewey's and Schön's theorizations of reflection. Dewey's and Schön's views were similar in that reflection is thought of as an important thought process involved with meta-awareness, learning, and growth that is practiced throughout the writing process. The four criteria central to Deweyan theories of reflection are: (a) reflection promotes knowledge transfer, (b) reflection is systematic thought, (c) reflection is interactive and communal, and (d) reflection can only happen when students have an attitude of growth (Rodgers, 2002). For example, Dewey (1933) defined reflection as "active, persistent, and careful consideration of any belief or supposed form of knowledge in light of the grounds that support it and the further conclusions to which it tends" (p. 9). Dewey's definition of reflection has influenced the field to make reflection goal-oriented: Reflection is a rational activity—a way of engaging in critical thinking about a situation or belief system that causes a shift in perspective.

Schön, likewise, considered reflection as rational: a cognitive process that emerged from a question/answer dynamic between teacher and student to promote critical thinking about a situation in progress. In his seminal text, *The Reflective Practitioner: How Professionals Think in Action*, Schön (1983) distinguishes "reflection-in-action" from "reflection-on-action." Reflection-in-action occurs when someone uses reflection within a moment to shape that same moment, while reflection-on-action happens when someone reflects retroactively so that they can improve a subsequent, similar event. This distinction of timeliness is particularly useful for considering reflection's rhetoricity: Chronos affects how we name, identify, and categorize different types of reflection. Schön's work pushes us to consider how students reflect within action to shape current action.

Though Yancey was inspired by Schön's theories and was clear in her definitional adaptations that reflection can occur throughout the writing process, Lennie Irvin was right to suggest in *Reflection Between the Drafts* (2020) that compositionists have neglected the importance of prompting reflection in the *during* of the writing process. Irvin wrote: "The kairotic moment after writing that occurs in the portfolio cover letter represents the paradigm for what reflection means in our field, shaping our more authentic evaluation of writing" (p. 59). Returning to Schön's reflection-in-action terminology, Irvin argued that we need to "allow a more considered acknowledgment and negotiation of all the forces of the writing situation while the situation is still in play in what Schön calls an 'action-present'" (p. 70).

Contemporary scholarship most often gravitates toward a Deweyan understanding of reflection—that of reflection upon past activity—using post-process interviews or portfolio critical reflections as emblematic of reflective rhetorical activity. In *Naming What We Know*, for example, Kara Taczak defined reflection as "a mode of inquiry: a deliberate way of systematically recalling writing experiences to reframe the current writing situation" (2016, p. 78). This description of reflection—a purposeful cognitive practice done to transfer writerly skills into a new context—is certainly one way we see reflection described in the field; reflection researchers have been excited about reflection's role in knowledge transfer (Yancey et al., 2014). Yet, as Tessa Brown so thoughtfully pointed out in her critique of the way that reflection is discussed in *Naming What We Know*, this kind of treatment of reflection can "[suggest] that writers' own theorizations of their writing practices are only personally valuable and can't contribute to broader understandings of writing and literacy" (2020, p. 608). I agree; seeing reflection as something that can teach a writer only about their own writing process is problematic. We know that there are rich histories of reflection that exist outside this narrow view—and these histories represent the kind of reflection often practiced by marginalized and underrepresented voices in the academy. I argue that it is important to recognize that reflection can—when practiced in the ways that scholars in rhetoric and composition often define, name, and practice it—help our students articulate their writing process and create pathways for transfer (Taczak & Robertson, 2017; Yancey et al., 2014), and yet it is just as important to acknowledge how reflection—at least on how we traditionally identify, name, and practice it—asks students to enact Westernized values and discourse. In the next section, then, I propose a new term for reflection teachers and researchers: reflection-in-motion.

A Proposed Definition of Reflection: Conceptualizing Reflection-in-Motion

When I use the word "reflection" in this book, I adopt a broad definition—a definition that I hope can encapsulate the robust ways that students and teachers are using reflection in the FYW classroom. Reflection is the intentional consideration (of activity, perspectives, or ideologies) that emerges from a rhetorical context and results in rhetorical action(s). As with past definitions of reflection offered from a variety of theorists, I am careful to emphasize that reflection emerges from a rhetorical situation, one with a multitude of factors that play into whether reflection results with rhetorical activity. When considering reflection, it is imperative we recognize reflection-in-motion. Reflection always involves the distributed agency of how the time, current events, materials, affects, emotions, dispositions, past experiences, interpersonal relationships, and so on play a role in shaping reflective activity. Though I do use the phrase "intentional consideration" to describe reflection, which could suggest that reflection is only possible when the rhetor is aware of the reflection occurring and doing it purposefully, it is important to emphasize that the agency of reflection is not solely dependent on the intentionality of the rhetor. Instead, agency for reflection is distributed among the varying entangled factors within a rhetorical situation. They work together, distributing agency, to create the collective intentionality.

My definition of reflection builds from current scholarship because of my emphasis on the rhetorical nature of reflection; it accounts for how reflection emerges from rhetorical context and results in rhetorical action. Yet, the definition also purposefully diverges from how reflection has been traditionally described by leaving open:

- the time reflection takes place
- the mediums and modalities that reflection embodies
- the rhetorical activity that results in reflection

In leaving the time, mediums and activities, and rhetorical effects open, I purposefully make space for all the ways that reflection can emerge and result. Reflection can happen at a variety of times, whether it be alongside an activity that is being reflected upon; as a form of projection; retroactively; or some combination of past, present, or future timeframes. Reflection can take place through a range of activities: interactive languaging, moving, listening, artistic interpreting, meditating, writing, and so on. Like all rhetoric, its effects can be wide ranging. Examples might include considering an alternative perspective, creating and transferring knowledge across contexts, investigating closely held beliefs, analyzing a current or prior action, ruminating on identities, projecting future connections to current or past happenings, or sitting with difficult emotions. Reflection, at least in this broad way that I am describing here, invites new research methods that honor reflection-in-motion; it suggests that we should learn from and trust that bodies have ways of knowing and doing reflection long before compositionists or other theorists have started theorizing or researching it. The following book overview explains how I will do this work.

Book Overview

In this first chapter, I have given a brief overview of reflection research to set up the problem that my book addresses: Reflection research has overwhelmingly centered its analysis upon pre-identified instances of reflective activity that researchers saw as consistent with mainstream reflection definitions in the field. These mainstream definitions of reflection were inspired by understandings of reflection theorized by John Dewey and Donald Schön. And though these ideas of reflection are representative of some practices of reflection, they are certainly not representative of all histories of reflection. Dewey and Schön represent Western views of reflection that rely heavily on rational understandings of reflection, closely aligned with critical thinking, metacognition, and transfer. This attention inadvertently ignores the breadth of reflection practice that might be associated with practices of meditation, mindfulness, and reflexivity. In this book, I purposefully center the experiences of students and teachers in MSIs so we can hear from underrepresented

TABLE 1.1. Data collection overview for this research project

Type of Data	When	How
Ethnographic notes	Daily	Notebook
Ethnographic audio recordings	Daily	Tape recorder
Ethnographic video recordings	Daily	GoPro video recorder
Focal student interviews	Three or four times per quarter or semester	Notebook and tape recorder
Focal student genre analysis	Texts discussed in focal-student interviews	Photos and/or downloads
Focal teacher interviews	Three times per quarter or semester	Notebook and tape recorder
Surveys (all students)	Once—end of course	Paper-Based Survey (completed in class)

viewpoints about how reflection works in the writing classroom. Learning from such a diverse group of students, I hope we can better serve the needs of our increasingly diverse student population (Barrios, 2023).

In Chapter 2, I overview my research sites, my methods, and my methodologies. I also describe the ways that I gathered data, the sites from which the data was gathered, and how that data was analyzed. Table 1.1 is an overview of the data I collected during the research study, along with when and how I collected it.

While studying reflection-in-motion, I adopt a "mosaic" approach (Evans-Winters, 2019) to help me gather a variety of data in a way that centered participants' lived experiences and embodied knowledge of reflective activity. I surveyed, interviewed, and observed twenty students and five teachers at three institutions, all while engaging with "feminist ears." Feminist ears, a term coined by Sara Ahmed, are used when a listener observes with a critical stance what is both said and not said. I adopt feminist ears by employing feminist rhetorics methodology of rhetorical listening. Inspired by Jacqueline Jones Royster's "When the First Voice You Hear is Not Your Own," Krista Ratcliffe theorized rhetorical listening in *Rhetorical Listening: A Trope for Interpretive Invention* (2005). Ratcliffe coined the term "rhetorical listening" as the "code of cross-cultural conduct" signifying "a stance of openness that a person may assume in relation to any person text or culture" (p. 17). Ratcliffe and Kyle Jensen later theorized it as a feminist concept-tactic, something that could be used to describe a methodology of listening to "deeply sedimented scenes with hauntings" (2022, p. 82). Through using rhetorical listening, researchers can listen openly, learn from others' perspectives, and tell the story of those perspectives. I layered my rhetorical listening to participants with real-time observations of what they described: sitting in, taking notes, and videoing each session of two classes at each institution.

Employing intersectional and/or Black feminist methods and methodologies allowed me to critically reconsider the "foundational assumptions, values, theories, and methods" (Chávez et al., 2012, p. 1) of reflection research, all while acknowledging rich rhetorical traditions of social justice–oriented versions of reflection. In a world where we so desperately need to learn from students as they acknowledge deep-rooted ideologies, consider alternative perspectives, and move across difference, I hope that my research on reflection can start to do the work of showcasing the important role that reflection can play in these important pedagogical aims.

I also spend time in Chapter 2 discussing the ethics of doing research at MSIs as a white researcher. As Heidi A. McKee and James E. Porter argue, it is of utmost importance that feminist researchers are aware of "one's own position, gender, and status," staying "attuned to the dynamics of power in all phases of a research project" (2017, p. 155). Of course, as Glenn explains,

> absolute objectivity is impossible and claiming it irresponsible. For that reason, claiming objectivity in our research is much less important than striving for research transparency as we rhetorical feminists gather and analyze information (knowledge). Whether we locate the subjects of our research in the library, the archives, or the face-to-face interview, our goal is respectful interaction and rhetorical listening. (2018, p. 97)

In Chapter 2, I sit with these ethical complexities, outline my methodologies, and offer a reasoning for them. My goal in this research was to listen and learn from my research participants, rather than to immediately pass judgment of whether past scholarship would identify those moments, texts, or conversations as reflective. In prioritizing participant-identified moments of reflection in this project, I hope to offer new methodologies for researching reflection. Chapter 2 then overviews my research methods, especially methods that are meant to be inclusive and intersectional—which means that I carefully and purposefully invoked Black feminist research methodologies. I invoke a Black feminist qualitative research method that Venus Evans-Winters calls a "mosaic": when researchers collect both traditional and nontraditional texts to create a full view of a complex research problem (2019, p. 24).

In Chapters 3 and 4, I invoke feminist storytelling as methodology to share accounts of students and teachers practicing reflection daily, all while amplifying the robust and varied definitions and practices of reflection within the writing classroom. Reflective storytelling, and personal narrative more broadly, are rhetorical strategies for feminist rhetoricians because they welcome rhetorical empathy. Like bell hooks explained, "If I wanted to write theory, especially feminist theory that would be read across the boundaries of race, gender, class, and educational levels, I would need to provide a common entry point" (2009, p. 51). Queer, feminist, and critical race theorists have long since used storytelling "to trouble or destabilize claims" (Condon, 2012, p. 141). I hope to join in that tradition to share the stories of my participants, whose lived experiences can better illuminate a capacious definition of reflection with exciting implications for pedagogy.

In Chapter 3, I showcase findings to paint a complex picture of where, when, and how teachers hope that reflection is identified and practiced in their writing classroom. Using grounded theory on both the interview responses and the survey results, I explore how teachers and students name, identify, and practice reflection in their specific contexts. Generally, participants reported: reflection-for-introspection, in which reflective agents consider their own internal selves; reflection-for-learning, in which reflective agents described considering a past experience and learning from their actions within that experience; reflection-for-mindfulness, or when reflective agents discuss becoming more attuned to themselves or their surroundings; reflection-for-awareness, in which reflective agents analyze their thought process currently and/or retroactively; and reflection-for-perspective, in which reflective agents considered reflection to be a kind of rumination for the purpose of reconsideration. According to focal students and teachers, there were two larger patterns regarding in what genres reflection can be found: written genres (like journaling, scrapbooks, social media, and reflection assignments associated with assessment) and speech genres (like interactions with mentors, group work, whole-class discussion, or conversations among friends about class material). I discuss the teacher's definitions of reflection at length and the activities they offer as opportunities for reflection in their classroom as a result.

In Chapter 4, I share how student definitions and contextual factors play a role in the selection, refusal, and subversion of teacher-intended reflective practice, along with students' self-prompted reflective activity. Students' stories demonstrate so clearly what a beautiful mess reflection is. Students do not reflect simply because they're asked to, nor do they reflect because they want to. Instead, students identify reflection with varying rhetorical effects built from their own definitions of reflection. For that aspirational rhetorical effect to occur, it must emerge from the complex interaction of contextual factors that align just so: the time, the affect, the emotions, the materials, the people. Students' past experiences with reflection are instrumental in the definitions of reflection they have, the rhetorical effect they associate with reflection, and the contextual factors that are favorable to that activity. Students provide a window into how much reflection they do that is not accounted for in their classrooms. They also admit to performative moments of supposed reflection that are not actually reflection to themselves, along with explaining creative ways they subvert teacher-mandated reflection activities that do not meet their needs. In this chapter, students give incredible insight into the rhetoricity of reflection.

Finally, in Chapter 5 I offer potential pedagogical implications and ideas for further research. I want reflection to do more for our students. I hope it will inspire new pedagogy that recognizes and encourages reflective practice as our students identify, name, and practice it, because reflection can help us work toward so many of our goals and reasons for teaching composition. Do we teach composition to demystify the writing process? Reflection can help illuminate the thought and consideration of writerly choices. Do we teach composition so that we can disambiguate the academic discourse community? Reflection can help navigate the complex emotions about joining a new discourse community. Do we teach composition to invite historically marginalized students' home literacies in the academy? Reflection can investigate how systemic racism plays a role in linguistic discrimination—and navigate emotions about joining a new discourse community. Do we teach composition to help bridge high school and college experiences—and then build connections to their desired majors or future careers? Reflection can work to transfer knowledge. Do we teach composition so that we might help students become critical thinkers and civic participants? Reflection can inspire deeper consideration about deeply held beliefs. I hope this book can inspire that change. To do that work, I asked research participants to define reflection and direct me to its activity. Then, I looked for it within the daily observations of FYW classrooms. In doing so, I learned how reflection emerges through the complicated relationship between university and classroom context, teacher training and pedagogical aims, materials and technologies, student dispositions and pedagogical memory, and others.

I see this book being of interest to a variety of readers. Research done at MSIs is comparatively less than at other institutional settings—and research that is done about MSIs is often ignored (Gilyard, 1999). In this book, then, I rely on participant-identified moments of reflection-in-motion, or how reflection emerges from complex rhetorical situations for varying rhetorical effects. Throughout the book, I document how practitioners and teachers practice name, identify, and practice reflection for varying rhetorical effects. This book offers insight into the important work done at MSIs—and will thus be of interest for those who teach or hope to teach in these settings. Given its topic of inquiry—reflection—it also will be of interest to all those teachers and scholars who are interested in how reflection works, especially according to reflective practitioners themselves. My hope is that the next four chapters will give a sense of all the different ways that students and teachers have identified, named, and practiced reflection so that we, as composition instructors, can:

- recognize the diversity of students' reflection definitions
- recognize the multitude of factors in the rhetorical context that play a role in the potential emergence of reflective activity
- recognize the various rhetorical effects of reflective activity

My hope is that the following chapters, and the stories told within them, will work to broaden our conceptions of reflection, all while honoring how complicated it is for reflection to emerge.

In this book, then, we will consider my participants' stories, written in coordination with the brave participants who shared their ideas about reflection and let me in their classrooms. I ask that as we read them, we engage in rhetorical empathy, *listening* to the participants without immediate judgment of whether we agree or disagree with their assessment of what reflection is and can be. As Lisa Blankenship (2019) explained, "Rhetorical empathy does not ask that we silence our own perspective but rather that we foreground our emotions and responses to Others' stories and ask how power is circulating and functioning in every speech act and rhetorical situation" (p. 119). I am excited to tell more stories in the chapters that follow—pausing purposefully between the telling and the analyzing so that we can hold space for the participants' knowledge and what we can learn from them before sharing my own ideas about what I think the stories can tell us. Let's get started.

2

Feminist Methodologies for Researching Reflection-in-Motion in Writing Classrooms

March 2017—Urban State University

I walk into the "CIC" (Urban State U's colloquial term for their computer integrated classrooms, two rectangular, windowless classrooms in the basement of a beautiful brick building that frames the school's most famous view). It's only 2 minutes before the class begins. I am decidedly not a morning person, and it is going to be a struggle for me to get to the class every day by 8:30 a.m. I'm a dissertating graduate student, still in my 20s, and I often stay up past the middle of the night to work. I had been up even later than usual last night spending time with my boyfriend, Brett (who, unbeknownst to me now, would later become my husband). It was only after Brett went to sleep that I stayed up for a few hours more to get some writing done while his dog, Cameron, curled up on my feet. Though Urban's campus is only a 15-minute drive from my house, driving is not cost-effective on my graduate student stipend. So, my commute starts a full hour earlier than when I need to be on campus (that's the minimum time allotment for completing a half-mile walk, then a train, and then another half-mile walk). Despite giving myself plenty of buffer for train delays, I'm still lucky to get to campus on time. I'm out of breath from my quickened pace that ended with a slight jog down the stairs.

https://doi.org/10.7330/9781646426942.c002

I walk in and smile a "hello" at the instructor, Grace, as I rush to an available computer pod. I settle in the second row of computer pods on the right-hand side of the room, taking in the surroundings. Overhead lights glare, a harsh contrast from the filtered sunlight that I enjoyed throughout the cloudy, misty commute. I wish there were windows in the room. Even from the brief encounter with Grace where we chatted about the project and she agreed to let me pitch it to her students, I get the feeling that Grace is the kind of teacher who would keep the fluorescent lights off in favor of letting natural sunlight illuminate the room.

The room is spread out with small clumps of computers, trios of computer desks arranged such that the students face each other in groups of three. Though the focus likely was intended to be the other students—given how desks face toward one another instead of in rows toward the teacher station—students' more obvious (and perhaps unintentional) focus seemed to be their monitor. Atop each desk is a computer monitor so large that students must roll their office chairs and peek between each other's monitors to get a glimpse of their podmates. The classroom's desks are large computer desks and immobile, so the office-style chairs (that allow students to rotate and roll) are the only way that students can shift their purview. This seems helpful because there is still a traditional "front" of the classroom with a podium, white board, overhead projector, and teacher desk (with a monitor and computer equipment) along one wall of the classroom.

Grace stands at the front of the room, saying "hello" to each student that enters, a warm smile on her face and an ever-so-slight Southern accent that seems to welcome students even more than her already disarming nature. She wears a flowy blouse, jeans, and booties—hair down in soft curls with natural-style makeup—which in this city means she is decidedly dressed up. In fact, I'm impressed that she's so put together. I remove my damp rain jacket to reveal my comfortable outfit that meets the city's lowkey fashion sense: high-tops, leggings, and an oversized sweater.

I reach into my backpack to get the essentials: consent forms for students, a notebook for observation notes, a tape recorder so I can listen back to intriguing moments later for analysis, my phone that doubles as a camera and backup recorder, a GoPro so the wide-view lens can easily show my perspective and the full view of the room, and chargers for all the technology. (I am observing Grace's section and then Kevin's immediately after—same room and course number, different teachers and students—and I need to be ready to go for both sections since I can't make it home and back—let alone to my office in this misty rain—and be ready to pitch my research to both sections.)

"Deep breath," I think, remembering the slow breathing technique that I practiced with my therapist when I'm in anxiety-provoking situations. Gosh, I hate how hard it is for me, as a person with clinical anxiety, to do qualitative, in-person research. As a researcher, I value the experiences of others and want to learn from and with them—but it is so hard to put myself out there like that, on display (especially in this CIC classroom where I know that I will usually have a GoPro blinking on my forehead for me to capture the room well [rather than the mini tripod I could use in a traditional setting]). I'm as ready as I ever will be for the research to begin.

March 2021—Rural Community College (Zoom)

My daughter, 11 months old, plays with the water table that I have set out. It might be March, but it's hot. That's the thing about living in Tallahassee, a swamp now covered with suburbs. It feels like we could drink the humidity with the straw. I'm barefoot in the grass, wearing what I like to think of as my "warm weather mom" ensemble: athletic shorts, oversized t shirt, hair piled at the crown of my head. Not the way I would have ever dreamed of introducing my research at Rural CC, but we're on Zoom and I'm without childcare. It's the best I can do.

I finished my research at Urban State U, wrote my dissertation, moved across the country for a tenure track position at Florida State University. A few months later, I got married, paused my research plans due to a medically complex pregnancy and postpartum period, and then postponed it again due to a global pandemic. So, here I am, March 2021, finally able to add research to the data I gathered at Urban State. Though my dissertation only looked at one school, Urban State, I had always hoped the project would be a multi-institutional study so that I could shed light on how students with different experiences and backgrounds with reflection did the work differently.

Now that I'm able to start doing the research, the circumstances are different than those at Urban. Rural is only offering asynchronous online courses in their writing program due to Covid-19. Also, I have an extra person with me today: my daughter. Our daycare is waiting for their teachers to get vaccinated before accepting new students—which I totally understand and support—but I really wish I had a better solution for today's research introduction to Jess's class.

I precariously balance my phone atop the umbrella of Parker's water table, angling the camera so the class can see me. I'm sitting atop the patio stairs, delicately balancing my notebook on my knee. This way, I think, Parker won't try to play with my phone and accidentally disconnect me from the Zoom room, and I can still take notes because she will be busy playing with the water table. I get ready to unmute myself, turn my video on, and tell the class about how I'll be following along with their class on Zoom and Canvas for the remainder of the quarter. First, I triple check to see the "recording in progress" note on Zoom, and that my handheld recorder is recording, as well. Then, I look at the preview of my video: flyaway hairs have tightened into curls, my makeup-free face glistens with sweat, and my white-T-shirt-clad shoulders peek out before the rest of my body is hidden from view. While it's not exactly the professionalism that I was hoping for, at least I figured out a way to do a live meeting with Jess's class at Rural. Though her course is asynchronous, Jess has optional Zoom sessions each week where she goes over the plan for the week and her students can ask questions. She's invited me to the second one so I can introduce my research after she's used the first meeting to establish her class culture.

The meeting starts. Jess's video turns on, and her face lights up the screen: a person among a sea of black boxes. I'm struck by her style and her affect: her artisanal earrings, winged eyeliner, and red lips show an excitement about playing with art, but she's not much into playing with the contouring and eyebrow filling we often see in contemporary makeup ads. The look instead reads like a cool aunt that you want to take to your next concert (especially if it's a punk one—because we can see the top half of a punk band shirt peeking out before the camera cuts her torso off). Though her style choices might invoke a relatively louder break-the-rules kind of vibe, her easy smile and softer, calm tone makes it clear she is kind—and that kindness is genuine. She welcomes the class, and then immediately invites me to speak.

I take a calming breath (that strategy still helps me), and then I begin. "This semester," I explain,

> I will be researching reflection in the writing classroom, learning from you all about how you define, identify, and practice reflection. Your instructor, Jess, has agreed to work with me, and I hope that I can talk to some of you as well. I'll be here for the informal mini lecture each week, lurking, like y'all, muted and video off.

I pause, hoping for a laugh at my attempt at a joke, but hearing none and seeing no reactions, I continue. "I'll be taking notes on what I see and hear. Then, I hope to chat with a few volunteers who agree to be a 'focal student.'"

Knowing that most of the students are first-generation and may have never been invited to be a part of a research program, I go off script to elaborate:

> "Focal student" is a fancy way of describing someone who I get to focus on in my research by learning about them in more detail through interviews. We do not always get to hear from our students in research, and I hope that my research project can amplify your voices so your younger friends and family will have teachers who better understand how to teach them. As a focal student, you'd interview with me every couple of weeks throughout the course.

I'm trying to indicate to them how I hope the research will be as ethical and reciprocal as possible.

I continue,

> In exchange, I offer free tutoring of any writing-related class or task. And, upon completion of all the interviews in the quarter, I'll give you fifty dollars. Shoot me an email if you're interested at jfiscus@fsu.edu. I'll drop it in the chat. For everyone else, just know that I'll be here in these optional weekly class reviews, and I'm an observer on Canvas. The goal in doing this research is to help teachers better understand how and why you define, identify, and practice reflection—and how they can best support that practice. Thanks for letting me learn from you! Does anyone have questions?

I stare at the black screens with the white letters listing various names. I know from Jess that her students vary in age from dual-enrolled high school students to forty-year-old first-generation college students who want to get their degree so they can change careers. Most of them identify as Chicanx students—this is an HSI community college in a rural area in the western United States—but all I can see are the little squares on my phone that are supposed to represent those people, those people that I desperately want to know and connect with, the ones I hope to learn from.

After a minute of awkward silence that feels like a lifetime, Jess thanks me, and encourages her students to join the research project. (I smile when she says, "So often researchers stay at big universities to learn about and talk with those students; take advantage of this opportunity to talk to Jacki.") Then, Jess starts her overview of the course for the week, explaining what weekly activities she has created and where they can find them, and how those activities and goals scaffold toward the overall goals of the course.

After class, I journal about my first experience researching at Rural. I'm excited that we will have some synchronous time, despite it not being mandatory for all students (nor mandatory for those present to reveal their video—something she doesn't require because many of her students are taking the video from a location they are embarrassed to share, or they are unable to share their background because they listen into class while helping with family or working). I need to ask her about that in her interview the next day. (I do, and Jess tells me that she offers these optional meetings because she sees her job as both teaching first-year writing and how to be a college student. Since nearly all her students are what the field considers nontraditional—whether that be because they are students of color, or because of their first-generation-student status, their age, or their class—Jess sees it as her job to help them navigate college student life, especially now that everything [the classes, the resources, the community support] is entirely online.)

September 2021—Southern HBCU

I pull into the parking spot at Southern, nervous about standing in front of students to pitch my research. The last time I was in person with students, I was 34 weeks pregnant and the WHO had officially called Covid-19 a global pandemic. Now, 17 months since I've been physically in a classroom, I need to inform three sections of L.J.'s classes about my research project today. It is a cross-institutional project where I observe classes of FYC daily and learn about how students and teachers name, identify, and practice reflection. I'm hoping that at least one section will accept my presence and that some will decide to become focal students. I have completed research at Urban State U in person and Rural CC online—and I've noticed that there is just this general sense of being overwhelmed among students and teachers during the pandemic. I had 10 focal students at Urban State U pre-pandemic, and I've only had three focal students commit at Rural CC. Of course, the circumstances have changed a bit (online vs. in person, asynchronous vs. synchronous, a white researcher in a majority Latinx/Chicanx classroom vs. a white researcher at a PWI), but I feel like the Covid slump has something to do with it too.

I read L.J.'s email for the third time, and according to my interpretation of L.J.'s email, I think I'm probably (I hope, maybe?) parked in the right place. This campus is beautiful. Rolling hills, towering trees, brick buildings. Students are walking with each other; they seem happy, content. I frankly have not seen so many happy students in a while. Our country has been in lockdown, and it both delights and scares me to see so many folks walking close together, masks off, gesticulating, laughing, and hugging before going a different way at a sidewalk juncture.

This is also my first time on an HBCU campus. I feel every single cell of my white skin prickling. I wonder if this is what it feels like every time my husband (who is Black) or our daughter (who, at three, tells us she's "Black like daddy") walks through a predominantly white space. I wonder too if that's how my students of color feel at my own institution, which is a predominantly white institution (PWI).

I follow a couple of girls up the stairs to find my classroom, one's braids bouncing on her back, while another's locks sway to the beat of our footsteps. I find the classroom; it's hot, the lights are off, and I sneak into the one remaining seat next to the door while we wait for L.J. to arrive. I feel like the awkward, old white lady in the corner, but the students are welcoming. They assume I'm a student in the class; they offer me the QR code to scan to join the class's GroupMe (an offer that I try to politely decline, but probably just confuse the invitees by refusing).

I take a big inhale. I've been unconsciously holding my breath with my nervousness. Time for that deep breathing again.

L.J. comes in, a flash of color and confidence, and says, "Hey, y'all, how's everyone doin'?" in one breath. I start to rise out of my seat to introduce myself but hesitate for a moment in indecision (it's two minutes after class was supposed to start, and I don't want to be a nuisance).

Thankfully, just then, L.J. looks in my direction and says, "Before we get started today, I'll have Doctor Fiscus-Cannaday introduce herself and her research." I do another deep breath and start passing out informed-consent forms as I say my spiel, on autopilot, about the research project.

(This is my fifth time doing it; just last night I had made a recording for Heather's class, another asynchronous class at Rural CC that has agreed to do my research project.)

Upon finishing the introduction of the project, I stop and stand still: "Do y'all have any questions?" I ask. One student's hand extends almost immediately, and I say, "Yeah, what's up?" to call on them.

The student asks, "Are you only looking at HBCUs? Or are you looking at white schools too?"

I'm thrown off guard for a moment; though appreciative of the student's straightforwardness, I have never been asked this question.

I give myself a beat by immediately responding, "Good question."

I breathe, then try to talk out an answer.

I'm observing classes from all over the country, at all different kinds of universities: big research schools, community colleges, liberal arts schools—all are welcome. My priority is working with what folks call "MSIs," a governmental designation for schools that serve students of color. I'm really hoping that I can learn from y'all so teachers who read this work can be better, more inclusive teachers.

I take a beat. The student is gazing at me still, and I realize I never really answered their question.

"Yeah, so to answer your question: right now, y'all are the only HBCU, but that might change. My other schools are an HSI and AANAPISI right now."

The student nods, but their body language seems like they're not entirely satisfied.

"Any other questions?"

I look first toward the student who asked me the question, who shakes their head. Then, I look at the class. The students sit in awkward silence, most not deigning a glance my way. I wait the requisite minute in painful silence, and then say,

> Okay! So, you have my information. If you have any questions, please reach out. And, please, please, don't hesitate to ask me to stay out of your class. At the end of the day, your education and your needs are most important. I'll see you again if all y'all are comfortable. No worries if not. Thank you for your time!

I gather my things and scoot quickly out of the room.

It is only once I get home, writing in my research journal and reflecting upon my day, that I realize I should have answered what the student was really asking: "Are you just another white person coming here to benefit from Black culture and knowledge? Why should we help you?"

Just then, I glance down; my phone is buzzing. The student texted me asking that I not observe the class. I text back immediately, letting the student know that I will of course honor their request. I let L.J. know that I will no longer by observing his first morning class.

Then, I take a beat to journal about whether I should continue researching at Southern at all; L.J. has welcomed me to observe in all three of his sections, and there have been no objections in his mid-morning and afternoon sections. My initial reaction is to pull out of this site entirely. The student is right that white people have historically used Black people as research participants for their gain, often at the detriment of Black people. Should I be doing this research at all?

Questions and rationalizations swirl in a dialogic pattern in my brain, and it comes out in bits and pieces on the paper.

How is my research design circumventing this pattern of gathering research at the expense of Black folks?

I am not doing research on Black folks to benefit myself. I am doing research to benefit Black students. Research is privileged at R1 institutions, institutions that are overwhelmingly built for and serve white students. Writing studies faculty, who are overwhelmingly white, often do research in the classrooms at their home institutions (and thus inadvertently amplify voices from students enrolled at PWIs). I purposefully selected MSIs as sites of inquiry so that I can center marginalized student voices in this research. Working exclusively with students at MSIs, especially at MSIs in different geographical locations and institutional types, was a purposeful choice.

And how is my research helping students of color?

The project centers student voices in its methodologies. I am adopting rhetorical listening with a feminist ear in all my observations, interviews, and surveys. Students' perceptions of reflection shape what I identify as reflection. I hope that the range of what students identify as reflection will in turn influence readers' inclusivity of what reflection might look like.

What can students and teachers gain in taking a part in this research?

I've offered to share my research findings with each focal teacher and student. I've offered to be a peer reviewer of any work that the focal teacher needs an extra eye on, from articles to grant applications to writing assignments. I've offered to pay focal students upon completion of the semester-long study and provide them with at least equivalent tutoring time to their interview time in the meanwhile. Students, both focal students and class students, will likely get a taste of what qualitative research looks like, which might get them interested in doing research projects of their own.

What do they risk in taking a part in this research?

Students risk anonymity. It's possible, even with the pseudonyms and disclosing only what they want audiences to know, that their identities could be compromised. It's possible, too, that they may feel uncomfortable being in a class with me. Perhaps they will not get as much out of their class, given my distracting presence.

How is my research helping the communities of these classrooms in particular?

My book itself highlights these communities' stories, which is important in systems that have historically (and still!) marginalized their epistemologies. It's possible that reading the book might help teachers see reflection differently, both at their schools and more broadly.

It's a comforting dialogue. I know that I have tried to enter this work from an ethical perspective, but I also know that I'm gaining more than my participants ever could from this research project. Their participation ensures the data that I need to write a book, a book that will help get me tenure, that ensures financial security. Everything the research participants might gain is all just so small in comparison. The student is right: I am a white researcher benefiting from the labor of Black and Brown scholars, students, and teachers. It is a power dynamic that I must recognize and sit with. And, to help me navigate the ethics of this situation, I need to talk to the community partners and go to the literature.

*****

Gesa Kirsch and Patricia Sullivan define methodology as "the underlying theory and analysis of how research does or should proceed" and a method as "a technique or way of proceeding or gathering evidence" (Kirsch & Sullivan, 1992, p. 2). In this chapter, I detail the methods of my research, along with the reasoning and support for the methodologies used to analyze the data gathered. I focus on both because this project adopts new methods and methodologies for researching reflection, and I want to be sure to give plenty of insight into my choices along with how that changed my ability to research reflection. As I discussed in the last chapter, I am less interested in what *compositionists* have identified as reflection and then doing research on those texts and more interested in understanding where, when, and how *practitioners* name, identify, and practice reflection. Being able to understand how practitioners (both teachers and students) name, identify, and practice reflection, inherently involves different methodologies for researching reflection—methodologies that allow for rhetorical listening. The first section, then, overviews the methods and ethical considerations of the methods, and the remaining sections work to unpack the methodologies and their ethical considerations as well.

Method Overview

Research methods hold the values of the cultures that value them—and they often work to reinscribe white epistemologies and reinforce white supremacy. This is in part because research, as we know it in the academy, emerged from white scholars using Black and Brown people as unwilling and/or coerced participants, often to fulfill racist agendas (Scharff et al., 2010). In Patricia Leavy and Danielle Harris's *Contemporary Feminist Research From Theory to Practice* (2019), they list the qualities of intersectional feminist research as ethical, reflexive, reciprocal, inclusive, intersectional, and activist. Intersectional feminist researchers are cognizant of the ways that research puts communities at risk or exploits them, all while being cognizant of the complex power relationships between research participants and the researcher. Researchers employing intersectional feminist methods should ask themselves questions like: How can I be aware of the power relationships between me and my research participants? How can I mitigate risks to the community? How can I make sure that my research is representative of the community's ideals and values? And how can I be sure my research is accessible for the community that I am researching? Researching with this kind of ethical, reflexive lens usually results in a reciprocal approach to research—a consideration of how to benefit the research participants and their community, along with a sharing of personal experiences from the researcher so the research process is not so one-sided. Intersectional feminist researchers pay specific attention to the layering of identities—being careful not to flatten the description (and thus the understanding) of a whole person (and consequent societal problem). I see my inclusive, reciprocal, and reflexive research practices, along with my attention to antiracist pedagogical implications, as key methodological implications for reflection research. Feminist research methods, in this project, looked like: designing for accessibility and equity in the data-collection period, practicing recursive self-reflexivity about my positionality as a researcher, and humanizing research participants in the research process (see, for example, best practices of this in Paris & Winn, 2013).

When I took up qualitative research methods like interviews and ethnographic observations, I employed what Sara Ahmed (2021) referred to as "a feminist ear," or a way of listening to both the rhetorical silences and the "sharpness of . . . words" and "how . . . and to whom they point" (p. 7). This open-hearted and thoughtfully present listening was especially helpful in developing relationships with research participants so that I could accurately and authentically record their perspectives. As Ahmed (2021) wrote, "It [means] sharing the work. It [means] becoming part of their collective. Their collective became ours. I think of that ours as the promise of feminism, ours not as a possession but as an invitation, an opening, a combining of forces" (p. 7). Feminist ears encouraged an attunement to research participants, a kind of solidarity with them, that encouraged on ethical and attentive reporting of their stories. Additionally, feminist ears inspired a self-reflexive and self-aware listening; it helped pause judgment and tries to open the eyes and soul for learning with a community—a community of experts. Ahmed first introduced the term in *Living a Feminist Life* (2017), and scholars have since used it as a type of method in writing studies (Thompson et al., 2022). Thompson et al. explained, "Feminist ears pay attention towards unexpected vibrations, vibrations that are not only vocally uttered but also to vibrations that manifest in other ways, such as bodily, spatial, visual, and ephemeral reverberations" (Thompson et al., 2022, p. 42–43).

Using feminist ears, then, relies on deep, embodied listening—a reliance on what Krista Ratcliffe called *rhetorical listening*, a term coined by Ratcliffe (2005) in *Rhetorical Listening: Identification, Gender, Whiteness* to explain a purposeful, mindful listening with suspended judgment. As explored in Krista Ratcliffe and Kyle Jensen's *Rhetorical Listening as a Concept-Tactic Approach* (2022), rhetorical listening can be a useful method, particularly in analyzing rhetorical situations, because it allows the researcher to recognize their own positionality and account for the ways that it aids, limits, and complicates their analysis (Ratcliffe & Jensen, 2022, p. 24). As in the work by material rhetoricians (e.g., see Cooper, 2016; Jarratt, 2001), Ratcliffe and Jensen (2022) were interested in the ways that rhetorical situations are subject to the audience and the rhetor, influenced by histories and future possibilities, and informed by the complex intersections of agencies between all rhetorical agents. Ratcliffe and Jensen, then, were interested in the "personal, discursive, cultural, and material" agencies at play in a rhetorical situation (p. 82) and wanted to theorize a method that might attend to the "deeply sedimented scene with hauntings" (p. 82). Rhetorical listening requires researchers to orient themselves in an open stance that generates curiosity, suspends judgment, and encourages generous interpretations (p. 24). I argue that rhetorical listening, especially done with a feminist ear, helped me see a fuller picture (both in breadth and in detail) of the rhetorical situations that I was studying—all while encouraging my own reflexivity about how my positionality influenced my understandings and interpretations.

While this project draws from both the Black feminist method of mosaic and intersectional methods of listening, I want to be clear in defining the ways that Black feminism is distinct from intersectional feminism. Black feminism refers to the "long tradition of women's intellectual labor and community endeavors in the U.S. and across the African Diaspora" (Evans-Winters 2019, p. 12). Intersectional feminism refers more broadly to contemporary understandings of feminism that "systems of race, social class, gender, sexuality, ethnicity, nation, and age form mutually constructing features of social organization" (Collins, 2000, p. 299). Intersectional feminist methods and methodologies can and do take up Black feminist methods and methodologies, as the two inform one another, but I elected to explicitly adopt a Black feminist research method so I could purposefully center antiracist research methods in this project. This was especially important to me as a white woman doing research about Black and Brown students. In designing my methods and methodologies, then, I was careful to follow Venus Evans-Winters's Black feminist research practices; these include: "(1) musings about knowledge and knowing, (2) how one interacts with participants throughout the research process, (3) one's understanding of the context where the study takes place, (4) the body of literature reviewed, and (5) interpretation and analysis of data" (Evans-Winters, 2019, p. 15). I discuss how I incorporated each of these qualities in the upcoming sections, beginning in the next section with how adopting a Black feminist mosaic approach to gathering data helped shape what knowledge I was privy to, my relationships with research participants, and my understanding of each rhetorical situation.

PIECING TOGETHER A BLACK FEMINIST "MOSAIC"

In this research project, I adopted a Black feminist "mosaic" method: a mixed-method approach gathering a variety of traditional and nontraditional texts, listening deeply to the stories of those in the community being researched, and engaging in personal narrative. While describing the approach in *Black Feminism in Qualitative Inquiry*, Evans-Winters (2019) reminded us that a "mosaic as an artform is the process of creating images with an assortment of small pieces of colored glass, stone, or other objects put together to create a pattern or picture." (p. 15). Likewise, a mosaic method utilizes a mixed-method approach—and recognizes that it is only through reading the data together that conclusions can be made. Evans-Winters suggests that doing so allows for a "collaboration with the self and the most vulnerable in society," which in turn can "bring us one step closer to intellectual emancipation" (p. 60). Therefore, Evans-Winters suggests Black feminist mosaic methods are particularly well suited to be adopted by Black women researchers to do research about Black women, especially young Black girls. As a white feminist researcher, I chose to adopt the method because I thought it modeled how to take up a Black feminist theoretical standpoint in my data collection and analysis, as well as offering best practices for researching marginalized communities. I therefore prioritized the experiences of students at three MSIs, observing the daily happenings of seven sections of first-year writing (FYW) classes at three schools: Urban State U (an AANAPISI and R1, two sections), Rural CC (an HSI and community college, three sections), and Southern HBCU (a mid-size HBCU, two sections).

My goal of adopting a Black feminist mosaic method in this research project was to capture reflection-in-motion, or reflection as it occurred in real time, according to the participants in the project.

Throughout the course of this project, I selected three institutional sites as locations of inquiry. At each, I used the same methods, following International Research Bureau (IRB) protocol and approval.[1] First, I solicited focal teachers via email a month before classes began. Upon discussing the research process and getting agreement from them to become focal teachers, I worked with them to introduce the research project during the first week of the course. I explained the project to students and asked for permission from all students to observe daily class happenings and document my observations with photos, tape recordings, and videos, so I could do follow-up analysis of participant-identified reflective activity. If all students agreed to be part of the research project and the teacher was still interested, I then solicited focal students, within the first few weeks of the course, to do interviews in exchange for compensation. Next, I conducted three interviews with focal students and focal teachers throughout the quarter or semester. These interviews gave me a sense of participants' definitions and experiences of reflection, along with insight about exemplary experiences of reflection in and about the course I was observing. Finally, I invited all enrolled students to take part in an end-of-course survey about their views of reflective activity so they too could shape what I researched as examples of reflection. In adopting these research

---

1. IRB approval numbers: Study00001613 and Study 00002003.

methods, I aimed to provide a layered, multifaceted approach to understanding how identities and experiences influence and shape reflective practice.

Feminist compositionists have successfully used methods like ethnography, interview, textual analysis, and more to understand the roles of identity in literacy (see Blair & Nickoson, 2018, for examples). To emphasize both personal perspectives and capture motion, I was drawn toward sensory ethnography, interviews, and storytelling—methods that could help see the layering communication that happened throughout interaction because of and in relationship to the context. In my research project, one piece of my mosaic is daily ethnographic observations of class happenings. I adapted practices of what Sarah Pink (2015) described as sensory ethnography, a feminist research method that is "a way of thinking about and doing ethnography that takes as its starting point the multisensoriality of experience, perception, knowing and practice" (p. xi). Scholars have used ethnography to study motion (Clifford & Marcus, 1986), and I selected sensory ethnography because it has been identified as a feminist research method (see, for example, Leavy & Harris, 2019). Though it could be argued that ethnography has always had an attention to the senses, Pink (2009) argued that an attention to the sensorial is a new paradigm or view for how to do ethnography (much like past ideas of how ethnography can be gendered, embodied, and/or visual). As Pink explained, "There is now no standard way of doing ethnography that is universally practiced" (p. 4). She continued, "Ethnographic practice tends to include participant observation, ethnographic interviewing, and a range of other participatory research techniques that are often developed and adapted in context and as appropriate to the needs and possibilities afforded by specific research projects" (p. 4). Some of these additional methods can include video, photo, and other technological tools. Since I saw agency as distributed across interrelationships between human and nonhuman factors (Barad, 2007), my sensory ethnographic observations allowed me to account for both human and nonhuman actors that were relevant in the interaction of actants affecting reflection within the space. In being particularly attuned to the context from which the activity emerged, I accounted for "thing power," or the "curious ability . . . to animate, to act, to produce effects dramatic and subtle" (Bennett, 2010, p. 6).

To add in shades and variation for my research mosaic, I took notes on my observations, along with collecting tape recordings, videos, and photographs during my observations. I took seriously the advice that "taking notes and recording is helpful, but also learning to smell, feel, hear, taste, and see rhetoric all around is necessary because otherwise ephemeral and material rhetorical devices remain unnoticed" (Endres & Senda-Cook, 2011, p. 278). In my case, I took on-the-fly notes during my observations and then used those to create weekly summary notes, reflexivity notes, and interview questions. I took notes and tape-recorded every class session, and I invited participants to direct what I should review during their interviews. I later re-listened to certain moments because of focal participant interest. I also used a GoPro for videos, taking advantage of both its wide lens and its unique ability to capture my researcher perspective, and my iPhone in wide-lens mode for photos so I could try to capture the rhetorical situation each day. My hope was that the combination of observations, notes, recordings, videos, and photos could help me learn about and be able to recount the complex rhetorical situations from which reflection emerged.

Another piece of my mosaic was focal-student and focal-participant interviews. I conducted four interviews of focal teachers and students during the duration of the term (Urban and Rural were on the quarter system, while Southern was on the semester system). I layered interviews with observations because they "highlight participants' words and value their subjective knowledge" (Leavy & Harris, 2019, p. 138). As reflection researcher Kevin Roozen (2016) suggests, "Reflective interviewing provides researchers with a means of viewing literate activity from the writer's perspective and making visible the writing-related knowledge practices identities and dispositions writers bring to bear on engagements" (p. 255). Like Roozen, I analyzed any reflective texts that participants brought to or mentioned during their interviews.

My interviews were semi-structured; I had set questions, but I did see interviews as a reciprocal space. I used the opportunity to respond to their contributions, occasionally asking follow-up questions or adding my own anecdotes to build rapport. Mostly I took the interviews as an opportunity to *listen* with an open heart and mind. In Jacqueline Jones Royster's "When the First Voice You Hear is Not Your Own" (1996), she drew attention to the importance of this practice, especially for white listeners to people of color. She wrote,

> The goal is not, "You talk, I talk." The goal is better practices so that we can exchange perspectives, negotiate meaning, and create understanding with the intent of being in a good position to cooperate, when, like now, cooperation is absolutely necessary. (p. 38)

I relied on the interviews to hear more about what participants did as reflection in the writing classroom—and how those practices came to be named, identified, and practiced as such.

For a final piece of my mosaic, I offered a survey to the entire class so they could inform me about their experiences of reflection if they chose to. Surveys can give an anonymized perspective of students who are not willing or able to be a focal student. My hope in offering them to the entire class was that the survey could give voice to all those I observed, maybe even to the students resistant to reflection that may feel less inclined to be a focal student. However, only Urban had a high response for survey completion, so I did not rely heavily on this data in my analysis.

I started this project at Urban State U, doing daily in-person observations of Grace's and Kevin's sections of in-person, 4-day-a-week 50-minute classes of first-year composition with a "multimodality" focus. During my in-person observations, I always used a tape recorder for the entire class session. I also took notes in my ethnography observations journal to note interesting class happenings—and took photos or videos to capture my viewpoint or perspective of those moments. While doing observations, I tried my best to move my body around the classroom so I could see and hear different perspectives. To gain insight from participants, I interviewed Kevin and Grace, along with four focal students from each class. Out of the eight total focal students at Urban State U, six identified as minoritized students (five identified as Asian and one as Hispanic). In return for their time and labor, I offered all of the students peer tutoring on any writing assignment, and I offered teachers peer review on any writing they were doing for publication or coursework. I did not offer these students financial incentives because at the time I was a graduate student and experiencing financial duress. At the end of the semester, I asked all students to participate in a survey about their reflection habits.

Upon gathering data, I planned to add two more case studies at new MSI institutions to my data so I could hear from a more inclusive representation of faculty and students, but I postponed so I could prioritize my mental health during my first year as an assistant professor—and then postponed again during a medically complex pregnancy. A few weeks before I gave birth, the WHO named Covid-19 a global pandemic, and shortly thereafter the IRB required researchers to cease nonessential in-person research projects. Therefore, I next observed two asynchronous online courses at Rural CC (rather than my original plan of in-person observations). The two instructors, Heather and Jess, made me a Canvas observer for their courses so I could follow along with class happenings like I would have if they were in-person, synchronous classes. Both Rural CC teachers used Canvas to host their FYC course, using a mixture of Canvas announcements, assignments, discussion boards, and readings to accomplish class happenings and learning; I was privy to all the public-facing posting from instructors and interaction from students. I also attended Jess's supplementary, optional weekly Zoom sessions and recorded them. Jess designed these synchronous meetings to give students an opportunity to meet with her weekly, allowing an opportunity for relationship building and live questions. She began her meetings with an overview of the goals for the week and the coordinating Canvas assignments, then asked for questions, and ended with light conversation with all her attendees.

My research methods at Rural CC were necessarily adapted due to the asynchronous nature (I did remote observations on Zoom, rather than in-person observations in each live class), but I did maintain the same research approaches: recording class happenings (using video and photos as necessary), along with interviewing focal teachers and students—and inviting students to participate in a survey at the end of the semester. Perhaps due to the collective burnout during Covid-19—which disproportionally affected BIPOC—along with my distance from students (giving the asynchronous nature of our interaction), I did not get as much student input. I had offered the same incentive to focal students (free peer tutoring) with an additional incentive because I was now faculty and financially secure: Focal students received $100 upon completing the four interviews. Only three focal students agreed to be in the study (all of whom were white), and one of the students had to drop the study before the semester was over due to being "too stressed because of the Pandemic." Additionally, at the end of the semester when I invited all enrolled students to take a survey, no students decided to participate. Though Rural CC did lack the student input that I hoped for, observing the classes and talking to the teachers (along with one student in each class) did give me a new perspective of what it meant to be doing reflection in a non-normative space, amid a worldwide shutdown. The data was not as representative of the students as I hoped, but the teachers taught me a lot about how adapting to tech-only communication affected their reflective pedagogy in an unprecedented time.

Once vaccinations were made available to the public in the United States, the IRB lifted the pause on in-person research. I did observations of two sections of in-person classes at Southern HBCU. Because in-person observations were again an option, I reached out to the teachers who had originally been interested in the project the year prior. Two of the three opted out because of safety concerns, but one (L.J.) was willing to continue with the research. He suggested that I sit in the back of the class since he encouraged students to sit toward the front; this arrangement would make it more likely to give students distance if they would like it. I adopted the methods from Urban State: I attended each class session in person, tape-recording and note-taking at each, along with taking videos and photos throughout my data collection. Like my time at Rural CC, I offered free tutoring and the $100 incentive to all focal students because I had financial security myself at that point to do so. For the safety of the students and the teacher, I also gave focal students and L.J. the option of meeting on the phone, over Zoom, or in person for their interviews. Most opted for phone calls, but I had a few Zoom calls and in-person meetings as well. I was lucky to work with L.J., along with 10 focal students (all of whom were Black), for which I was especially grateful since it was during a tenuous time for in-person research.

Throughout this research process, then, I adapted to the shifting contexts—which shaped and reshaped what "observation" looked like. At each site, though, I knew that the research needed to be able to capture *motion* because of the nature of the project. Reflection, in this project, was not predetermined by me as the researcher. This meant participants could mention all sorts of activities as reflective; they may point to a writer's memo or portfolio cover sheet—but they also might talk about group work, student-teacher conferences, or peer review. Therefore, I needed to be able to account for what participants were *doing*, as opposed to only investigating the static texts that were *done*. Though I was willing to review a reflective text that students or instructors pointed to as exemplary moments of reflective activity, I also wanted to be able to analyze interactive, dynamic, and multimodal moments that happened at different times in class. In the next section, I consider the importance of doing research at MSIs—and conclude with the ethics of engaging in research at MSIs as a white researcher.

PRIORITIZING MSIS AS SITES OF INQUIRY

MSIs can be R1, private, public, two-year, four-year, university, college, or community college. AANAPISIs make up about 8% of the US's total accredited institutions (Rothberg, 2020), HSIs make up about 12% (Burke, 2021), and HBCUs make up about 3% (Jackson et al., 2019). MSI research is incredibly important; as Jimesha Relerford (2012) explained, "These stories should be told, and they must be told, if we are to move toward a richer, more diverse, and more historically accurate understanding of our field, our scholarship, and our students" (p. 126). Yet, because of the often-increased teaching and administrative commitments at MSIs, scholars at these institutions cannot always find time to conduct research or report on programmatic success at their institutions. Even when they do, they are often ignored: In Iris Ruiz's *Reclaiming Composition for Chicano/as and Other Ethnic Minorities: A Critical History and Pedagogy*, she argued that composition scholars have repeatedly ignored contributions from traditional understandings of composition history (2016, p. 3). Some journals try to encourage research from scholars at MSIs by creating more accessible publications (see, for example, *Composition Studies*' FEN blog, *Peitho*'s "Recoveries and Reconsiderations" articles, or *Kairos*'s Praxis wiki)—and committing to special issues about MSIs (see, for example, special editions like the *College Composition and Communication* volume 50, issue 4 [1999]; *Reflections* volume 10, issue 2 [2011]; *Composition Studies* volume 44, issue 2 [2016] and 49, issue 2 [2021]; and *Spark*'s volume 2 [2020]). Though well-intentioned, these special issues and alternative publication venues do not solve the underlying problem. Research from scholars of color remains underrepresented, as are research projects that highlight contributions from minoritized students and MSIs. This is problematic because we are failing to learn from the smart work happening at HBCUs, HSIs, and AANAPISIs.

Research at and about MSIs is such an important area of inquiry in writing studies because MSIs purposefully center the literacies of students of color. Academic literacy was traditionally thought of as a right of white people (Prendergast, 2003), and racism has infiltrated the ways we have traditionally taught reading and writing in the academy—especially at PWIs. In "Chicanx/Latinx Rhetorics as Methodology for Writing Program Design at HSIs," Aydé Enríquez-Loya and Kendall Leon (2017) explained: "Many institutional spaces were not designed for students of color. This is especially true in rhetoric and composition programs, perhaps even more so than literary studies, and even truer when we focus on composition programs and their administration" (p. 212). Even once students of color were permitted into academic spaces, the institutions committed "cultural and linguistic genocide" (Love, 2019, p. 28) to those students of color, insisting they perform whiteness as part of their studenthood. Quite frankly, it is no surprise that "simply put, many of our schools function as spaces of dark suffering" (Love, 2019, p. 15). Yet, we do know that inclusive pedagogy can make institutions more equitable for all students (Baca et al., 2019; Jackson & Jackson, 2016). J. Estrella Torrez, for example, suggested that a pedagogy of love (which is theorized and practiced by Chicanx feminists) can create safe spaces that are community- and activist-centered in otherwise hostile academic spaces (2015). MSIs largely enact inclusive pedagogies like this, and research shows that they can be adopted into PWIs with relative success. As such, I hope my work can both celebrate work done at MSIs so that other MSIs can emulate their successes and learn from their struggles while also giving us ideas about how to make PWIs more inclusive spaces.

Southern HBCU, Urban State U, and Rural CC all amplify voices of students of color, as well as showcase a multitude of institutional types. Urban is a PWI and R1 school, but it is also an AANAPISI that welcomes a relatively large percentage of international students; 25% of students at Urban State U reported being Asian, Pacific Islander, or Native, and 15% of students are non-resident aliens. Rural is a community college and an HSI, but it far exceeds the requirements for HSI designation: It is also a Latinx/Chicanx-majority school, with over 80% of students identifying as such. Southern is a mid-size, highly ranked public HBCU, with over 80% of students identifying as Black. Compositionists have repeatedly called for more research on students of color, particularly those who attend MSIs (Kynard & Eddy, 2009), because mainstream scholarship often neglects vital perspectives from students of color, along with the instructors and administrators who serve them (Gasman et al., 2015). Faye Spencer-Maor and Robert Randolph (2016) claimed that "HBCUs are, perhaps, one of the last frontiers for sustained feminist praxis" (p. 179)—and I extend that argument to all MSIs because of their relationship to underrepresented students and teachers of color, along with the goals of the research. Even though research at MSIs is important, what is more complicated is whether it is ethical for me, as a white researcher, to participate in that research—and if so, how to do that work well. I discuss this phenomenon in the next section.

ETHICAL CONSIDERATIONS OF DOING REFLECTION RESEARCH AT MSIS AS A WHITE RESEARCHER

In bell hooks's (2015a) *Ain't I a Woman: Black Women and Feminism*, hooks comments upon the problematic nature of well-meaning white feminists engaging in scholarship about Black women. Using Gerda Lerner (author of *Black Women in White America: A Documentary History*) as an example, hooks agrees that Lerner's research is important but questions whether Lerner should be doing this research. It is possible, hooks posits, that Lerner's research may have just been a way of achieving capital gain rather than genuine interest in the topic matter. Regardless, hooks notes the double standard: white researchers can claim research areas investigating Blackness, but the reverse is rarely true. Hooks writes, "It is significant that in our society white women are given grant money to do research on black women but I can find no instance where black women have received funds to research white women's history" (2015a, p.10). This phenomenon still exists today. White scholars often specialize in and about cultures, literacies, and histories other than their own; yet the reverse is not often true.

As Karen Keaton Jackson, Hope Jackson, and Dawn N. Hicks Tafari recommend, writing studies should do better to support teacher-scholars at HBCUs to be the primary researchers for MSI research—recommending the field work toward increasing funding opportunities for research conducted by HBCU faculty, improving representation of HBCU faculty in national organizations and editorial boards, recruiting HBCU colleagues for coauthoring opportunities and writing support, and supporting HBCU-sponsored professional development. I agree, wholeheartedly, with Jackson et al.'s recommendations to support HBCU scholars and create partnerships with their institutions. Researchers who work at MSIs will have their own unique viewpoints shaped by their lived experiences. Undoubtedly, they will have a better sense of how to develop research that would give not only to the field but to the institutions themselves. It is imperative to support and prioritize MSI-housed researchers doing research at MSIs. In fact, I think writing studies should extend their argument to apply to research practices at MSIs more broadly. Writing studies scholars can and should mobilize for better funding resources and professional support for MSI teacher-scholars in our field and form partnerships with researchers at MSIs.

At the same time, I think that researchers at PWIs who have the research support to have robust research agendas can and should use their position to amplify the voices of students of color and support community-engaged research in marginalized communities. While they do that, they should recognize that their lived experiences shape their standpoint as researchers; the kinds of questions they ask, the methods they select, and the insights they might glean, are all shaped by their worldview. In other words, both things can be true: we can and should support MSI-housed researchers—and we can and should support more research at MSIs, as a field, generally. As an intersectional feminist, I believe it is irresponsible to investigate writing classroom phenomena only within PWI institutions, contributing to the hyper-prevalence of research about PWIs. We need to encourage more research at MSIs—and this research can be done ethically and responsibly when researchers adopt antiracist and reflexive stances. As Frankie Condon discusses at length in *I Hope I Join the Band*, performative antiracist allyship of white scholars is complicated:

> There is work to be done in resistance to racism and there are ways to share the work. But how to be and become an ally is not self-evident. We who are raced white have to learn to unmake our selves in order that we might make allies of ourselves. (Condon, 2012, p. 144)

As Jackson et al. themselves rightfully lament, even with the growing attention to the important conversations about Black literacies, "absent from this conversation in any consistent way are conversations about writing programs at historically black colleges and universities (HBCUs)" (2019, p. 185). Research at MSIs, especially HBCUs, is often underrepresented due to underfunding and intensive teaching and service expectations in these spaces. Yet Jackson et al. highlight why it is imperative that writing studies commits to more research at HBCUs: Researchers developing pedagogy for Black students

> should want to spend extensive time working with faculty and students in majority black classrooms to engage in what Paulo Freire calls true praxis, where the theory and research inform each other's stories from these institutions connecting scholars who do research about students of color with students of color. (p. 207)

To do that work, they encourage "*normative, intentional and long-term dialogue* involving race as well as cross-boundary discourses within the field of composition" (p. 192, emphasis in original).

I agree with these recommendations, and I have tried to take them up in this research project.

Research at MSIs is an important contribution to our growing conversations about antiracism in writing studies. It is in this spirit of antiracist scholarship that I decided to continue with my research plan, continuing to make a concerted effort to ask each school, teacher, and student about how I can give back to them and their community—and follow through. Through creating these connections and fostering relationships, I can best listen to students and teachers involved in the research project about how they want to be represented in the research, how they may want to reframe our relationship as research partners in the future, and how I can give back to the community in the meantime. In the next section, I share who I had the privilege of learning from during this research project.

Focal Participant Overview

Given my site selection, I had a robust group of focal participants to learn from. I was honored to speak with focal participants from a variety of backgrounds and positionalities. Throughout the course of the project, I talked with twenty-five different focal participants, five of whom were teachers and twenty of whom were students (eight from Urban State U, three from Rural CC, and nine from Southern HBCU). Students and teachers across the schools generally showed the various constituencies present at each school with the exception of Rural CC's student population. I only had the opportunity to speak to three white students (albeit local to the area) at Rural; the school is a majority Chicanx, and I had hoped to have a more representative student sample. I'm sure my status as an out-of-area, white researcher whom students have only met on Zoom heavily influenced my ability to connect with students. If the context of when research was collected could have been different, and I could have been present in their classes, I would have hoped to gain the trust of students and make them feel more comfortable participating in the project. This was the case, for example, at Southern. Though only three students volunteered to discuss being focal students on the first day, six more students decided to join the project by the deadline, 3 weeks into the semester. Once I was able to build rapport with students in the classroom, students were more comfortable working with me as focal participants.

In an effort to describe my participants in a way that felt authentic to them, I asked each focal participant to tell me a bit about themself for the purpose of introducing them to the reader of my research project. The table that follows organizes some common trends of the ways that participants described themselves: age range, racial/cultural identity, pronouns, and area of scholarly inquiry. It is important to note that Table 2.1 uses identifiers in the same ways that the participants communicated them to me; the terminology is the participants' own. Throughout the project, I refrained from ever having set questions of my focal participants like: How old are you? Or what is your sexual identity? Asking pointed questions such as these about a participant's demographics felt like an invasion of privacy—a way of boxing them in, like filling out a census form. Instead, I asked focal participants about what they thought

TABLE 2.1. Focal participant overview with basic demographics

Name	Age	Race/Ethnicity	Pronouns	Positionality	Disciplinary interests
URBAN STATE U—CLASS 1					
Kevin	28 y/o	Hispanic	He/Him	Graduate student instructor	Poetry
Conan	18 y/o	Korean American	He/Him	First-year student	Undecided
Mia	18 y/o	Chinese American	She/Her	First-year student	Computer science
Rachel	18 y/o	White	She/Her	First-year student	Psychology
Serena	19 y/o	Chinese American	She/Her	First-year student	Undecided
URBAN STATE U—CLASS 2					
Grace	30 y/o	White	She/Her	Graduate student instructor	Affect theory
Alan	19 y/o	Hispanic	He/Him	First-year student	Mathematics
Autumn	19 y/o	White	She/Her	First-year student	Engineering
Julie	19 y/o	South Asian (Indian)	She/Her	First-year student	Computer science and business
June	19 y/o	South Asian (Indian)	She/Her	First-year student	Business
RURAL CC—CLASS 1					
Jess	32 y/o	Chicanx	She/Her	Full-time lecturer	Chicanx literature and composition
Francis	18 y/o	White	He/Him	First-year student	Undecided
Ryann	18 y/o	White	She/Her	First-year student	Education
RURAL CC—CLASS 2					
Heather	50 y/o	White	She/Her	Tenured faculty	Rhetoric and composition
Jennifer	18 y/o	White	She/Her	First-year student	Nursing
SOUTHERN HBCU—CLASSES 1 AND 2					
L.J.	30 y/o	Black	He/Him	Adjunct faculty	Af. Am. Lit. and Literacy studies

continued on next page

TABLE 2.1.—continued

Name	Age	Race/Ethnicity	Pronouns	Positionality	Disciplinary interests
Angel	18 y/o	Black	She/Her	First-year student	Undecided
Colby	18 y/o	Black	He/Him	First-year student	Sociology
JoAnn	18 y/o	Black	She/Her	First-year student	Undecided
King	18 y/o	Black	He/Him	First-year student	Pre-med
Maya	18 y/o	Black	She/Her	First-year student	Pre-med
Miles	20 y/o	Black	He/Him	Third-year student	Engineering
Paris	19 y/o	Black	She/Hers	Second-year student	Psychology
Tracy	19 y/o	Black	She/Hers	Second-year student	Accounting
Vanessa	18 y/o	Black	She/Hers	First-year student	Music

would be important for the audience of this research to know. I wanted them to decide if and how they would represent their multifaceted identities—and I wanted them to do that in ways that felt like ethical and accurate descriptions. All of us hold identities as teachers and students—identities that come into play as students, teachers, writers, and reflectors in the FYW context. Below is an overview of the participants that I was lucky to work with (all of whom are identified by a pseudonym, in accordance with the IRB).

Table 2.1 gives a brief snapshot of the identities of focal participants. Three of the five teachers identified as people of color (e.g., identifying themselves as Black, Chicanx, and Hispanic), while the other two self-identified as white. Five students identified as white, and the remainder were students of color (one Hispanic, ten Black, three Asian American, and two Indian international students). The focal teachers represented the breadth of writing instructor positionalities: adjunct, GSI, lecturer, and tenured faculty. Most of the focal students were 1st-year students, but they ranged in intended disciplinary focus (e.g., five students with STEM majors, three students on the pre-med/nursing track, three "undecided" students, three students interested in social science fields, two business-school-hopeful students, one educator, and one music major). Though students did not readily disclose their gender identities, participants overwhelmingly used femme-identifying pronouns, a few used masc-identifying pronouns, and no one selected "they/their" to signal gender nonbinary identities.

In addition to what is organized in the table, many participants shared things like their hobbies, athletic background, sexuality, family structure, economic background, and hometown. Focal participants came from all geographical areas in the United States (e.g., the West, the Midwest, the Southwest, the Southeast, and the Northeast). I also had two international students from India. About two-thirds of focal students mentioned being first-generation US citizens, multilingual or multidialectal speakers, first-generation students, or some combination of those identities. Four focal participants mentioned that they were part of the LGBTQ+ community. Three identified as being neurologically atypical and one identified as having a physical disability. Generally, participants represented a variety of different socioeconomic upbringings and family backgrounds (e.g., different relationships to caregivers, number of living caregivers, marital status of caregivers, number of siblings). I've decided not to list every quality that I learned about them because, like my participants, I worry about their privacy. Instead, I will share generalities about participants important to the collective group, with permission from the participants.

Across participants, hobbies seemed to play a role in their relationship with reflection. Religious participants talked about the ways their experiences influenced how they reflected in prayer, religious services, or religious practices. One self-identified Christian participant, for example, talked about how their daily prayers made them understand reflection as a way of seeing how they could make the world a better place. A self-identified Buddhist participant talked about the ways their religious views shifted how they saw reflection as being integral to the interconnectedness of the living and spiritual realm. Students who enjoyed music tended to have a genre that inspired reflection; one mentioned classical music while another mentioned rap. Exercise, like rowing or weightlifting, seemed to play a role in the ways that students found time to let their mind wander. The hobbies they shared with others (e.g., sharing a phone call with a parent as they walked to class) seemed instrumental too.

Despite the swath of focal students that I was grateful to talk to, I did miss a subsection of our students that would be incredibly interesting to learn from: Students resistant to reflection. It makes sense that these students are not represented; even though I encouraged focal student participation with incentives like free tutoring and monetary compensation, resistant reflectors may not want to talk to someone who is so clearly invested in the reflective process. This leaves me with lingering questions: Can resistant reflectors be converted into active reflectors if they see new benefits to the practice? Does the resistance of some reflectors shift the potential reflective practices of those around them? In failing to talk with self-identified people who resist reflection, I am unable to consider these questions (and others like them). In the section that follows, I overview what I did learn from these focal students about where and how they practiced reflection.

Also important to the work of reflection was the relationship that participants had with writing or reflection. About 60% of the participants saw themselves as reflective, purposefully making time to practice it daily, weekly, or biweekly. For example, they pointed to moments like talking to a mentor, teacher, friend, or family member about choices or goals; internal mental exercises like meditating, praying, and introspection; and various hobbies (e.g., baking, cleaning, walking, yoga, journaling, listening to music) that they used for reflective activity. The remainder were more apt to reflect when the situation emerged but did not set time aside for the activity specifically.

All teachers saw themselves as reflective in some capacity and tried to incorporate reflection into their pedagogy, which made sense given that they allowed me in the classroom space daily (which was such a big ask; what a debt I owe them). The student participants were much more mixed. I think that future researchers can and should make themselves more approachable throughout the research to solicit insight into the reasons that folks are resistant to reflection. Perhaps they could (and should) target talking to teachers who are resistant to reflective activity to see how that identity shapes their reflective practice in the writing classroom. Could an instructor resistant to reflection still provide moments suitable for students to take up reflection in their classroom? Despite these shortcomings, I think that the methodologies of the project, discussed in the next section, work to give a thorough analysis of the intricacies of how students and teachers take up reflective activity in their everyday moments.

Methodology Overview

Upon engaging in daily observations, focal participant interview, and whole class surveys, I selected feminist storytelling as my methodology for this project. Feminist methodologies, more broadly, are particularly well-suited for this project because they "[intervene] by asking what if? What if we approach the questions that guide our work differently? Or what if we ask different questions entirely?" (Blair & Nickoson, 2018, p. 3). Feminist storytelling in particular is especially helpful because it allows for me to more fully represent how participants defined, identified, and practiced reflection in the daily happenings of their writing classes. The next section details the methodology.

FEMINIST STORYTELLING AS METHODOLOGY

Storytelling is an increasingly popular methodology among feminist scholars because it disrupts the academic/personal binary that feminists often find themselves in (Hesford, 1990, p. 20). I choose to engage in storytelling because it allows for the inclusion of life histories and personal accounts in research. Feminist scholars Rosa de Nooijer and Lillian Sol Cueva explain feminist storytelling as a methodology in their chapter of *Feminist Methodologies: Experiments, Collaborations and Reflections* (de Nooijer & Sol Cueva, 2022). De Nooijer and Cueva's chapter, entitled "Feminist Storytellers Imagining New Stories to Tell," explains how storytelling is a culturally rooted and multimodal phenomenon: "Storytelling is a customary practice of transmitting histories, knowledges and cosmologies and has historically been done in various ways" (p. 233). When taken up by feminist researchers as a methodology, storytelling becomes "a way to challenge dominant narratives which erase, oversimplify and universalize women's voices and experiences" (p. 234). In de Nooijer and Cueva's work, they specifically name stories about women as emblematic of feminist methodology, but not all feminist researchers nor all who engage in feminist storytelling as methodology agree that feminist researchers use this methodology for women and women alone. In the introduction of the edited collection that de Nooijer and Cueva's chapter is a part of, editors Constance Dupuis, Wendy Harcourt, Jacqueline Gaybor, and Karijn van den Berg explain that feminist methodologies are used for more than women and/or feminist agendas. Researchers can use feminist methodologies with a range of research participants and for a variety of research goals; they explain simply: "Feminist methodologies are thus engaged as counter-narratives to dominant traditional models of research and science, as well as through foregrounding the experiential and embodied nature of doing research" (Dupuis et al., 2022, p. 4).

Storytelling, generally, is often done to highlight the stories of the underrepresented—often written as autobiographical narratives from scholars and/or students of color in rhetoric and composition. Although incorporating methods that invite the personal was historically frowned upon, there is growing acceptance of personal writing and narrative methods in contemporary scholarship (Spigelman, 2001, p. 67). The rise in the adoption of ethnographic methods in the 1980s allowed researchers to deeply contextualize their data and be more attuned to how identity shaped their findings—and this in turn made room for methodologies that incorporated narratives. This has been especially true among antiracist and feminist researchers in rhetoric and composition. As Kaisa Ilmonen writes simply, "Storytelling is a focal part of any critical work" (2020, p. 347). One such method is counterstory, which Aja Martinez explains as both a method and methodology in *Counterstory: The Rhetoric and Writing of Critical Race Theory*. Martinez credits counterstory as "a methodology in scholarly publications" that emerged from critical race theorist Richard Delgado as a way for "minoritized people to intervene in research methods that would form 'master narratives' based on ignorance and assumptions about minoritized people" (2020, p. 21). Martinez traces the emergence of counterstory in rhetoric and composition, all while giving a tutorial about how to invoke such methodologies. Another method, what April Baker-Bell calls "Black feminist–womanist storytelling" in "For Loretta: A Black Woman Literacy Scholar's Journey to Prioritizing Self-Preservation and Black Feminist–Womanist Storytelling" (2017), is

> a methodology that weaves together autoethnography, the African American female language and literacy tradition, Black feminist/womanist theories, and storytelling to create an approach that provides Black women with a method for collecting our stories, writing our stories, analyzing our stories, and theorizing our stories at the same time as healing from them. (p. 531)

Storytelling can be an especially useful methodology for academics of the global majority, who often invoke personal narrative and autoethnographic reflective writing as a "hush space" (Kynard, 2010) to cope with the field's overwhelming privileging of whiteness. Storytelling too can be a way that white researchers engage in self-reflexivity in allyship. As Aja Martinez writes, using Frankie Condon as an example, "Whites can and do tell counterstories" (Martinez, 2014, p. 51).

In my work, I hope storytelling can function like a counterstory to traditional understandings of reflection because they work to "cast doubt on the validity of accepted premises or myths, especially ones held by the majority" (Delgado & Stefancic, 2001, p. 144).

My goal in taking up storytelling as methodology is to share what reflection meant according to my participants, which at times affirmed traditional understandings of reflection, but also complicated and pushed against mainstream understandings of the practice as well. As Robert Nash and Sydnee Viray (2013) discuss in *Our Stories Matter*,

> Throughout recent history, feminist, queer, and critical race theorists have used narrative to create visibility for the underrepresented; to break the silence and shame surrounding the identities of the "outsiders"; and to promote a collective voice among "outsiders" in the academy. (p. 35)

This gave me the flexibility of attending to the nuances of my students' identities and more holistically represent the complex stories they shared with me. It too was beneficial for evoking a clearer image of what reflection looked and felt like, according to my research participants. It also attended to "the dynamics and difficulties created by living in and moving through relationships and communities stratified by intersecting systems of injustice" (Guy-Sheftall, 1995, p. 103). Telling stories is important because "students' responses in classrooms are always conditioned by their social and cultural backgrounds and the institutions in which they express themselves" (Kynard 2016, p. 128). My goal in using storytelling as feminist methodology is to explain how the complex relationships between human and nonhuman agents, emotions, histories, futures, and sensorial input shaped and reshaped reflective activity. I took special care not to flatten the rhetorical situations from which reflection emerged, or worse yet, lose the complexity of my participants' contributions to our understandings of the rhetoricity of reflection.

Though storytelling is now a generally accepted feminist methodology, it emerged as a Black feminist practice. As Sarojini Nadar explains in "Stories are Data With Soul—Lessons From Black Feminist Epistemology" (2014), "the epistemological foundations of African and Black intellectualism have always been based on narrative" (p. 22). Black feminists have commonly engaged in storytelling because of its value on the personal but also because of its readability. bell hooks (2013) explained, "If I wanted to write theory, especially feminist theory that would be read across the boundaries of race, gender, class, and educational levels, I would need to provide a common entry point" (p. 51). That entry point was often narrative writing. Black feminists gravitated toward storytelling as method because there is a deep-rooted history of oral storytelling in African American rhetoric. In *Digital Griots: African American Rhetoric in a Multimedia Age*, Adam Banks (2010) detailed the history of griots, or storytellers in Western Africa that traveled to villages with songs of historical accounts, contemporary news, and political commentary. He argues that

African American rhetoric has always been influenced by oral storytelling. Western Africans were not alone in this tradition: Each group in Africa had a name for a storyteller (e.g., "Akewi" for the Yoruba, "Moroka" for the Hausa, "Imbongi" for the Xhosa). When white Europeans enslaved Africans and brought them to the United States, Africans brought with them oral storytelling traditions of their homelands, at times adapting stories to meet their new rhetorical situation or creating new stories. In fact, African Americans used this kind of storytelling as a form of advice-giving, remembrance, and resistance during slavery. Black storytelling is still popular today; As Gwendelon Pough argued in "Personal Narratives and Rhetorics of Black Womanhood in Hip-Hop" (2004), storytelling is a rhetorical tradition in contemporary hip-hop performances by Black women.

Feminist storytelling as a methodology is broadly practiced as a feminist methodology because Black women are not alone in their use of storytelling as literacy practice. *Testimonio*, for example, is a reflective genre of writing with roots in Latin America (Menchú, 1984/2010) and often taken up as a Chicanx/Latinx feminist methodology (Latina Feminist Group, 2001). In Mónica González Ybarra's "Testimoniando: Chicana/Latina Feminist Reflections on Embodied Knowledge, Literacies, And Narrating the Self," Ybarra explained that testimonio is "a critical literacy practice that reveals what has been silenced and unseen within marginalized communities" (2022, p. 255). Testimonio is the "text" and "testimoniando" is "the practice of sharing and generating testimonios" (Ybarra, 2022, p. 251). Though testimonios typically document personal experiences, the stories shared connect to overarching sociopolitical concerns to show a humanized perspective of the problem (Delgado et al., 2012)—and the sharing of testimonios works to inspire activism and change (Brabeck, 2003). Testimonio works to disrupt Westernized ways of knowing and doing because it moves "beyond quantitative versus qualitative methods" (Delgado, 1998, p. 555) by granting power to the person's personal experience, validating it as important data (Cruz, 2012). As Christina Kirklighter explained in the foreword to *Latina Leadership: Language and Literacy Education across Communities* (Gonzales & Kells, 2022), Latinx people have been "excluded" from academic spaces and thus the tradition of testimonio has been too; its incorporation will make "academic research and writing so much more powerful, accurate, knowledgeable, and honest" (Kirklighter, 2022, p. xii).

Throughout this book, then, I take up storytelling as feminist methodology—all while acknowledging and honoring the rich histories of storytelling that came before me. I hope that in doing so I can share the rich and nuanced ways that my research participants experience reflection. My goal in sharing these stories is to paint the robust settings from which reflection emerged and to honor what participants said and did—sharing that as I saw them. I hope, as well, that storytelling can help me recount the stories about reflection shared with me as they were told, not just with their words but with their bodies. In the next section, I discuss the history of taking feminist methods and methodologies in composition and rhetoric—especially intersectional and/or Black feminist qualitative research practices.

RHETORIC AND COMPOSITION—AND FEMINIST METHODS AND METHODOLOGIES

"Feminism" is a slippery term, but one used often in academia—especially when describing participant-centered methodologies. "Feminism" emerged from the French word *féminisme*, associated with French suffragists in 1805 (Baumgardner & Richards 2020). Though we typically describe feminism as an activist movement with first, second, and third waves—beginning with the US suffragist movement—it "configures a story that honors the lives and activities of white, middle-class, (presumed) heterosexual women in the Global North and overlooks the activities of women situated otherwise" (McCann et al. 2021, p. 8). Instead, contemporary feminists tend to see feminism as a transnational movement that works toward the equity of all people; or, as bell hooks puts it succinctly, "Simply put, feminism is a movement to end sexism, sexist exploitation, and oppression" (2015b, p. 1).

Rhetoric and composition have been influenced by feminism and its theories since the inception of our field (Stenberg, 2015). "Feminism has long been interested in bridging theory with practice" (Kafer, 2013, p. 15), so it is unsurprising that feminist teachers started considering how to bring their feminist values in the classroom. It was not until the 1970s, though, that feminism explicitly entered the academy under the guise of women's and gender studies departments (Sullivan, 1992, p. 37). At around the same time, composition and rhetoric scholars were increasingly frustrated by the sexism in the field and repeated feminization of writing studies (Miller, 1991). In 1972, for example, Janet Emig published an "Open Letter from Janet Emig, Chairwoman, NCTE Committee on the Role and Image of Women," in attempts to encourage women teacher/scholars to testify about any discrimination they faced within the discipline and the academy at large as well as encourage readers to nominate themselves or others for the committee that would fight against these inequities. Meanwhile, feminist scholars in rhetoric and composition were increasingly interested in recovering feminist rhetoricians, honoring women's ways of knowing and doing, and incorporating feminist theories into their pedagogies.

Two complementary and often overlapping subfields emerged: feminist rhetorics and feminist composition pedagogies. In the hopes of mentoring scholars in the emerging field, Kathleen Ethel Welch gathered colleagues Marjorie Currie Woods, Winifred Bryan Horner, Nan Johnson, and C. Jan Swearingen to create an organization aimed at mentoring feminist scholars in rhetoric and composition; together, they created and signed the constitution for the Coalition of Feminist Scholars in the History of Rhetoric and Composition (CFSHRC) in 1989. CFSHRC has become increasingly influential in rhetoric and composition writ large, sponsoring a mentoring network, Feminisms and Rhetorics Conference, a peer reviewed journal (*Peitho*), and an annual meeting at the College Composition and Communication Conference (Enoch & Fishman, 2015). Though some scholars focus on recoveries and reconsiderations of the rhetorical canon, putting their energy into contributions for rhetorical theory and practice, many rhetorical feminists are interested in feminist pedagogy. As Glenn explains in the "Pedagogy" section of her *Rhetorical Feminism and This Thing Called Hope* (2018), "For rhetorical feminists, teaching is hope embodied. It is a forward-looking endeavor, one that has power to change lives—our own, our students'. To pretend otherwise is irresponsible" (p. 125). Feminist pedagogy has always been central to feminist rhetorical work.

Feminist rhetoricians added to the growing scholarship among feminist compositionists (see, for example, *College English*'s special issues in 1971 and 1972). It was not until "the late 1980s," though, that "a regular, visible presence" of feminist composition emerged in rhetoric and composition (Stenberg, 2015, p. 27). Pamela J. Annas's 1985 "Style as Politics: A Feminist Approach to the Teaching of Writing" and Elizabeth Flynn's "Composing as a Woman" (1988) were immensely popular examples of emerging feminist composition scholarship. The late 1980s seemed to be a watershed moment for an influx of feminist pedagogy publications that continued the next decade (Ritchie & Boardman, 1999)—and many of these publications began using research methods and methodologies that they identified as "feminist."

When selecting research methods and analytical tools in this project, I gravitated toward intersectional and/or Black feminist methods and methodologies because I thought they could most ethically tell the stories of my participants. Kimberlé Crenshaw, a Black feminist theorist, coined the term "intersectionality" in 1989 as an analytic for lawmakers, but it has been taken up as a theoretical concept adopted by feminist researchers who want to attend to the identities of their research participants (Crenshaw, 1989). Crenshaw used the term "intersectionality" as a way of accounting for the ways that Black women faced their own forms of oppression, distinct from white women or Black men. At the time, Black women could either file discrimination lawsuits based on their gender or their race, but not as their unique positionality as Black women. Though Crenshaw coined the term, intersectionality is not the brainchild of Crenshaw alone; it is "a term rooted in black women's intellectual production" (Nash, 2019, p. 2).

Black feminist rhetors have articulated their unique forms of oppression historically; bell hooks lovingly refers to Sojourner Truth, Anna Cooper, and Mary Church Terrell as the "19th century sisters" (Hull et al. 1982/2015, p. 196) that lay the foundation for Black feminist thought. Black feminists like Frances Beal, who discussed "double jeopardy" in 1969 to explain what it was like to be a Black woman, and Deborah King, who discussed "multiple jeopardy" to explain how Black women experienced discrimination relating to other identifiers as well, made way for intersectional feminism. Yet, as the editors of the canonical Black feminist text *But Some of Us Are Brave* explain, "Because of white women's racism and Black men's sexism, there was no room in either area for a serious consideration of the lives of Black women" (Hull et al. 1982/2015, p. xxi).

In the 1970s and 1980s, feminism saw a proliferation of publications from women of color calling out mainstream feminism for ignoring the positionalities of women of color (see, for example, work by June Jordan, Audre Lorde, Alice Walker, Gloria Anzaldúa, and the Combahee River Collective). In closing remarks given at the National Women's Studies Association Convention, Barbara Smith challenged her colleagues to do better, saying,

> The reason racism is a feminist issue is easily explained by the inherent definition of feminism. Feminism is the political theory and practice that struggles to free all women: women of color, working class women, poor women, disabled women, lesbians, old women—as well as white, economically privileged, heterosexual women. Anything less than this vision of total freedom is not feminism, but merely female self-aggrandizement. (Smith, 1980, p. 48)

Mainstream feminist movements centered white women's issues and civil rights movements centered racism, but neither met the needs of Black women. Crenshaw hoped to explain how Black women's unique positionality made them oppressed in ways that neither white women nor Black men could quite understand.

Since its coining in 1989, intersectionality has largely been taken up by the feminist movement, propelled by coalitions of women of color—Indigenous feminists and Chicanx feminists, as well as feminists coming together in organizations (e.g., the Combahee River Collective) or publications (e.g., *This Bridge Called My Back*)—to disrupt the white hegemony of mainstream feminism. This makes sense because Chicanx feminists, like Gloria Anzaldúa, have "always been intersectional" (Hurtado, 2020, p. 29) despite never using the term. In fact, Hurtado argues "borderlands theory expanded intersectionality by incorporating social identity theory as embodied in the master statuses of gender, class, sexuality, ethnicity, race, and physical ableness" (p. 148). Intersectional feminists, generally, acknowledge that all too often women who fell outside the identities of white, upper-class, able-bodied, and cisgender were pressured to ignore parts of themselves to join a movement that at times actively attacked identities they held. Intersectional feminism hopes to center feminists of color—and their theoretical and methodological contributions. It is somewhat complicated, though, to take up these methods and methodologies authentically as a white researcher. I explore this phenomenon in the next section.

ETHICAL CONSIDERATIONS OF ADOPTING BLACK FEMINIST AND/OR INTERSECTIONAL FEMINIST METHODOLOGIES AS A WHITE RESEARCHER

It may be hard for some readers to believe that I can take up intersectional feminist methods or methodologies ethically. There is a general distrust of white women among feminists of color because "White Womanhood has functioned as the maternal arm of empire" (Hamad, 2020, p. 235). In *White Tears/Black Scars: How White Feminism Betrays Women of Color* (2020), Ruby Hamad detailed the ways that white women have played a role in naming Black men as sexual assailants, serving as catalysts for murder in the name of white supremacy. This is not just a phenomenon in the United States but globally.

It is not just white women that are suspect; white feminists themselves are culpable for enacting dangerous racist rhetorics throughout history. In *From the Suffragettes to Influencers and Who They Leave Behind*, Koa Beck (2022) deftly explains white feminism, or the feminism embodied by white, privileged women who so often centered their own concerns at the detriment of feminists of color and marginalized people. Kyla Schuller, for example, details the ways that famous white feminists, often lauded only for their "accomplishments," held deeply racist, classist, homophobic, and ablest views that they not only espoused but worked toward affirming (2021). Elizabeth Cady Stanton, for example, invoked white fear by encouraging white men to vote for women's suffrage so that they could quiet newly enfranchised Black men. Though known for her organizing for access to birth control, Margaret Sanger was a racist eugenicist who hoped to curtail reproduction of marginalized populations. It was not just as if these women were the only racist white feminists; they were simply the most egregious racist white feminists. These are just two examples from her long, detailed, and persuasive history of white supremacist values supported by white feminists. Over and over again, mainstream feminism in the United States prioritized concerns of white, privileged women. Though this is but one book detailing this history in depth, scholars of color have been concerned about this phenomenon throughout the feminist movement—perhaps the most popularly known of which is the 1977 Combahee River Collective Statement. Most recently, Mikki Kendall detailed white feminism's persistent exclusion of women of color's needs and values in *Hood Feminism: Notes from the Women that a Movement Forgot* (2020). Her book works as a sort of manifesto outlining the needs of poor women of color, who are often ignored; Kendall provides explanations of why feminisms should organize activism about the rights of sex workers, elimination of food deserts, the racism embedded in beauty standards, the sexualization of girls of color, the maternal health needs of women of color (e.g., the increased maternal mortality rates, forced sterilizations, and inadequate preventive care measures), gun safety, housing insecurity, and more. Upon doing so, Kendall concludes, "the fundamental problem with white feminism has always been that it refuses to admit that the primary goal is shifting power to white women" (2020, p. 256).

Given feminism's whitewashing, and especially my own positionality as a white woman who is therefore a white feminist, I feel it is imperative to pause here and say: I understand the hesitancy in hearing that I, a white woman, can really employ an intersectional and/or Black feminist method or methodology. And, the truth is, I can only promise that I take up self-reflexivity as a constant practice to check in with my success of using these research practices authentically. I read broadly from intersectional and Black feminist theorists to understand the intersectional feminist theories that underpin my methodologies. Like Inoue, I am wary of the "white racial habitus" of the field, or what "might be thought of as a dominant set of durable and flexible dispositions to read and write in English" (Inoue, 2016). Intersectional and Black feminist methods and methodologies can help me be aware of my own white racial habitus (which I inhabit as a default standpoint as a white woman), as well as the field's—especially by helping me re-see the literature through a new light, which is an affordance of feminist method, more broadly (Sullivan, 1992, p. 41).

Intersectional and Black feminist methods and methodologies can also help me avoid white, Western, and masculinist values. As Jacqueline Jones Royster and Gesa Kirsch surmise, feminist research methodologies, or "the guiding assumptions and theoretical principles that underlie all research," influence "what counts as data, how we gather and interpret data, what role researchers play in relation to participants, what ethical stance they assume, and so on" (Royster & Kirsch, 2012, p. 29). Reflection—with its deeply sedimented, hegemonic rhetorics—is especially ripe for feminist intervention. In Jennifer Enoch's interview of Cheryl Glenn, Glenn argues that "feminist questions" can help scholars "rethink traditional topics" (Enoch, 2014). In *Rhetorical Feminism and This Thing Called Hope*, Glenn explicitly calls for more research on the rhetorical traditions of "silence and listening," like the site of "reflection," because of its potential to show how rhetoric is for more than the power of persuasion (2018, p. 83).

Throughout my data collection, I was (and still am) concerned about falling into the trap of the "white feminist," or "someone who refuses to consider the role that whiteness and the racial privilege attached to it have played and continue to play in universalizing white feminist concerns, agendas, and beliefs as being those of all feminism and all feminists" (Zakaria, 2021, p. 1). My research methods and methodologies are not intersectional just because I adopt a Black feminist qualitative methodology. I lean into Patricia Hill Collins's sentiment when she says that "nothing in a research methodology is inherently white or black, male or female. Certain methodologies can be coded as white and/or male and thus work to disadvantage Black women" (Collins, 2000, p. 297). I worried about coming into MSIs as an observer, oblivious to my whiteness. I worried about the ways that my research might be voyeuristic—with more gain for me than for the communities that I was observing. It is my responsibility as a feminist researcher to be ethical and reflexive, regardless of the methods that I took up.

Because of that, I think it is important to be transparent: I still worry about the voyeuristic qualities of this research. I, as a white compositionist, purposefully went out to learn from and with students and teachers of color at MSIs. I did so with good intentions: I wanted to highlight the stories of students of color, especially at institutions that are underrepresented in our field. And yet, I still profited off the labor of Black and Brown students. This book ultimately is much more beneficial for me than whatever they got out of this project. Like I shared in one of the stories at the beginning of the chapter, a student at Southern specifically called me out on it. His question ("Are we the only HBCU you're looking at?") still sits with me. Though I tried to mitigate the risks for my students and emphasize the reciprocity of this research, it might not be enough. The students that agreed to be focal students are not representative of all the students at MSIs. Sometimes participants will refuse research because of the colonizers' gaze (Paris & Winn, 2013). Though I constantly pushed myself—asking questions like How can research be more inclusive, more accessible, and more ethical?—and made changes accordingly, I readily admit that there are flaws in my study. There is an unavoidable and problematic power relationship learning from MSIs as a white researcher. Even if I have good intentions—I hope to disrupt the way we look at reflection so we can serve all students—I am still using my privilege as a white, tenure-track professor to capitalize on the contributions of people of color.

One way I addressed this very real problem was avoiding being, as April Baker-Bell (2020) so candidly wrote, another "hit it and quit it researcher" (p. 141) where I capitalized off Black and Brown knowledge and then left the community. I tried to make relationships with students, so that they might take me up on my offer to reach out throughout their academic careers whenever they needed an extra eye on writing or mentoring. I always prioritized giving back to my research participants—at first with time and later (when I was financially secure) with money. I purposefully tried to include them in how they were identified and represented in the book. I asked participants to share only what they felt comfortable with, I shared my chapters with all those interested so they could provide input and make corrections, and I shared with them my own experiences with reflection—many of which I have included in this book, as a way of acknowledging how deeply personal reflection is and what a trusting act it is to share these stories. I also tried to write this so that teachers, students, and the broader communities that they came from could find this book engaging and accessible. In other words, I tried to act with an "ethic of personal accountability" (Collins, 2000, p. 265). I conclude, next, with implications of incorporating these methods and methodologies for reflection research.

Conclusion: Implications of Intersectional and/or Black Feminist Methods and Methodologies for Reflection Research

This chapter explains the methods and methodologies of this research project. As discussed in the previous chapter, all too often composition researchers have determined what reflection is and where it exists in the writing classroom, largely focusing on retrospective, written texts. In doing so, we have been unable to learn how students and teachers name, identify, and practice reflection through their daily interactions in class. We know, though, that reflection can move across genres and modalities (Fiscus, 2017). Michael Neal (2016) explained, for example, that reflection often "appears in written form, but it's also contemplative, visual, spatial, gestural, or multimodal" (p. 65). Past research methods have largely included qualitative research methods: Researchers tend to isolate specific texts as exemplary reflective activity, and then analyze those texts and/or interview reflectors about those texts. Instead, the intersectional and Black feminist methods and methodologies in this project put an emphasis on the experience of the participants: Their personal experience is valued and accepted as relevant and important insight into understanding what is named, identified, and practiced as reflection. As Jennifer Esposito and Venus Evans-Winters explained, "Intersectionality takes as a core claim that lived experiences are important sources of data" (2022, p. 27). This project follows in that tradition of valuing personal experiences by engaging in both sensory ethnography of daily happenings in class and interviews of research participants.

Researchers often adopt critical lenses for research in the composition; theories of alterity and difference (e.g., critical race theory, feminist theory, disability theory, queer theory) are important theoretical lenses for composition research because they push against normative assumptions and allow for new conclusions. Feminist research methods have been instrumental in understanding pedagogical practices differently. In *Integrating Mindfulness into Anti-Oppression Pedagogy: Social Justice in Higher Education*, for example, Beth Berila (2015) links feminist pedagogy and antiracist pedagogy as intersecting pedagogical strategies that are often used in conjunction with one another in "diversity classrooms" (p. 154). One such intersection is the incorporation of "self-reflection and critical analysis" (2015, p. 154). As Berila (2015) explained,

> Feminist and anti-oppression pedagogy mark self-reflection as a central ingredient for a transformational learning process. In this context, self-reflection usually means examining our own positionality

> in society, our role(s) in power systems, and an evaluation of how issues affect our personal lives. (p. 20)

This kind of reflexivity emphasizes the ways that individuals have played a part in systemic oppression—and how our systems of oppression influence our lives. Reflection is most frequently defined as a way of explaining writerly choices, so researchers have been apt to use that definition to shape their selection of reflection. Yet, other theorists have connected reflection to critical thinking about ideologies and critical self-awareness—qualities essential to antiracist pedagogy. In *I Hope I Join the Band* (2012), for example, Frankie Condon wrote: "There is no antiracism with deliberation without reflection, without self-examination and critique" (p. 10). As a feminist researcher and pedagogue, this potential rhetorical effect was particularly exciting to me because antiracist and feminist pedagogies have similar goals and strategies.

Though the primary goal of this project is to hear how reflective practitioners define, identify, and practice reflection, I do think that this project can seek to enlighten others about reflection's emancipatory potential. Horst Rittel and Melvin Webber (1973) noted that some problems are so complex (like racism, sexism, classism, and phobia) that they are "wicked problems," reliant on so many interdependent and layered beliefs, laws, and ideologies that they are difficult, if not impossible, to solve. Working through these kinds of wicked problems requires a first step of awareness of them as problems; often they are so ingrained in society that it is difficult to see or disrupt them. Reflection helps illuminate these wicked problems through rhetorical listening, or "a stance of openness that a person may choose to assume in relation to any person, text, or culture" (Ratcliffe, 2005, p. 1). This kind of openness can help develop rhetorical empathy, which is a process of "considering motives behind speech acts and actions; engaging in reflection and self-critique; addressing difference, power, and embodiment" (Blankenship, 2019, p. 20). Since rhetorical empathy is a possible rhetorical effect of reflection, reflection can be antiracist; it can have a capacity for social justice. To me, then, in leaving the bounds of what "counts" as reflection up to the practitioners of the rhetorical activity itself, I have made space for a more capacious understanding of reflection: one that has the potential to illuminate the antiracist potential of reflection but is not required to. In the next section, I explain how I weave all the findings from this research project together via storytelling as feminist methodology.

3
Reflection-in-Motion

Emerging Rhetorics of Reflection Within the Writing Classroom

May 2021—Rural CC

I finish Parker's naptime routine, rush up the stairs to the guest room with the baby monitor in hand, plop down on my stomach on the bed, and open Zoom. I carefully select a background. The colorful bookcase that I chose makes it look like I might be leaning forward on my arms, sitting in a position that is a little closer to the camera than what's flattering. I know it is super awkward and unprofessional to be lying down in an interview, but like many during Covid-19, I'm making do with my complex working reality. I'm hiding from a child who is stuck at home with me because of childcare closures, and the guest room is the only option (despite not having a desk). Meanwhile, I'm suffering from an injury: a hip labral tear from Parker's birth. I cannot sit longer than a few minutes unless I'm on ice (something I do not have access to upstairs).

I feel so embarrassed as I get ready for my interview, waiting for Jess to enter the waiting room. I check the time and realize I have a few minutes yet. So, I try to shake my nerves (and, frankly, my embarrassment) aside. The methods of this project have had to shift dramatically since I started at Urban U. I've gone from in-person meetings in a cramped TA office to a Zoom meeting recorded from an actual bed.

https://doi.org/10.7330/9781646426942.c003

As I hear Zoom "ding" to indicate I have someone in the waiting room, I quickly ensure my video only shows a too-close version of my face and let Jess in the meeting room. Jess looks much more professional and put together than me. She wears her typical teaching ensemble: an oversized punk band T-shirt, fashionable winged eyeliner, and some sterling silver artisan earrings that peek out of her overgrown pixie cut. (Jess later tells me that she's taken to cutting her hair herself during the pandemic, and it's hard to keep up with it.) She smiles, waves, and says, "Welcome to my office!"

I smile and appraise her background. Jess is surrounded by her real home office, no telltale blurriness of choppy outlines around her hair when she moves. Jess's books—both for pleasure and for school—pepper the bookshelves behind her. Interspersed with her wide-ranging book collection, Jess has various fun pops of color; Chicanx art, a Mexican flag, Funko figurines of Black and Brown superheroes, and a Progress Pride flag are easily visible among her reading materials. Her two dogs are playing on the floor with a toy behind her.

"Thanks for having me over," I say cheekily, and we both laugh. We exchange our pleasantries, and then we get down to business. I remind her of the project methodology: We will be meeting three times throughout the semester via Zoom; all our conversations will be recorded.

Jess and I start our interview with get-to-know-you questions. I tell her that one of the things that is important to me as a researcher is that I be able to create a picture for my readers that represents how they view themselves as a person. I explain that I will start first by modeling what I would want to share about myself so that readers could picture me. I say:

> I'm a 30-something-year-old woman who walks through the world with an incredible amount of privilege, appearing straight, cisgendered, and able-bodied. I'm queer and neurodivergent, but those identities are largely invisible to most. I'm married to a super loving and supportive husband who moved to Tallahassee for my job. He's a Black man, working in tech, and living in a small city in the South, which is a huge sacrifice for him. Together, we've built a little family together with our two dogs and our daughter, Parker, who was born about a year ago. She is the absolute light of our lives. I identify primarily as a mom right now, as I'm the primary caregiver in our home at the moment—and it's by far the best, hardest, and most important job that I've ever had. I'm also a feminist and antiracist compositionist. I'm an assistant professor at Florida State, and my favorite part is

teaching our super thoughtful students in our undergrad and grad programs.

I pause for a breath after speaking my truths. Perhaps I overshared a bit, but I did so purposefully. I wanted to honor how incredibly personal it is to talk about reflection; I acknowledged that by giving of myself too. "So, that's me," I conclude. "How about you?" I ask. Then I rush to qualify, "You totally don't have to share the same things about yourself that I did, but you could if that felt right. What do you think is important for the audience to know?"

Jess smiles and says,

> Like you, I'm in my 30s. I am Chicana, ethnically and culturally. And, racially, I'm a white mestiza. I don't think my students see me as straight; I'm a very queer person who happens to be married to a man. I'm proud to be a teacher in the community that I grew up in. Rural CC is not just a school that I went to, but an integral part of the neighborhood that I grew up in.

She pauses, and I echo back what she's said to me, confirming I understand what she'd like to share.

Then, I say, "So you're both a native to the area and a lecturer at Rural. Tell me more."

Her tone is earnest, thankful even, when she starts talking about her job at Rural.

> Teaching at Rural is my dream job. I was a PhD student, ABD [all but dissertation], when I saw the job posting here. Even though I wasn't done with my diss[ertation] yet, I applied because I always wanted to go back to my hometown after graduation. I actually went to Rural as a [dual enrollment] student, and being a student here gave me the confidence I needed to apply to college. I only applied to one—and that was after a lot of encouragement from faculty here. I knew that I really wanted to get back home after grad school, and I especially wanted to give back to the school that made such an impact on me.

I congratulate her on landing her dream job. I also add that I think her students too are lucky to have her: After seeing her first meeting with her students, I can already tell how invested in her students, how caring she is. Though Jess is struggling with the pandemic like everyone else, Jess makes it a priority to offer unrequired weekly synchronous meetings for her asynchronous class. These meetings allow students to have regularly scheduled times to check in with her and learn about the course for the week.

"I appreciate that," Jess says. "I feel like those meetings are so important because every single resource for our students has moved to an online platform."

I nod, and Jess continues, "The thing about being a teacher of first year comp[osition], especially at Rural, is that my job is not just teaching writing. It's about teaching students how to be college students. Most of my students do not know how to navigate college, and many of them do not have family or friends they can ask. I see it as my job to introduce them to our campus—being sure they have the knowledge and confidence to use the resources we have so they can succeed at their goals."

Her tone is sincere—no trace of bragging or criticism. Jess genuinely cares about her students; she wants to do what she can to have them succeed. It reminds me of the way Laura Gonzales and Michelle Hall Kells talk about how "familismo" is central to education in HSIs.

"I love that you treat them like family," I say. "I bet your students appreciate it."

She smiles, and says, "Of course I do. They are family."

I transition us to our next interview topic (her teaching) with a question: "So, can you tell me a bit about your teaching philosophy?"

Jess begins her response in a more practiced way, giving me what I assume is the "elevator pitch" version of her teaching philosophy, the one she might use during a job interview. Jess talks matter-of-factly, arms down at her side—using only varying intonation to keep her voice engaging. Her elevator pitch teaches me that Jess is an antiracist pedagogue who works to create "an equitable and inclusive pedagogy" via "culturally responsive teaching practices."

"Tell me a bit more about that," I say. "How do you enact that kind of teaching philosophy day-to-day?" I lean in even closer to my screen with an expression that I hope looks like genuine curiosity.

Jess's more professional demeanor shifts to excitement; she cares about teaching.

"I think that I'm really compassionate," Jess says. "I want to be that all the time. Compassionate and responsive and supportive." As she shares this, Jess's hands gesticulate so much that they go in and out of the range available for her Zoom screen. She continues,

My most important goal is for my students to be more confident as writers and readers. How can I make you more confident and capable? I've been thinking about this as punk pedagogy. I see myself as a punk, and in a rhet-comp [rhetoric and composition studies] context, it comes out as doing whatever I need to, breaking all the rules to help students succeed.

"Punk pedagogy," I say. "That'd be a cool title for an article. You should totally write about that."

"With what time?" she jokes.

We both know that she teaches three classes a quarter, takes on more service positions than are required, participates in all the antiracist pedagogy research projects on campus, and still makes time for publications and conferences. We share a commiserating laugh, and I remind Jess that part of being a research participant means that I will be giving her at least equivalent time in copyediting or peer response; perhaps we could use that for her to develop something about this teaching approach.

"That's true," Jess says. "Well, maybe one day I'll get to it and hit you up then."

"I hope you will," I say, transitioning back to the interview. "So, tell me to what extent—if at all—does reflection connect to your punk pedagogy approach?"

Jess responds, animatedly,

> I think that the work of reflection is like an incredibly necessary component in my punk pedagogy—or I guess what mainstream compositionists might think of a way of culturally responsive approach to teaching—because reflection can be integrated in low-stakes ways. And we know that this helps them name and practice an integral part of the writing process: here's what I'm learning and here's how or why I'm learning it. It might be low-stakes in terms of assessment, but high-impact for pedagogical gains.

As she talks, Jess's voice takes on an intensity that I hear so often in her teaching: an excited buzzing kind of energy. It's not bubbly or saccharine; the tone just signals how genuinely present she is. When she uses that tone in her class's synchronous check-ins, I always imagine her students leaning in and really hearing her, a natural response to engage with someone who clearly just *cares* so much about their success. (There's no way to know for sure, though, because she is repeatedly the only one with her video on during those optional weekly synchronous check-ins. However, I do know from the one focal student who has agreed to work with me from her class this semester that they notice this energy from her too. As Francis, a 1st-year student from the class, says, "It's just so easy to try in a class where I can tell that Jess is trying so hard too.")

"Okay," I say. "So, you incorporate reflection because it's important to you and your teaching philosophy. Can you tell me a bit about how you define reflection?"

"Sure," Jess tells me.

> I'd define reflection as that act of looking in the mirror. It's pausing to look at yourself or your actions and having that time to break down what you see. So that's what I'm trying to create in every first-year writing class that I teach. I'm trying to have my students pause and look—on their identities and experiences, on everything.

As she answers, I can see her palms face up, oscillating between each hand for emphasis as she lists "identities," "experiences," and "everything."

This sparks my interest. I write a note in my journal: "Intrinsic motivation?" Though Jess is intrinsically motivated to do reflection, she does not assume that is the case for her students. Instead, she creates opportunities for her students to do reflection within daily moments of her pedagogy, along with bigger assignments.

I keep my observation to myself, though, jotting it in my notes, before asking my next question.

"And can you tell me the story of where that definition comes from?" I ask, curious about how she learned to have this view of reflection: as something integral to writing, especially learning, but also malleable to the context.

"I was born in the nineties," she says, "so the movie *Mulan* was super popular." I arch my eyebrows questioningly to prod her forward. She grins and says her punch line. "Mulan's practice of stopping to look and processing herself was definitely a formative influence in my interpretation. I sang her song 'Reflection' a lot as a kid."

We share a bout of laughter. As our laughter quiets, she says, "But seriously, I do see reflection as this pausing to look at yourself or your actions and having that time to break down what you see—and I've been doing it as long as I can remember."

For Jess, reflection was not something that she specifically remembers learning. She identifies as introspective. Jess tells me that reflection is something that she does constantly throughout her daily life; whether she is making lunch, watching TV, hanging out with her dogs, or listening to music, Jess is constantly reflecting. Jess continues telling stories about her habitual reflections, inspired by her "naturally reflective identity." Her reflection definition comes from her childhood memories, her lived experiences.

"Great, thank you. Can you give me some examples of what this practice of reflection looks like in your class, then?" I ask.

"Of course," she says with a nod, her mouth forming into a slight smile. "In the class that you're observing, there is not as much reflection as I should have [included], to be honest," she says, and her slight smile turns into a grimace.

I'm used to this kind of disclosure. Focal students and teachers are often apologetic about how much they reflect, sometimes voice self-doubt about their definitions and practices of reflection, and occasionally admit to adding in new or extra reflective practices just because of my presence in the class. Before I can get into my well-practiced version of "I'm just interested in what you do, and what you do is enough" speech, though, Jess begins to elaborate with the examples of what she does do.

"We do have the reflective essay required as the midterm," she says.

> I try to ask really clear questions, so they understand that kind of reflective rhetorical rationale as central to their writing process. And there's lots of reflection in the self-assessments I assign throughout the quarter, like the process reading notes I require for each reading throughout the class or the get-to-know-you mixtape assignment that we're doing right now. I also try to cue for reflection in our weekly meetings, conferences, and even in the scaffolding work for their projects throughout our quarter.

I'm writing down notes as she talks, and she can hear my keys clicking, so Jess takes a breath before saying, unprompted,

> My goal in doing assignments like these is to show students that we're always describing the way we're writing and making connections across our learning contexts; it's just part of the writing process. I think that if I were in a face-to-face setting, or if the affect online was a lot different, I think I'd have students do reflective posts doing that work clearly and concretely more often. I think that kind of reflection should happen in class. But, with the time these students are living through, and where they are emotionally because of it, constant asynchronous online reflection would just feel like busy work. Like when

I teach it typically, we have journal writing or conversations where we talk about: "What did you learn this week? What skills do you feel confident in? What do you feel like you want to work on? What questions do you have?" But with Covid, I feel like it's just not in the cards. Students are so overextended, and I need to honor that.

"That's super smart," I comment, as I jot down, "Very strategic about showing students the how and why, and super aware of student affect in response to Covid." Upon finishing this note, my eyes peripherally notice the time. We've gone well past our goal of 30 minutes. I want to respect her time and wrap up right away.

I say, "Wow, I've been having so much fun learning from you that I just realized we're way over time. Thank you so much for talking to me today. I look forward to learning from you throughout the semester. We can pick up here next time. Do you have any questions or concerns for me in the meantime?"

Jess shakes her head and enthusiastically agrees to meet again. We say our pleasantries and disconnect.

I spend 15 or so minutes writing in my ethnography journal after we disconnect; I hurriedly write down notes before my babysitter hits her allotted hours. I'm left feeling inspired by Jess; she's an instructor that cares so deeply about her students, one that feels like it's her role to serve as an ambassador to the college experience. Jess is purposefully and thoughtfully engaging in reflective pedagogy, according to her definition of reflection, and then even adapting that definition to both the local and global context. Yet, to me at least, Jess is selling herself short in saying she does not have "enough" reflection. She does have various reflective assignments in her carefully curated Canvas modules.

In fact, students are currently engaged in an incredible reflective activity—the "mixtape" assignment. Jess asks students to introduce themselves to her and their classmates with at least five songs, along with their thick description of why those songs are representative of their individual identities. As Jess writes in her prompt, students are asked to "set the scene, tell the story, and just make sure that you are being specific and clear about why you have included this song in your mix." This introductory assignment sets the stage for reflection incorporated throughout the course: students will return this mixtape assignment, creating a new mix that represents their experience in and beyond her course this quarter. Jess uses reflection to understand her students' lived experiences and embodied knowledges as she asks them,

"What do you want me to take away from this mixtape? What impact do you want these songs to have on me as your audience? What do you want me to feel or think about?" Additionally, she cues for reflection in so many ways in-between: in discussion board posts, reflective course assignments, rhetorical rationales, and optional synchronous meetings with students, both in large group meetings and conferences (neither of which Rural CC requires her to do for an asynchronous class).

Her interview leaves me wondering: What can we learn about how teachers define reflection—and then how they incorporate potential reflective activities in her pedagogy? How does their understanding of reflection and consequent pedagogy add to, complement, and disrupt what the field knows about reflection as a rhetorical practice in the writing classroom?

*****

In Chapter 2, I described methods: I worked with three MSIs, observing two sections of FYW at each school. Along with my daily observations of each class, I interviewed a total of twenty students and five teachers three times throughout their course. I also distributed a survey so I could hear the experiences of all students who were able to offer their experiences with reflection. In this chapter, I take up my methodology, feminist storytelling, to share findings from my research. This chapter works to explain how reflection emerges from the distributed agency of contextual factors within a rhetorical context and then results in rhetorical effect. Like everything rhetorical, many contextual factors come into play during reflective activity; time, materials, technologies, affect, emotions, sensory reactions, identities, relationships, and more all play a role in how reflection emerges from distributed agency in a rhetorical situation. Throughout this chapter, I will share examples that demonstrate this, focusing on the focal teachers as example subjects. Throughout this chapter, I will discuss how teachers define reflection—and how those definitions influence the way they invite students to do reflection within their pedagogy, all while being responsive to each institutional context. This chapter, then, serves as an overview of what the teachers intended students to take up. This sets us up for the focus of the next chapter: what students reported upon doing with reflection (sometimes in the ways that teachers hoped, but often in subverted, new, or repurposed ways).

Teaching for Reflection: How Teachers Define, Practice, and Offer Opportunities for Reflection

In this section, I report on how teachers say that they define and practice reflection in their own writing and teaching practices, along with how they hope to offer opportunities for reflection for their students. Using grounded theory to see emerging patterns of how focal teachers and students defined reflection, I found that participants associated reflection following rhetorical effects: reflection-for-awareness, reflection-for-introspection, reflection-for-learning, reflection-for-mindfulness, and reflection-for-perspective. For example, in this chapter's opening story, Jess shared her definition of reflection: "pausing to look at yourself or your actions and having that time to break down what you see." Given Jess's definition of reflection, I identified Jess's understanding of reflection as "reflection-for-awareness," or reflection that results with an analysis of decisions or choices. Jess associated reflection with a particular rhetorical activity—awareness—and she incorporates this kind of reflection in her own writing processes, as well as her pedagogy. Reflection was a key part of Jess's own writing and learning processes, as it helped her write with rhetorical awareness. Her instrumental experiences involved her reflective nature, which she remembers as being part of her identity, even in childhood.

Though she did honor those experiences and her own experiences with reflection, Jess was careful to adopt her reflective pedagogy to the context that she specifically teaches within. As she explained, "I think that if I were in a face-to-face setting, or if the affect online was a lot different, I think I'd have students do reflective posts doing that work clearly and concretely more often." Though she typically had students reflect via conversation and low-stakes personal writing during class time, Jess knew that students were "overextended," and translating this to discussion board prompts would feel "like busy work." Therefore, she incorporated pedagogy, but differently: with intermittent reflective writing assignments designed to dovetail with their writing assignments. In doing so, Jess hoped that students could adopt that same careful thoughtfulness in their writing process that she values, all while meeting her goal to provide them opportunities to understand how reflective practice can serve as a form of strategic awareness of their rhetorical situation. Jess's identification of reflection as a form of awareness was common among the teachers: I identified three of the five as associating their definition of reflection to awareness using grounded theory. In Table 3.1, I present

TABLE 3.1. Teacher definitions of reflection

Name	Reflection type	Definitions of reflection	Fundamental memory	Examples
URBAN STATE U—TEACHER OF CLASS 1				
Kevin	Reflection-for-learning	"To me, reflection is that making of the transition of working to thinking, to really look at what do I know, what have I learned from the gathering and the absorbing, and then what can I take with me in the executing. When I'm teaching, I often make opportunities for reflection that happen in the space between thinking and doing."	Reading an article that he read in a textual studies course	1. Free writes 2. Group work 3. Peer review
URBAN STATE U—TEACHER OF CLASS 2				
Grace	Reflection-for-awareness	"So, reflection basically for me is just the tracking of logic behind the decisions but having to kind of scoop that out of wherever it came from. It's almost subconscious at times, but [it's] just developing the awareness of that."	Practicing yoga and learning about mindfulness, particularly using self-awareness of the breath within exercise and meditation	1. Conferences 2. Course assignments 3. Group work 4. "Reflection" assignments 5. Whole class discussion
RURAL CC—TEACHER OF CLASS 1				
Jess	Reflection-for-awareness	"I'd define reflection as that act of pausing to look at yourself or your actions and having that time to break down what you see."	Ruminating is part of her introspective personality and her writerly process	1. Class assignments 2. Discussion board 3. Internal practice 4. "Reflection" assignments

continued on next page

TABLE 3.1.—*continued*

Name	Reflection type	Definitions of reflection	Fundamental memory	Examples
RURAL CC—TEACHER OF CLASS 2				
Heather	Reflection-for-awareness	"So, the way I've come to see it in the writing classroom is that reflection is a kind of metacognitive process that is integral to the reading and writing process."	Identifying as a "reflective" person and then taking up that interest by learning about it in her graduate school education (and further professional development opportunities since then)	1. Class assignments 2. Internal practice 3. "Reflection" assignments 4. Verbal processing 5. Whole group discussion
SOUTHERN HBCU—TEACHER OF CLASSES 1 AND 2				
L.J.	Reflection-for-introspection	"Reflection is a process to work on the interior and assess my blind spots. Like, what are the things that you knowingly overlooked? What are the emotions that you didn't want to engage with? Why? Reflection helps people stay grounded."	Being a writer, because writing itself (to him) is a "process of critically engaging who you are" and "engaging in dark spots"	1. Class assignments 2. Class community building exercises 3. Whole group discussions 4. Writing

the definitions of reflection that teachers gave me during our first interview, along with where they tended to associate reflection in their pedagogy.

In Table 3.1, we see each teacher's definition of reflection provided in their first interview, the code of what kind of rhetorical effect is associated with the definition, and examples of where the focal teachers hoped that reflection would live within their pedagogy. Three of the five teachers (Grace, Heather, and Jess) identified reflection as a kind of awareness, citing it as an integral part of the reading and writing process. Grace, for instance, described reflection as "tracing the logic" of decision-making, and Heather described reflection as a "metacognitive process." While Jess saw reflection as related to metacognition but not identical, Heather and Grace saw metacognition as synonymous. Grace pulled from her personal life the yoga studio and how she has learned to be aware of her breath. Heather succinctly explained reflection to me initially as "a kind of metacognitive process that is integral to the reading and writing process," but she layered onto that definition with a suggestion that reflection can be a kind of "rhetorical listening" to oneself, a way for someone to understand why and how perspectives are built. The other two instructors, Kevin and L.J., defined reflection differently. Kevin saw it resulting in learning, noting that it is the mental process of translating cognition into a kind of physical manifestation, what he called "the space between thinking and doing." Kevin's definition is inspired by an article he read in graduate school about learning. L.J., whose definition of reflection is influenced by his identity as a writer (and as one who engages in a lot of personal writing), saw reflection as a practice of examining the self (especially the parts of the self that we would rather avoid).

Each teacher's definition was inspired by a specific, foundational experience. This experience, then, shaped their definition of reflection—and in turn influenced the rhetorical effect that they imagined reflection should have for both them and their students. Since all the teachers saw themselves as "writers" (though they may have a complicated relationship with it), they often saw reflection as being involved in their own writing processes—and in turn viewed reflection as important to incorporate in their writing pedagogy. When incorporating reflection into their pedagogy, each teacher was careful to translate reflection to something that they thought would work for their context in particular. In the next sections, I explain each rhetorical context (Rural CC, Urban State, and Southern HBCU)—along with how the teachers adapted their activities of reflection to meet the specific pedagogical needs of their students at those institutions.

Rural CC Overview

Rural CC is an HSI, which by definition "enrolls at least 25% undergraduate, full-time equivalent Hispanic students" (U.S. Department of Education, n.d.). It is also a Hispanic/Latinx majority school: About 60% of students are Hispanic/Latinx, 30% of students are white, and the remainder of students identify as other nationally minoritized groups, according to school-reported statistics. As Aydé Enríquez-Loya and Kendall Leon explained,

> [HSIs] are not all the same . . . Students are not always multilingual, low income, or high risk at HSIs. Some have pride in their Spanish-speaking, others have internalized racism about being multilingual. Some have and are proud of dual-citizenship, others insist about their American-ness as paramount (or only identity). (2017, p. 212)

Though students hail from different backgrounds and have different relationships with language and identity (Kells et al., 2004), HSIs generally "attract students whose access to higher education is limited by financial, sociological, academic, and cultural circumstances" (Kirklighter et al., 2007, p. 18). This is true of Rural CC. Nearly 80% of its current student population identifies as first-generation, or students who do not have any family members who have earned a post-secondary degree. Meanwhile, about 75% of the residents in the town surrounding Rural CC have their high school diploma or GED, 19% have their bachelor's degree, and 9% have a graduate degree.

Rural CC is the local postsecondary institution in a smaller town with a largely agricultural-based economy. The historically Indigenous hunting and farming area was stolen by white Americans in the 1850s because of its fertile lands and abundant hunting and fishing. The area has remained agricultural. It is known now for its fruit produce and vineyards. Farming in the area has been supported by Mexican migrant farmers since the 1930s. According to 2020 census data, about half of the 95,000 people living in the city are Hispanic (most of whom likely identify as Chicanx but are not able to stipulate as such on their census forms, since government-issued communication only leaves an option for "Hispanic").

Rural CC opened its doors in the 1920s. The school prides itself as a teaching-oriented institution that can support a wide variety of learners. It offers certificates (the most popular being medical-related), associate degrees (the most popular of which are liberal arts), and bachelor's degrees (the most popular of which are business or teaching)—as well as community outreach programs, especially for English-as-a-second-language learners. Since its opening, the school's goal has been to provide education opportunities to those in the surrounding city, along with the nearby farming communities. Students typically attend Rural CC as degree and certificate seekers—and some come for dual-enrollment opportunities as high school students. Instructors at Rural CC are made up of about 50% part-time faculty, 20% full-time non-tenure-track faculty, and 30% tenured/tenure-track faculty. I had the opportunity to speak to two instructors: Heather, a tenured professor who has taught at Rural for over a decade, and Jess, a full-time instructor who has taught at Rural for 3 years. In the following subsections, I discuss Jess's and Heather's reflective pedagogy.

JESS: AN OVERVIEW OF PLANNED REFLECTIVE ACTIVITY IN HER CLASS

Spring 2021—Zoom, Rural CC

We're 6 weeks into the 10-week quarter, and our synchronous meeting follows the established pattern: Jess welcomes us all to the meeting, and says, "Okay, I'm going to get started. As a reminder, I'll be recording for folks that can't make it. I'll give you a space to ask questions when I'm done with my mini lecture." Jess begins the overview of the week, screensharing the corresponding Canvas module to her discussion. A few minutes into her description, she gets to the discussion of what is called the "Music Project Presentation," which seemed to me (when I read it earlier on her Canvas site that day) to be a kind of peer review that also helped scaffold students toward being able to write their required rhetorical rationales of their music project.

She says, "So what you're doing is, by the end of the day on Wednesday, May 5, you are going to submit your Music Project Presentation, right?" Though about 20 students are in the synchronous meeting, Jess gets no feedback from them on her question. All the boxes remain black screens; no one chooses to make a reaction or put a comment on the chat. She continues, "And all you need to do for this is open up that Canvas discussion box and write a Canvas presentation post." Jess uses the screenshare feature to model each step that she walks through next. She says,

> And so in this presentation box, you'll put the title (so if you have a title, you'll put that there; if not, this will prompt you to come up with a title), the genre (like an essay, a zine, a collage, fan art, video, a hybrid genre—there might be a couple together, that's cool), the purpose of your work (so what kind of impact did you want to have, what did you want people to learn, what did you want people to think, what did you want people to feel, what did you want people to do after they kind of read your project, saw your project, or listened to your project) and then what do you want the audience to pay attention to (so if there's anything [where] you're like, "Hey, check it out, this is like a cool part of [the] project, or this [is] a choice I made that I really want people to think about." This is again kind of you thinking rhetorically). So, you'll write that post and then you'll attach a version of your project like this.

Upon finishing modeling the steps, Jess stops screensharing, and transitions back to just talking to students.

"So," she says smiling,

> If you're done with your project already, you can attach or put in a link to your project in that post. If you're not done, or you only have part of it done, you can attach or link [to] what you have so far. And, in your little comment you can say you know this isn't all the way done. You can say something like, "There's still some stuff I need to do, but here's like a preview or an excerpt, right?"

In my ethnography journal, on the observation side, I make a note. "No required point of completion for this project before refl[ection] assignment. Ss [students] have agency!" I'm struck by this bit here; students are not required to complete the draft in its entirety before doing the reflective work. Instead, they are tasked to do the reflection by the deadline of the homework prompt, which occurs before the deadline for the completed draft of the project. The amount of drafting—and when their reflection and peer review is done within that drafting—is up to them. This makes space for either what Kathleen Yancey calls reflection-in-action (reflection throughout the drafting process) or reflection-in-presentation (reflection for another to explain a completed draft).

As I'm writing, Jess continues,

> Oh, also, if you've written something kind of personal, or something that you're taking some risks with, you can kind of pick or choose part of your draft. Like, um, if you wrote a poem, you could be like, "Here's a quote from my poem." Or if you're doing a zine, you could be like, "Here's one page from my zine." You don't need to share the whole thing. If you're doing a video or podcast, you might just share the outline or script, because you're probably still working on the production of that. Whatever you have done, share that or an excerpt of that. Just so that way your peers have kind of an idea of what you will do for the completed project. You can put that in a note to your peers via the section of what you want your audience to know.

Another note in my observations. "Attn [attention] to student disclosure! Ethics of reflection about personal writing?"

Jess pauses for a moment, letting her audience regroup before continuing.

"So again," she says, "Take a look at this sample. It's short. Here's what I made, here's what my purpose was, here's what I think is cool, and then I attached my zine as a comment."

Upon completing the description of how to do the assignment, Jess switches to instructions on how to do the response part of the assignment. "I expect to see three responses with either a compliment or connection. We are not peer reviewing. We are making connections to other people's posts. Or, telling them something we like."

I make myself a note to remember how she describes this activity as "not peer reviewing." It seems like Jess is cautious about peer review. I should follow up with her about that.

Jess continues,

> What might happen is that you might compliment or share connections that you realize you might want to talk about in your rhetorical reflection. You know someone gives you a compliment on something like, "I really like the use of color in my zine"; you might think, "Oh, I didn't even write about the use of color in my zine in my rhetorical reflection. I should maybe talk about that as one of the rhetorical features." So, I purposefully spaced it a couple of extra days out so if there are other things that you realize from reading that feedback, that positive feedback from everyone in class, you can build your own analysis of your work for the rhetorical reflection you're writing with the full draft. So that's why there's that little gap, okay?

I make a time stamp note of this dialogue in my notebook to re-listen to. I'm really interested in how transparent Jess is about the goals of her pedagogy; the explicitness of this dialogue is worth another listen before our next interview.

Meanwhile, Jess closes her monologue.

"So again for the music project itself, the creative part."

She holds up her fingers to show the number one.

> Remember, it can be any genre about anything related to music. We've looked at comics, listicles, fan art, photography, painting, illustrations, podcast, zines, etc., in class. Grading for this portion of the music project is credit/noncredit. It just needs to be modeled or inspired by readings in the course for it to be complete.

Jess then moves her fingers to show the number two. "The second piece is the rhetorical reflection. It's the piece that's kind of, well, it's the most complex piece of writing that we've done together this term."

I write quickly in my notes, "Jess is placing a high value on rhetorical rationales."

Jess continues, "So, when you're looking at the rhetorical reflection, you are required to answer these questions in an MLA formatted essay that goes with your creative piece."

Jess pulls up the prompt for the rhetorical rationale, screensharing the questions, and reading them verbatim:

> What is the project about? Why did you focus on it? Why did you choose the genre or genres that you did? The genres of your project. Who is your audience? Who are the ideal readers of this? Who did you want to impact with your work? What is your purpose? Or how did you want to impact them? And what are *at least* two specific rhetorical choices that you made in creating your project? What is one reading that inspired your work, something that you modeled your work after? And what else do you want people to know?

Jess leaves the screenshare up but stops reading directly, paraphrasing the rest of the directions, "Then this section," she circles the area with her cursor,

> breaks down and helps you focus on what to write. Like this list gives you an idea of features that again you might be using in your work. Go down this list it might be helpful. You want to be really specific, signposting like, "This is an example of pathos because X, or this is an example of repetition because Y." And whatever your reading is that you're citing, you want to include that in a works cited. As a reminder, there's a handbook on MLA formatting on module one. If you go to module four, we have the sample music projects. And module three has sample rhetorical reflections. Don't stress about that; just make sure you're answering the questions listed here. It's basically you talking about your own work and your own process. I'm really excited to read them, and I know your classmates are too. Later on, you will be responding to each other's posts because we can learn a lot from reading about each other's process. More on that next week.

After, as I review my notes, I journal and collect my thoughts and reactions. I'm struck by the way that Jess has overviewed the project, explained the importance of the project, given resources and samples for the project that students can refer to, and elevated the value of doing this kind of reflective work by assigning it twice in very different formats (an interactive discussion board and a rhetorical rationale) with different audiences (classmates and her). I'm also struck by the very specific questions she gives students, which suggested that she views it as her responsibility to explain and scaffold for reflection. And I'm particularly struck by the way she notes how vulnerable it is for students to engage in reflective work.

*****

Jess was a local to the community surrounding Rural CC—leaving only for undergraduate and graduate school. Jess, though, did attend Rural CC, as a dual-enrollment student during her high school years. When she moved away from the town for undergraduate and graduate school, she always knew that her goal was to come back to her home community and teach—preferably at the community college that she attended as a part of her dual-enrollment experience. Jess was a self-described "punk" in her 30s, a "white Mestiza—a culturally and ethnically Chicanx—who [was] very, very queer but happens to be married to a man." Jess was in her last year of her PhD program when Rural CC posted a lecturer position that fit her qualifications. She applied, got the job, and completed her dissertation all while teaching three courses each quarter, as well as taking on more service than required of her position and volunteering for a variety of campus initiatives.

Jess went to graduate school to study Chicanx literature but decided to specialize in both composition and Chicanx literature because of her passion for inclusive and antiracist pedagogy theory. Her scholarly interests in culturally responsive, sustainable, and antiracist pedagogy were central to her pedagogy, but Jess's own experiences as a local student in the area are too. Combining these, she approached her classroom with what she has come to think of as "punk pedagogy," or "breaking every rule that you need to break to make to make your pedagogy as compassionate as possible." Her students viewed her as "kind" and "compassionate," embodying the "familismo" characteristics so often employed in HSIs.

Though the context could have been a sterile Zoom room with a nondescript green screen background, Jess was always careful to invite us into her own home, her piles of books and art surrounding her, and her dogs playing in the background. We saw glimpses of her tastes in music, reading, and art because of this. She almost always had a band shirt on—and local and fan art was clearly visible among the Chicanx literature and antiracist books on her bookshelf. A pride flag was predominantly displayed, and we saw a peek of a Mexico flag too. Jess's weekly synchronous check-ins were optional to students, but most students chose to attend. Jess always arrived in the Zoom room with her camera on, sharing her live backdrop (her cozy home office) before screensharing anything of importance. She used this same, authentic office background in all her videos for students as well. It's almost like she was trying to humanize herself and the course through her purposeful video choices.

Jess never encouraged students to share their videos, leaving it up to them whether they felt safe to disclose their location, and no student ever opted to turn on their video cameras. Jess always used the first 10 minutes or so to create a live recording of her explaining the weekly goals and corresponding assignments, so that those who were unable to make the live session would still get the benefit of hearing her explanations later. When Jess completed her review, she stopped the recording feature and announced that the floor was open for questions. She often used that question time as a space to build community, calling on people in the group who didn't raise their hand to ask a question—inquiring about students' social and emotional health, complimenting students about recent work, and/or talking about how they might tackle the project. Students were at times stilted in response, but Jess always persevered with a kind, genuinely inquisitive tone. She built as much community as she possibly could with a collection of black screens.

This community-building was central to how she hoped students might take up reflection in her class, which she felt was dependent on building a relationship with students and establishing trust. As she explained,

> I'm always trying to do reflection-in-action with my more "performative" reflection, so it's integrated into the writing process. I try to frame reflection and describing our own processes as something we just do; we always describe the way we're writing—framing it as part of the writing process. But likely students perceive it as more of a "here's what I did, let me show it to you," even if I try to not make it like that.

Reflection-in-presentation, for Jess at least, was something she tries to avoid. "The field defines reflection as the kind of thinking that exists in portfolio cover letters," she said, "but I want to do it differently." She explained:

> During grad school, I was at a huge R1 school in a metropolitan area. A lot of my students knew how to do college—or had the confidence to do it (because their families have been, they've toured, they have the opportunity to engage with college readiness resources, etc.) and that's not true here. That's a sign of privilege. Academic with a capital 'A.' Here, our students are 70% first generation. A huge percentage are low income. We have a huge withdrawal rate and drop rate. And so, I see a big part of my job as an opportunity to take students by the hand

to show them college, build their confidence. First year writing here is not meant to be gatekeeping; it's trying to pull people through the door, grabbing students by the hand—like 'stay with me.' So, in my pedagogy, reflection is a huge responsiveness to this. I think reflection, when integrated in the day-to-day, through low-stakes activities, can be a way to help students articulate what they need. It helps students name what they're learning and how I can help them do that. That's why you see me integrating so much reflection-in-action, and something that I think is a lot deeper than constructive reflection. Take the mixtape for example. It doesn't quite go with the constructive reflection. Now, I'm just framing all literacies as belonging. Who are you, what is your history, how do you get here, and then you belong. And what are the ties to culture and art and community and family and how do you express that in the music that you listen to. It's not for me to gauge their learning, it's for them to do so. I'm just providing and offering a space for them to articulate themselves. Again, it's not for me.

Jess was so careful to adopt her reflective pedagogy to her context: a Chicanx-majority population at an HSI. She practices reflection differently than she did at a PWI, and she very purposefully broke rules to achieve her pedagogical goals.

Jess had memories as far back as early childhood where she was doing this kind of cognitive activity unprompted. Jess saw reflection as an important part of the writing process, perhaps in part because it's central to hers. In a later interview, Jess recounted how most of her writing time is spent thinking about the writing, rather than doing the writing. As she explained,

> I was always the kind of student who could sit down and pound out the paper before it was due because I was so busy thinking about it all week: while I cooked, while I cleaned, while I walked to class. I was constantly reflecting during my monotonous, daily activities. I'd reflect about the prompt, my response—things like what I should write, how I should support the ideas, etc. And all that work would be done even before I started typing.

Interestingly, though, she was careful not to assume that her own constant state of reflection is the same for her students. In fact, Jess was adamant about creating plenty of moments of scaffolding for her bigger assignments, scaffolding that does the kind of work that she herself does on her own prompting, in her head.

Perhaps that was because of her "punk pedagogy." Rather than being forced into the expectations of what college students "should" know or do, Jess was more than willing to "break all the rules" to ensure student success. Given that she was both a student and a faculty member at Rural CC, Jess takes care to meet the students where they are at. She adjusted her expectations to meet what students do, and thus Jess illuminated the reasons for what she was doing and why she was doing it. Perhaps that was why Jess was so responsive to her students' affect and their general malaise.

In interviews, Jess told me that she incorporates reflection through low-stakes class assignments, discussion boards, prompted internal practice in weekly synchronous meetings, and mandatory "reflection" assignments. One of the most common reflection exercises she assigned (something Jess incorporated as weekly assignments for her online course) was what I characterize as "pre-writing" reflective work. These low-stakes assignments asked students to articulate their reactions to readings and prompts along with the way their knowledge might move across writerly contexts; students saw these moments as potential avenues for practicing reflection. Another weekly occurrence for her class was what I call "cueing for transfer," or asking students to connect their knowledge across contexts, which her students also saw as reflection. Not only did her pre-writing assignments often do this, but Jess included written rationales for these assignments, which are viewable to students and articulated orally in weekly, synchronous meetings. In doing so, Jess modeled reflection (and asked students to follow her reflective thought) by explaining why an activity is important, what goals it helps them meet, and how it will scaffold toward the next writerly task for students. Reflection, therefore, was central to her course.

However, it is important to note that the asynchronous nature of her course, along with the contextual factors of a relatively stressed and consequently overwhelmed student population did alter how Jess typically incorporates reflection in her course. In past years, reflection was typically incorporated as a way of community-building as a class, relationship-building with her as a teacher, and an attention to personal growth. Even still, Jess began and ended the course with reflective assignments. In week one, Jess welcomed her students to class with a mixtape assignment. Students introduced themselves to her and one another with a list of songs that were representative of their identities, along with a reflection of why they are representative. Then she repeated the mixtape assignment at the end of the course, requesting they make a new mix with at least five songs that represent their journey in the class. This kind of reflection was what Jess loved to incorporate. Like we saw in the first story, though, she worried that the Covid-19 pandemic (and her honoring of students' resultant affect) made it difficult for her to do more. Instead, she had a higher frequency of more traditional kinds of "reflection" like we saw in the above story: discussion board assignments of rhetorical rationales of works in progress. Even then, Jess subverted generic expectations of what students should do for reflective rhetorical rationales.

In the above example, which is representative of the kind of assignment she requires of each major assignment in their course, Jess encouraged students to screen share descriptions of the multimodal projects that are in process (rather than doing it retroactively), only share what they are most proud of (rather than requiring they share the whole project), share these with the whole class via discussion board (rather than sharing just to her), and interact with their peers' reflections in some way (rather than keeping reflections as a performance only for their teacher's eyes). In subverting the genre conventions of a reflective rhetorical rationale, Jess still attempted to meet some of her alternative goals for reflection—all while working within the confines of her context—before engaging in more traditional reflective writing (the rhetorical rationale associated with the project). In doing so, Jess made space for traditional practices of reflection, as well as alternative modes of reflection that lent themselves to antiracist and culturally responsive applications of reflective activity. In the next subsection, I consider how her colleague, Heather, similarly reacted to the cultural context of Rural, but did so with different activities, intentions, and resultant rhetorical effect.

HEATHER: AN OVERVIEW OF PLANNED REFLECTIVE ACTIVITY IN HER CLASS

Fall 2022—Rural CC (Zoom)

I quickly let my hair down from my messy bun to try to look put together. I've been juggling teaching three courses at my institution, observing two courses at Southern and one at Rural CC, and interviewing all my focal students this week. Parker is typically in school now, but she came down with a fever. My husband and I have been taking turns caring for her, moving around meetings as necessary. With a quick finger brush, I realize I look even more unkempt this way. I put it back up quickly, as I let Heather into the Zoom room; Zoom has just alerted that she is waiting.

"Thanks again for rescheduling because of Park's fever," I say with a soft smile.

"Of course! Of course!" Heather exclaims. "It's hard for everyone in the pandemic, especially those with littles."

I nod gratefully, and say, "I really do appreciate your grace, though. And I don't want to keep you any longer than necessary because I know this isn't your first choice to talk. So, today, we're circling back to your definitions of reflection. So, last time we were talking about the ways writing instructors often use abstract terms and assume that everyone knows what they mean. We use terms like synthesis or reflection or whatever, and we think that everybody uses them in the same—"

Suddenly, I stop midsentence. My phone is ringing with an unknown number from my local area.

"Sorry, Heather, can you hold on one second? Someone is calling me, and I just need to make sure this isn't my daughter's doctor office. They told me a nurse would be calling me today because she might have something more serious. We need to watch for unknown numbers so we can get the lab results."

She nods, I mute myself and pause the recording, and I return 3 minutes later.

"Good news, Heather! Parker's fever is just caused by a regular bug! Nothing to worry about."

Heather lets out a wide grin, saying, "Oh good! So glad to hear!"

"Thank you!" I say with enthusiasm. I'm relieved. "Okay, back to us: I was re-orienting us to our previous discussions of reflection. Now, I want to ask: How are you defining reflection lately?"

"I kind of got into this last time," Heather says. "But I think I see reflection as different for me than my students."

I've heard this before; many instructors talk about how they reflect internally but ask students to do external processing, how they reflect through conversation themselves but have adapted their pedagogy to include written reflections because their program requires that modality, or how they were inspired by scholarship to incorporate a certain kind of reflective activity in class.

I smile encouragingly at Heather and say, "Interesting. Can you tell me more?"

> Well, mostly when I think of it, I'm thinking of it in terms of reading processes and writing processes and metacognitive awareness of what

they're doing in those processes. I took the Reading Apprenticeships. I'm not sure if you're familiar with it?

She pauses briefly to wait for me to react (I signal no with a small head-shake), and she quickly continues.

"Oh, so it's a course I took a couple years ago, which was great. Yeah, reading fits right with writing, who would have thought?"

We share a laugh.

"I don't know why I didn't figure this out before," she says, and then switches to a mocking, singsong voice: "Boy, practicing reading and being metacognitively aware with that skill helps just like it does in writing."

She laughs, and I smile to indicate my amusement.

> So, I tend to think about reflection as a metacognitive awareness. And really, for me, that means trying to get students to consider—well, I've framed it increasingly in terms of decision-making and trying to get them to think about—you know they may not appreciate the word "rhetoric" yet—but a rhetorical decision-making.

I nod, and she goes on:

> So, you know, I'm basically asking them: "How and why are you doing certain things to appeal to your audience? Who are you imagining in your head? How and why are you doing different things to achieve a particular purpose?" Even things like, "Why did you do this?" Before the [reading apprenticeship] course, I don't think I incorporated enough of the whole "Why did you do this there?" I wasn't clear on their logic, why elements ended up in their paper in the ways that they did. And now that I really ask students that, I see it. Maybe it didn't have that effect on me that you wanted, but yes. I could see what you were trying to do. Reflection makes space for my students to be active decision makers in their writing. And so, I try to use reflection to get them to stop and think about what we're doing, because a lot of time we don't, and we get kind of immersed in doing. If they think about what they're doing, then I know what they're trying to do. And sometimes they even tell me, like I wasn't making conscious decisions. But even that's helpful to know, and I can push them to think: "So how does this actually work for my intended purpose? Or did I just get so caught up in the doing of things that this actually doesn't serve my larger purpose, or serve my audience, or meet larger expectations, or even meet my intentions with what I was doing with my writing?"

I'm nodding along as Heather talks, taking notes about what I'm noticing: Heather is a teacher who uses reflection, metacognitive awareness specifically, to practice antiracist pedagogy. Rather than seeing their rhetorical rationales as a defense for what students write, she sees reflection as a way of them taking ownership as authors. I make a note that her approach reminds me of Min-zhan Lu's article (1991) where Lu pushes against Shaughnessy's perception of error: perhaps if we *ask* students what they intended, we might realize that what we perceived as "error" is a purposeful rhetorical choice.

Heather continues,

> Basically, I'm trying to teach them the concept of rhetorical listening. I guess it's a little different than what we usually do for that, because I'm teaching them how to rhetorically listen to themselves. But that's what reflection is in our class: reflection is kind of a way of doing rhetorical listening to yourself.

Then, she pauses, sighs, and unhappily says,

> There's a part of me that wishes you were watching my other class or just not watching me during Covid. In the class you're observing, I had to strip it down so much because we're online, and we really only do the whole reflection is kind of that writing about writing theory, where it's just a greater pedagogical awareness of what students are doing and with the kind of idea in mind.

I write down a note about this: both Jess and Heather have had to adjust their typical teaching methods in response to students' affect and physical realities during the pandemic.

Meanwhile, Heather is saying,

> I typically assign that kind of retrospective work so my students are able to transfer their abilities to different context. But I think reflection can make you be aware of how your experiences or your cultural background or how your biases even, how your personal history, and really just how all the things that you believe work as authorities in what you believe, what you do. Reflection can get us thinking about how do all my past experiences, identities, beliefs, how does all that effect how you see new information presented, how you react? And so, when you have strong reactions, instead of like reacting, reflection can help you spend a moment considering: "What is causing me to feel this way about a certain piece of information or, you know, what's causing me to feel this way about this conversation?"

I write another note: "Antiracist potential for reflection? Connection to reflection-for-introspection definitions? Or to potentially reflection-for-perspective definitions? Maybe making space for both in that introspection leading to a shift of perception?" The kind of reflection that Heather is describing here is closely related to critical awareness and thinking. The kind of internal rumination that can help various anti-oppression teacher-activists encourage to get their students to become aware of their own deep-rooted ideologies and disrupt them.

While I jot down observations, Heather explains why she is still incorporating this kind of reflection in her other class, but not the one I'm observing:

> I'm doing that in another course that's not first-year writing, and I do incorporate a lot of those kinds of conversations in my first-year writing classes, but I haven't figured out a way yet to productively adapt that kind of interactive, change your perspective kind of reflective conversations, to work in this online setting. Especially in first-year writing classes where we are tasked to do so much.

After we meet, I review my notes, and I notice she's articulating why I started researching reflection in the first place: I'm interested in what I think of as the "emancipatory nature of reflection"—how it can help us investigate deep-rooted ideologies, consider alternative perspectives, and work across difference. Heather really wants reflection to do this kind of work in her classroom. It seems, though, that the course objectives, the modalities, the affect, the class community, and so much more can really influence whether instructors will play with this kind of reflection, even if they are believers in it. I too hope I can learn from Heather in a future semester, but I'm interested to see if I can find glimmers of reflection that do different work than that "writing about writing" Heather describes as her fallback that she's incorporated into this class.

*****

Heather was local to the area and well-liked by her students, known for equitable and inclusive pedagogies. Though she never attended Rural CC as a student, Heather had always lived in the town, with the exceptions of quick stints for undergraduate and graduate school. Heather was middle-aged, and she identified as white. Heather was a tenured professor who had been teaching at Rural for over 20 years. Heather began her career as a K–12 teacher, but decided to go back to graduate school so she could teach college. As Heather explained to me in her first interview, she had "always been interested in multilingual, multicultural education and literature" because of her own difficulties of trying to navigate across languages in her community, as well as a study abroad experience as an undergraduate to a Spanish-speaking country. Given her research interests, she specialized in antiracist pedagogy in graduate school and still considered that her research area two decades later.

Heather's teaching philosophy too was inspired by her scholarly interests. As she explained, "Antiracist pedagogy is more than just inclusivity; it's a kind of dismantling too—a pushing against whole systems in service of my students." Despite her own beliefs about writing instruction, Heather felt a kind of "tension" in her pedagogy because "many of [her] students want these things that [she's] telling them not to want. They want to immerse themselves in the language of power and they might buy into the mythology that if you work hard you can succeed." She tried to balance her ideologies about writing with her students' beliefs and needs. Putting it simply, she concluded: "I'm not here to have an agenda, I'm here to serve students. There are revolutionaries, and I'm not one of them." Heather's students felt safe and welcome in her classroom, seeing her classroom space as a way of "illuminating academic writing and what is expected"—a difference from Jess's students who discussed realizing "writing can be different than what [they] have done before; it can be fun." Working with both Jess and Heather gave me insight into two different pedagogies: both done wholeheartedly in the interest of their students, but with different tactics and different effects. Their academic backgrounds, teaching philosophies, and identities shaped the way they took up reflection in their classrooms—and the opportunities that their students had for naming, identifying, and practicing reflective activity in FYC, even at the same institution with the same kind of asynchronous online instruction.

Heather's most incorporated, readily identifiable moments of reflection included very traditional reflective writing assignments: rhetorical rationales where students wrote about their own writing. With every assignment, Heather required that students turn in a retroactive, written reflection of what they wrote and why they wrote it. However, in the interview above, we can see that reflection in these genres was more than just having students be able to recount their writing process and rhetorical awareness. Her assignments were doing the hard work of fostering rhetorical awareness and encouraging transfer—but they were done for antiracist intentions; Heather also hoped they could boost confidence for students and make them feel like they have a say in how she would read their work. For students at Rural CC, mostly nontraditional students who were first-generation and/or multilingual, Heather felt this was important work. In her communication with students, Heather signaled the reasoning for these rhetorical rationales, in attempts to more clearly explain to them why these assignments are required of them, which may in turn change their perspective of what those reflective moments could do to better adapt to their own practices of reflection.

Like Jess, Heather found that the current moment had shaped her pedagogy such that reflection was no longer helping students do everything Heather knew reflection could do. Switching the course to an asynchronous, online setting made it difficult for Heather to incorporate reflection that might yield the other rhetorical effect: reflection-for-perspective. Heather typically used verbal processing and whole-group discussion in synchronous, in-person contexts to do that kind of work. With the new format, due to the Covid-19 pandemic, those activities were no longer an option. Heather, like Jess, worried about student affect and the modalities of her instruction, so she had "stripped down" her pedagogy. Also, like Jess, Heather gravitated toward "reflection" assignments (assigning rhetorical rationales with final drafts of assignments). However, in losing the dynamic communication with students because of contextual factors, other potential rhetorical effects of reflection were not as available.

Heather and Jess incorporated reflection differently in their classes, even with similar contexts, similar past experiences of reflection, and similar definitions of reflection. They both saw reflection as a kind of rhetorical awareness. They served the same student populations, taught the same course with the same modalities and programmatic requirements, and even recognized similar lethargy in their students. Yet, the two incorporate reflection in different ways.

Both Jess and Heather had similar values: they believed in antiracist and inclusive pedagogy. Their goals, as they told me repeatedly, were to engage in culturally responsive pedagogy. Both teachers reported having an interest in graduate school and doing extracurricular professional development recently about the topic. Yet, the two enacted these practices differently: Jess explaining her "punk" pedagogy that "breaks all the rules," and Heather felt a tension between "pushing against whole systems in service of my students" and students' wants. Though Heather agreed with Jess that teachers can and should disrupt white supremacy values in the academy, Heather balanced that personal objective with the very real concerns of her students: They wanted to have access to White Mainstream English and scholarly discourse communities. Due to that, Heather often (admittedly hesitantly) incorporated more normative or expected pedagogical practices in her course. Therefore, while Jess incorporated multimodal reflective practices with a wide range of rhetorical effects, Heather was more apt to latch on to genres that are accepted and commonly used within college writing. This was even more true because this course was held online asynchronously. The course format shifted Heather's ability to engage in the dynamic conversations with students that she had begun incorporating as a way of teaching what she thought of as rhetorical listening of the self, or a kind of introspective unearthing of ideologies and values so students could better work across differences. The pressure from students and administration about accessing language and discourses of power—combined with the global pandemic and all the emotions, technologies, and time constraints that came with it—resulted in her reverting back to integrating the smart but more normative rhetorically aware kinds of reflection she has historically done. In doing so, there was space for culturally responsive teaching, with reflection's antiracist potential left up to the students to engage in, if they chose to. Teachers at Urban State U, with different definitions and different contextual considerations, integrated reflection differently in their courses, which I detail in the next section.

Urban State U Overview

Urban State U was a large, R1 university located in a metropolitan area. The city surrounding Urban State U was around 750,000 people, 65% of whom are white, 15% Asian or Pacific Islander, and the remainder of the population identifies as Black, Latinx, or two or more races. Most of the jobs in the city at the time of research collection were business- or engineering-related, and the companies often provide internship opportunities for Urban students. White European settlers stole the land in the 1850s from Indigenous people native to the area to create a port town, with logging and fishing industries, but it has since become a technology hub on the West Coast. The city was a relatively wealthy and educated city in the United States, with the median income being $350,000, and with two-thirds of the population holding a bachelor's degree or higher. The surrounding city influenced the student population at Urban: Students are usually (though of course not unilaterally) wealthy, with a median of $110,000 family income. Most students at Urban aspired to enter a STEM-related field, with majors like psychology, engineering, mathematics, informatics, business, and computer science being among the most popular.

Urban State U was in the Pacific Northwest (PNW), which was a region known for being politically progressive in its voting and legislation. Yet, like most urban areas in the United States, the ideals of the majority city dwellers were at odds with the realities of the city itself: Racial segregation and economic disparities were rampant.

At the time of data collection, 45% of students self-reported to Urban that they were white; 25% reported being Asian, Pacific Islander, or Native; 15% reported being nonresident alien; and the remainder were Latinx, Black, or two or more races. These demographics made the school both a primary white institution (PWI) and an Asian American, Native American, and Pacific Islander Serving Institution (AANAPISI). Most of the students who attended Urban State U were multigenerational college students, though there were programs in place to help first-generation and underrepresented students transition to college. Most students matriculated within 4 years. Urban was consistently ranked in the top 60% of schools in the United States. Instructors at Urban State U were mostly tenure-track or tenured faculty, but the FYW program was supported almost exclusively by graduate students instructors (GSIs), with some lecturer or adjunct faculty filling in for courses that could not be covered by graduate student labor. I worked with two GSIs, Grace and Kevin, who were both 2nd-year PhD students in their 20s teaching FYW.

The FYW program at Urban was larger than the other two institutions, and they had more options for types of courses their students could teach: a writing across the curriculum course, a writing in the disciplines course, a literature-themed course, a service-learning course, and a multimodal writing course. Their sections were both multimodal FYC courses, something I was interested in both because of multimodality's relationship to reflection and because it offered a different context of inquiry: These courses were scheduled in computer integrated classrooms either full- or half-time. As a PWI, AANAPISI, and R1, Urban State has writing instructors with different contextual concerns than Rural CC. Rather than prioritizing the needs of Chicanx multilingual and multidialectal students that were mostly first-generation college students like Rural CC, Urban State teachers were tasked to support privileged, white, monolingual students; multilingual, upper-class international students; and multilingual, multidialectal, and/or first-generation students. Though the demographics of students differed from Rural, Urban writing instructors likewise adapted their definitions of reflection to Urban State's unique contextual considerations. In the next subsection, I discuss what this looked like for Grace, a PhD student in English who was teaching a multimodal FYC section in the computer-integrated-classrooms on campus.

GRACE: AN OVERVIEW OF PLANNED REFLECTIVE ACTIVITY IN HER CLASS

Spring 2017—Urban State University

During the first week of class, Grace had her students work in groups so they could work together to understand (and later present interpretations of) the writing program's mandated course outcomes. Today is the second day of group presentations of their translated outcomes. She begins class with a preamble, framing the course objective of the day: Students will understand course outcome "1.4." Grace paces in the front of the classroom, and most students shift in the seats, rotating and rolling them so they can see her and the projector screen, which is down but not showing anything just yet.

Grace explains that they have gone through the other parts of outcome 1 the day prior, but Autumn and Alan (two focal students) would be presenting the fourth bullet point today. This outcome, Grace explains, is about articulating writer choices.

"Please pay close attention," Grace says. "This particular outcome is really central to our course."

She invites Autumn and Alan to do their presentation; they oblige, but most students rotate their chairs back to their own computer screen rather than where the students are presenting at the front of the room. Realizing that students are having trouble concentrating this morning, Grace thanks Autumn and Alan at the end of their presentation and then changes tactics. Grace uses the projector to pull up the image from a Google search of a sound board but has no PowerPoint or guiding script.

As Grace lectures, she paces near the front of the classroom, like her movement when introducing the group activity, oscillating between standing next to the screen and gesturing toward it. She explains, "The fourth bullet point of outcome 1 is important because it is connected to something we call 'higher order transfer'—or a way of moving knowledge from one context to another."

Students begin rolling their chairs and rotating to look at her. Many look at her encouragingly.

Noticing their attention, she continues more enthusiastically: "It is something we are going to practice a lot in this course. I'm going to ask you to talk through your decisions a lot: in our conversations, during group work share out, conferences."

Noticing some nodding, she continues, pulling up an image of a soundboard.

"Alright, so we see this soundboard?" she asks. Students nod.

> Right, so. Let's imagine we've never used one before. If we wanted to make music, we'd need at least a basic understanding of what the different nobs were: what they mean, what they can do, and when we might want to use them.

She pauses, scanning for understanding. Satisfied, she continues.

> Alright so writing is kind of like that. You need to understand the way writing works to execute rhetorical and genre awareness in a new situation. So like, we need to understand how spatial arrangement works. Or maybe you need to understand the difference in tone or style. We do MLA formatting and academic writing in a philosophy paper while using a more breathable format—shorter paragraphs, hyperlinks for citation, an informal tone—for a blog post.

I write a note in my notebook: "Scholarly identity→Teaching philosophy?" It seems like Grace's insistence that contexts are permeable—in part because of her identity as an affect theory scholar who does public-facing scholarship—makes her classroom context inviting of situations found in outside contexts.

Grace then connects this idea of transfer to metacognition, concluding,

> So, for me, metacognition means being aware of the logic behind your choices, and for the purposes of this class, being able to say it in a way that other human beings can understand. Sometimes me, sometimes other people. And that just gets us in the habit so that this step becomes natural. It becomes intuitive.

She pauses, scanning the room, and decides to give another example to ensure her point is made. "Okay, so, does anyone here do yoga?" she asks.

Students stare blankly at her. No one nods.

Grace decides to joke. "Cool, cool. Just me. That's great."

Her students respond with laughter.

She continues:

> So, fun fact about yoga. You probably know this: That there's a huge emphasis on following your breath. You're going to be breathing no

matter what. Even if you're not paying attention. But when you're paying attention to it, then you can use the whole potential of that breath. So, for me, metacognition—articulating the logic behind your choices—is not you doing something that you aren't already doing, but you being aware of it. So, you can bust it out to its full potential, so you can use it in a variety of situations. In this class or any class, there's no way that we could experience every kind of composition task you could be faced with. There's no way. But we can work with, "What is the logic behind the decisions I'm making for the audience, my purpose, whatever?" and then having that awareness in everything you do—out of this classroom, out of this university, out of this town.

Class wraps up, and I head out to review my notes and reflect upon them in a summary note. As I do, I notice so many things happening in today's class: Grace sharing her own definition of reflection, using the same example she gave me days earlier in an interview. Grace trying to encourage students of the importance of this practice. Grace responding to the affect of the room to very clearly do an impromptu lecture so students would get her perspective when she felt like they weren't quite understanding the concept. It is especially interesting that Grace simply collapsed reflection and metacognition together in her class, likened it to a practice many think of as awareness, and then talked about its applicability to rhetorical awareness. It is almost as if the different rhetorical effects that others distinguished were a big, squishy, overlapping, synonymous ecology to her.

*****

Grace tended to have a more responsive approach to her teaching style, having general activities planned for the day but responding to the affect of the room in order to make adjustments that she felt would better suit her students in that moment on that day. At the time of data collection, Grace was studying for her PhD candidacy exams in English, with a specialization in digital humanities and affect theory. Grace was a "white, straight woman" who hoped to finish her PhD and then go on to do public-facing scholarship outside the academy. She had graduated with her MA a few years prior and taught at a vocational school for a year in between her MA and PhD. Grace's pedagogy was "182% individualization," which she saw as a "you do you" approach. She hoped that her classes provided her students an opportunity to be "the style of learner [they] think [they are]" and aimed to "just collaborate so that [she knows] what to do to help [her students] get there." Her pedagogy involved "a lot of openness. A lot of [her students] deciding what the rules are for them and what makes sense."

Therefore, Grace incorporated practices like open-ended prompts, being flexible with due dates and modalities employed in writing assignments, and generally "[encouraging] students not to compare themselves to the person next to them and to do their own version of a successful project." Because of her concern that each student processes information differently, Grace established a practice of "processing time" during class where students would digest information from a lecture or an activity in whatever they chose: chatting with a peer in their pod, writing by themselves on their computer or notebook, or something else that they deemed appropriate.

Additionally, Grace broke the norms of meeting with students: Rather than follow her class schedule of 4 days a week, she taught 3 days and then held weekly conferences with her students. During these conferences, Grace "[took the students'] lead" in what the conferences would entail. Grace knew from her own experience and interests that academic writing was not of interest to everyone. Therefore, she hoped her class would help students "figure out how 'so-called nontraditional composition' fits into their lives as students and people in the world and how they can bridge the gap between what they do in the academy and what goes on outside of it." Her primary goal was to help students transfer within and across both academic and public contexts.

In Grace's class, she provided a plethora of opportunities for what she thought of as "tracing the logic." For example, students had weekly conferences where they discussed their drafting process, along with composer's memos that assisted her assessment of the projects once drafted. Neither of these activities were required by the writing program, but they were important to Grace, so she worked within the confines of the required assignments and conferences to make things work for what she thought was important. In offering weekly conferences that discussed student work in various writerly stages (brainstorming, drafting, upon completing a draft, revising, etc.), Grace was able to practice reflection in dynamic and interactive ways throughout the entire writerly process. She incorporated these weekly conferences, despite it not being a programmatic policy. (In fact, she needed special permission to do it as a graduate student instructor.) Doing so allowed the rhetorical rationales she assigned with more finalized drafts, and again at the end of the quarter via program-required cover letters for student portfolios, to almost function like extensions of their informal conversations about their work—just done with different modalities in different mediums.

Within class time itself, Grace also adopted some interesting pedagogical choices to help scaffold for reflective activity. Though she was in a computer integrated classroom, Grace purposefully did not require students to use their computers daily. In an interview, Grace told me that she had formed her opinion on technology use in the CIC based on a conversation with students in previous quarters. In a roundtable discussion with students, students made a case for the educational benefits of using technology as a supplementary tool to look up concepts they did not understand. Grace, therefore, framed the available computers as a supplemental tool for students, not something they were ever required to use. Instead, she often did mini lectures followed by something she calls "processing time." Processing time was designed for open-ended reflection for students to take up however they saw fit. They were encouraged to ruminate internally, discuss with a peer, use the computer to do some writing or mind mapping, or do whatever else seemed appropriate to reflect in their classroom space. After the allotted time, students came back together for a whole-group discussion.

Grace's whole-group discussion had different conversational patterns than was typical. Most teachers adopt what linguists call an IRE speech pattern in whole group discussion, which stands for initiate, respond, evaluate. In this speech pattern, the teacher initiates with a question, the student responds to the question, and the teacher evaluates the student response. However, in Grace's classes, she disrupted that pattern; first she initiated, then students would respond, and next (rather than evaluating) Grace would respond with another question. Grace and her students did this repeated question/response/question/response turn-taking for four or more turns until Grace was satisfied. She signaled a neutral evaluation like "Okay, I hear that" to signal the question/response/question/response turn-taking should cease. According to Grace's responses in interviews, this unique speech pattern was Grace's attempt at making whole-group discussion a possibility for interactive reflection. Regardless of the topic in her course each day, Grace utilized her consistent questioning to encourage reflection. Her hope in doing this was to model the kinds of reflection students might do outside of the academy. Grace liked to "blur the boundaries between the academy and the real world," and she planned reflection to help her do that work—even within the act of reflecting itself. In doing so, Grace made space for students to take up different definitions of reflection, with various rhetorical effect. Her contemporary, Kevin, had a different definition of reflection and thus incorporated reflection differently in his classes, which I detail in the next section.

KEVIN: AN OVERVIEW OF PLANNED REFLECTIVE ACTIVITY IN HIS CLASS

Spring 2017—Urban State University

On day three of Kevin's course, he begins class with a description of what students will do for the day. Students are in long rows, facing the front of the traditional classroom. His class oscillates between the computer integrated classroom and a traditional classroom, equipped with long conference-style tables for students facing forward. Kevin starts the class the way he does in both spaces, with turning on the projector to share the Google slideshow for the day—always with a white and blue theme and a title slide that indicates the topic for the day. Today, Kevin's first slide reads: "Metamoment."

I jot down an observation note to myself; I've never heard of this term before, and I want to follow up with Kevin about where this activity and its title came from.

As I write "metamoment?" Kevin gives his intro: "So what we're gonna do—metacognition, has anyone ever heard of the word metacognition? Maybe you have encountered it. Maybe you've heard the pieces of this word before. Metacognition means 'awareness of understanding of one's thought processes and learning practices.'"

I add to my observation note, "link between 'metamoment' and metacognition? Is this his idea or did someone else model this?"

As I write, Kevin continues with his explanation, pacing at the front of the room by the projector and teacher station. Students are watching him, tracking with their eyes, but none take notes.

"So, it means basically stopping and thinking, 'Why am I learning this way? Why am I being asked to do this?' It's a level of self-awareness that will be incredibly productive throughout this class and well into the future."

I see a few head nods. Though it's an early class, Kevin has an energy that seems to demand students' attention.

> Building metacognition and having meta-awareness means knowing more than what to do, but [also] why you're doing it. It means reflecting on your learning and thinking processes in order to make those processes more flexible and more adaptable. So, the first step to really building metacognition is to step outside of that immediate task before you and start by asking yourself, "Why am I being asked to do this in the first place?" So that's what I'm asking you: "Why do you think I'm asking you to create a syllabus as your very first project?"

Kevin pauses, scanning the room for any hands raised for a question. Seeing no hands raised, just a sea of anticipatory faces, he then gives the class more insight on the activity for the day.

> Alright, so we're going to do this thing called a "freewrite." If you haven't done one of those before, you basically just respond to the question posed with whatever comes to mind. Don't worry about flow or organization or correctness. Just about getting words out. Immediate reactions. You can use whatever you want—computer, paper, whatever. Any questions?

He's met with blank looks from his students. No one moves. In my notes, I jot down, "Class is paying attention but quiet; how does context matter? Are they understanding what he asks?" I should follow up with my focal students.

Kevin takes a deep breath, looking hopefully and patiently across the rows of students while he waits the requisite 10-second pause for any nervous students to tentatively raise a hand. Then, with a nod, he says, "Okay. Just write. Let's give it five minutes." For those three that already have their notebooks out, they begin to write. The remaining students reach into their bags, two pulling out tablets and the remainder paper and pens. Kevin starts a timer that students can view in the upper corner of the screen. Students oscillate between gazing at the questions, staring into space, or attending to their writing.

After class, as I sit reviewing my observation notes, I sit thinking and writing my observation summary. I consider how important the naming of reflective moments might be—this idea of a "meta-moment," for example, seems something purposefully named to signal what kind of thinking Kevin hopes students will engage in. I wonder where the name came from, where the idea for the activity came from, and what students think of it. I need to learn more about this in my upcoming interviews.

*****

Kevin identified as a "Hispanic, gay man." He was a poet but did not see FYC as a place to have students learn about or practice creative writing. Kevin hoped his course would give students the skills necessary to become successful academic writers. As he explained, "I think what I have come to see as the goal for this course is to take seriously the idea of writing as inquiry." Kevin's emphasis on a skill-based approach affected the types of classroom activities he incorporated with his lesson plans and thus the type of activity available for students to participate in. He was more apt to take a structured approach in the classroom, creating closely linked lesson plans and using carefully crafted beginning and closing statements for each class that highlighted what they would learn (or had learned) and how that learning linked to other learning in the class, scaffolded for the upcoming assignment, helped with a skill necessary for a future assignment, connected to the course outcomes, and/or might help in daily life.

Most often, Kevin used his classes to teach and then have students practice specific skills necessary for the upcoming assignments. Because the genre, audience, and purpose are already fixed for all the prompts in his class, his lesson plans tended to be skill-based. As he explained,

> I still try to use these sorts of skills-oriented lessons. Let's say we're doing an abstract. I'll be like, if you look for these five things and you put pressure on every single sentence you can create a really strong 200-word abstract. And that skill is going to serve you.

He most often adopted an approach where he used the initial part of class in the computer classroom to lecture about a concept to students, and then used the remaining time to have students practice that skill with each other in groups through collaborative, computer-mediated activities. As an output of their group work, students most often contributed to the Google Slides for the day, which were either shared via verbal explanation at the end of the class period or the following day in the computer classroom, depending on the time needed for the activity. The days in the traditional classroom typically served as a follow-up to share out and discuss the group activity from the following day or to introduce a new topic that involved lecture, whole-group discussion, and/or freewriting.

Kevin's incorporation of reflection in his classroom activities was different from how he practiced it himself. This distinction between his own practice and his teacherly interpretation of reflection was made clear because he gave me a succinct definition of his own practice of reflection, which he then juxtaposed to how he taught reflection. Kevin described his own reflective practice as

> Reflection is that making of the transition of working to thinking, to really look at what do I know, what have I learned from the gathering and the absorbing, and then what can I take with me in the executing. When I'm teaching, I often make opportunities for reflection that happen in the space between thinking and doing.

Yet, he differentiated how he talked about reflection when he was teaching; "The program uses the word 'metacognition' so that's what I use." Kevin learned the term in orientation, and he noticed that it is in the required outcomes for the course. Therefore, he introduced metacognition to his students but still lets his definition of reflection influence his incorporation of reflective moments in his pedagogy. Kevin saw it as his job to model these things because he "doesn't have faith students can reflect on their own," and therefore Kevin saw himself as needing to prompt and shepherd students through reflective activity. Kevin often named freewriting, group work, and peer review as reflective activities because they could do that metacognitive work while also helping students linger in liminal spaces between thinking and doing.

As Kevin explained to me in an interview, "When you asked me if you could come to my class to study reflection, I thought, 'Wait, I don't do 'reflection' in my course.'" His air quotes around reflection signaled how Kevin thought I'd be looking for something in particular—the kind of thing that Kevin associated with the discussion of metacognition in his writing program's orientation. He had incorporated some reflective writing in the past with "artist's statements" that had "failed," so he doesn't incorporate them much anymore. "I got to be honest, though," Kevin said. "I totally called it 'metamoment' for you. I'd usually just call it a 'freewrite.'" As he explained to me,

> I wanted to be purposeful this quarter with how I incorporated reflection in ways that I actually believe it works, things like metamoments or freewrites or group work or peer review or whatever that are like, "Okay, what did you learn and how can you transfer it?"

Because Kevin's classroom was held in a computer classroom next to Grace's on Mondays and Wednesdays and a traditional classroom on Tuesdays and Thursdays, I noticed that the intended moments of reflection were influenced by the classroom spaces themselves, along with the materials available and his interpretation of them. In an interview, Kevin explained that he felt like he needed to use the computers as something within his lesson plans when his class was scheduled in the computer lab. When he first was assigned to the computer-integrated-classroom, Kevin recounted that he began with lofty goals of using technology like video annotation software, but after some negative experiences with technology failure in his first quarter, Kevin shifted to incorporating "programs and software that are more accountable so if [they] run into trouble [he] can troubleshoot them." Throughout my ethnographic observations, I noted that he used Google Drive products most often—students collaborated nearly every day with Google Docs and/or slides in the computer-integrated-classroom—but occasionally used other programs like Paint, PowerPoint, Adobe Illustrator, and Audacity.

Because of his view of technology, the computers in Kevin's classroom influenced reflective activity differently than Grace's: He tended to spend most of his time in the computer lab doing interactive group work or giving individual work time where students practiced a new skill or technology. Students in the traditional classroom were organized into long rows at long tables, each of which had space for three to four chairs for students. On the 2 days that he had "roundtable" discussions with students, Kevin did ask students to rearrange the room; the rows were reshaped into one large rectangle. Given the classroom was usually in rows, students generally faced the teacher station and projector where Kevin often stood. Sometimes the students faced a side wall or the back of the classroom, which made it harder for them to see the projection during lectures—a more common activity during the traditional classroom days. The large tables in the traditional classroom made student group work more challenging, as they usually chose not to move and remained in long rows, which made hearing and seeing all members in the group difficult. Yet, Kevin still engaged in it regularly. Therefore, even on the days when chairs faced away from the teacher station, students chose to sit in them, assuming the class would mostly involve collaboration with one another. Classroom context shaped Kevin's pedagogy quite distinctly, as he oscillated from computer room to traditional room. Yet, across the contexts, Kevin's pedagogy lent itself well to interactive, collaborative reflection—mediated by technology within the computer-integrated-classroom—with some opportunities for individualistic reflection in writing and internal rumination in both spaces.

Both Kevin and Grace were attentive to how reflection might work differently within the programmatic context. They both took up the word "metacognition" when discussing what they thought of as reflection, seeing reflection and metacognition as synonymous—and using the word "metacognition" in accordance with the expectations of the discourse community. They too were aware of their classroom context; both Kevin and Grace were thoughtful in their use of technology in the classroom, as well as the students' interest in multimodal writing. Yet, they were not as cognizant of (or at least they did not mention) how the demographics of the students themselves might shift their reflective activity offerings. This contrasts with the focal teachers at Rural CC; both Jess and Heather considered how reflection worked for the demographic of students they served, despite the students they served. In fact, they purposefully did reflection differently than they would have (or had done previously) at a PWI. Likewise, L.J., the focal teacher at Southern HBCU, shifted his pedagogy when he moved from a PWI context to Southern HBCU so he could better meet the needs of his students. We will discuss this in the next section.

Southern HBCU Overview

The city surrounding Southern HBCU was mid-sized; it had nearly 200,000 residents, nearly 95% of whom have completed their high school degree or equivalent, 30% of whom have completed their Bachelor of Arts and/or Science degrees, and 20% of whom have completed their post-graduate degrees. Although the area was historically Indigenous land, the most recent census data reports that the city is approximately 50% white, 35% Black, 10% Hispanic, 5% Asian, and 5% people of two or more races. The Native population was such a negligible percentage that it is not reportable in my averaged numbers created for anonymity. Spanish explorers stole the land from Indigenous people, and later the Spanish sold the land to the United States. At the time of data collection, it was home to government, healthcare, and university jobs. Southern HBCU was one of three post-secondary schools in the area—but the only HBCU.

HBCUs have a rich history in the United States. Before the Civil War, there were five institutions that welcomed Black students; they are now named Cheyney University (1837), Avery College (1849), the Miner Institute (1852), Lincoln University (1854) and Wilberforce University (1856) (Sias & Moss, 2011, p. 4). These schools, and others like Southern HBCU, opened their doors throughout segregation; they "were the main sites of higher learning available to people of color when all other doors of education were closed" (Sias & Moss, 2011, p. 5). As Karen Keaton Jackson et al. noted, creation of Historically Black Colleges and Universities, colloquially referred to as "HBCUs," was especially popular in the Reconstruction period after the Civil War to help previously enslaved Black people gain access to education (2019, p. 185).

There are over 100 HBCUs in the United States today. They played an integral role in the Great Black Awakening and have been successful in producing graduates who can go on to high levels of achievement from a general perspective (Sias & Moss, 2011, p. 5). Today, they continue to serve as institutions of educational excellence for students—contributing to "at least 40% [of college-degree graduates] in some science and engineering fields" and thus "[diversifying] historically white graduate and professional programs in

STEM fields, as well" (Lockett & Walker, 2016, p. 172). HBCUs often do more with less, as they are particularly affected by economic depressions (Daniel, 2016; Redd, 2003). Yet, composition research done at or about HBCUs is "most noticeably, and perhaps ironically, absent from this conversation in any consistent way" (Jackson et al., 2019, p. 185).

The kind of teaching done at HBCUs is unique: "Because HBCUs are inundated with difference and because writing instruction at HBCUs requires a type of critical creativity to address these differences, the teaching performed in these classrooms can be instructive to teachers invested in culturally sustaining pedagogies" (Green, 2016, p. 162). HBCUs have more first-generation students and speakers of Black English than PWIs (Jordan, 2012, p. 188). Some scholars who work with Black English speakers and some Black English speakers who are in rhetoric and composition, along with antiracist pedagogues, have worked hard to make linguistic diversity a priority in rhetoric and composition (see NCTE's "Students' Right to Their Own Language" and Smitherman [1999] for a thorough overview of the work that led to this statement)—and have continued to demand linguistic justice (Baker-Bell, 2020), as evidenced by NCTE's most recent "This Ain't Another Statement" (2020). Sometimes, though, HBCUs struggle to implement antiracist linguistic pedagogy because of the pressures within the institutions: Administration and students sometimes insist upon students' need to learn code-switching so they can enter and succeed in the fields that have systematically excluded Black students (Spencer-Maor & Randolph, 2016, p. 179). This is often compounded by the fact that many instructors at HBCUs are trained in literature or Black studies, rather than as compositionists (Spencer-Maor & Randolph, 2016, p. 179). Taking these two together, HBCUs sometimes (inadvertently) "[cling] desperately to the patriarchal and hierarchical skill development and deficiency model of writing pedagogy" (Spencer-Maor & Randolph, 2016, p. 180). Many do work actively to be safe spaces for their students—and succeed—by offering inclusive pedagogy for multilingual and multidialectal students, clarifying college norms to first-generation students, and celebrating a multitude of literacies (see, for example, Paris & Alim, 2017). Thus, scholars insist that HBCUs are important places of inquiry because they give us insight into how "Black rhetorical excellence has thrived at HBCUs" (Moss, 2021, p. 146)—and L.J.'s pedagogy gave me a front-row view into why. L.J. was a full-time instructor at Southern, who taught four classes a semester—three of which were FYW and one was Introduction to African American Literature. I observed two of his FYW courses.

L.J.: AN OVERVIEW OF PLANNED REFLECTIVE ACTIVITY IN HIS CLASS

November 2021—Southern HBCU

We're sitting in what feels like an office devoid of personality—plain white walls, university-issued furniture, fluorescent lighting overhead, and no personal effects in sight. L.J.'s office seems like such a contrast to the vibrant, fashionable clothing choices that L.J. wears each day that I see him in class. My guess is that L.J. does not use his office space often. We've walked together from class to his office, making small talk, and I've turned on my recording device—with his permission—to start our official interview. I've asked L.J. to tell me a bit about his teaching philosophy, and he's busy telling me how he has curated his pedagogy for Southern in particular. Though L.J. was trained "at a large R1 state school that privileged certain ways of reading and writing," L.J. knew firsthand that literacy was "not one size fits all."

As he explains to me, "I wasn't a person who liked to read. I would read for class, but because my dad was a coach, we just read for school so we could play sports."

I nod. I can relate to this. "I feel that," I say.

> I was an athlete growing up. Though I was always a book nerd, I know that plenty of my friends did just enough school to stay compliant for academic eligibility. Sometimes it just feels like academics is just an annoying prerequisite to doing what we're excited about. I wonder if what you were assigned to read had anything to do with it.

He gives a grimace. Then, he decides to disclose a childhood story:

> [I] remember being called 'obnoxious' in class by a teacher in elementary school. It was a competitive class. She kind of saw me being energetic. I told my mom, and it was a whole thing; she told the teacher that I had things to say, and we need to figure out a way for him to be able to express himself.

I lean in, saying, "I'm glad you had your mom."
He smiles and continues,

> So when I was a kid, I didn't read books, but I read other things. And I didn't learn the analytical part until I was here as a student at Southern. I learned to verbalize and think through my thoughts, using discussion. I know firsthand that the white page can be very, very intimidating.

It's interesting to hear this from L.J.; his pedagogy is making more sense to me now. In my class observations, I've made numerous notations about how much scaffolding he does before asking students to write. The scaffolding he does, though, rarely employs the traditional genres of pre-writing I would expect; there is no freewriting, outlining, student conferences, or peer review. Instead, he does a lot of whole-class discussions to model analytical thinking about the texts they read. In doing so, focal students have commented that they feel a real sense of community in his classroom; he has developed trust with his students. They report being invested in the class and his teaching methods. The whole-group discussions feel safe and approachable to them. Given his commentary, I write a note too about how this connects to the days he schedules for in-class writing time. Not only does L.J. create a safe space for exploring analytical thinking but he also relies on that trust to create a less intimidating space for students to start their papers.

As I start to connect my observations to his interview, he continues:

> And here [at Southern], just kind of understanding reading and writing have been particularly damaging and violent for Black and Brown students, they respond verbally. And I can tell that [my students are] a lot more honest when they're verbal. They're a lot more honest, and I think it's simply because the space is safe. Community-building is cool. But writing is not particularly safe to them. Even if they don't tell me that they've been told their writing is bad, I can tell that they have this experience. I try to give them a lot of support to do writing. And, after they do, I try to encourage my students by giving them an opportunity to read their work aloud—not for feedback but just for others to give witness to each other's work and to provide them a safe and convenient way to write and ask questions.

"Connection to culturally sustaining pedagogy?" I ask in my notebook. This reminds me of Django Paris's work; Paris offers a pedagogical approach for teaching students that respects and celebrates students' cultural backgrounds. This seems central to L.J.'s pedagogy. I create bullet points in my journal: "Purposeful builds from student incomes. Focus on emotional responses to writing. Emphasis on community." I draw an arrow. "Trust is integral to the kind of reflection that happens in this class." Then, I write, "Check with student reporting to confirm!" (Later, when I do, I see that L.J. is right: the majority of my focal students report that they do not traditionally enjoy reading and writing. This is, of course, not universally the case: Some folks explain that reading and/or writing is something that they have confidence in. But unilaterally, students agree that this class is different: It values their own identities, insights, and expertise.)

As I jot down notes, L.J. is busy telling me why he thinks that is the case. "I think they gravitate toward the verbal too because of 'nomo': an oral tradition in the Black community that is a form of literacy," he says.

> We know that there are ways that we can prove ourselves as literate outside reading and writing. We rely on the vocality. Geneva Smitherman, David Banks, Keith Gilyard—they emphasize the importance of the oral tradition and voice. If I don't lean into that oral tradition, I'd be doing my students a disservice. That's why we do discussion and then in-class writing assignments where they can use my support to do that translation work across modes—and we do both those things before I ask them to do the writing assignment on their own. I also assign things that they're experts on, things that are based on their own experience. They don't think about how this assignment is so long or so much work because they have a kind of personal experience to draw from.

I nod vigorously as he talks, and we wrap up our interview.

When I review my notes later and I write my observation summary, I write about how L.J. knows his students; he adopts his pedagogy to meet their needs and celebrate their strengths—and he tries to provide opportunities for reflection that are structured toward this rhetorical situation. Reflection supports his pedagogical goals for first-year writing, but he has also adapted the ways that he offers opportunities for reflection by making it responsive to the student population he serves and the institutional type.

*****

L.J. was in his 30s and a graduate of Southern HBCU's undergraduate English program before he went on to do his MA and PhD in African American literature and literacy at a large, state university. Like Jess, L.J. left the program as a PhD candidate to pursue his dream job; L.J. taught at Southern while finishing his dissertation. He too built community with his students, often sharing personal aspects of his life with them. As one of his students explained,

> Dr. L.J. is very relaxed and relatable. I really appreciate him sharing his college experiences with us; he's more than a teacher. He's always like, "Okay tell me how y'all feel," and he makes me feel safe to do that and be real.

In an interview with me, L.J. talked about why he tries to be such an empathetic teacher: He identifies as Christian, which shapes "how [he] interact[s], showing grace and empathy."

L.J. has a lot of empathy for his students because of his past experiences. L.J. went to a PWI and R1 for 1 year before attending Southern HBCU for the remainder of his undergraduate experience. During his first year of college, at the PWI, L.J. regularly found himself to be one of the only Black students in his classes, which caused him to feel "alone and misunderstood." The racism and sexism in the academy affected his typical scholarly practices. He left and enrolled at Southern HBCU, where he found a home. When L.J. was an undergraduate student, he had dreams of being a band director. Though he did start as a music major at Southern HBCU, he ultimately became an English major because it brought him joy. After his first English class, L.J. quickly realized that he wanted to learn more about African American literature. L.J. was so interested in African American literature because he wanted to write scholarship that "help[s] students and people back home learn about themselves." Music was still part of his life, though, even after pursuing his MA/PhD in African American literature and teaching literature and writing courses. "Hip hop is the soundtrack of my life," he said, and I saw that to be true in his pedagogy. He often included music in his classes; sometimes in more robust ways like teaching analysis, and others in smaller ways like playing music in the background during writing time.

L.J.'s definition of reflection was adapted for his specific context: Southern HBCU. L.J. went to a large R1 university for his graduate program, where he was trained to do reflection as a static, retroactive text via the process memo. Once at Southern, though, L.J. thought it was more important to consider "how to do the work of those process memos as a living and breathing thing—and instead do more of what I've done with reflection." As he explained, "Reflection has taught me about myself and made me reassess (as a student, writer, person)." Because of this, L.J. no longer assigned process memos but instead asked students to engage in other activities that were more dynamic and conversation-oriented. He often incorporated whole-group discussions that do community-building work. Five different times in the semester, for example, L.J. uses the entire class period to ask students to share what they are feeling as they adjust to college. Students shared their stressors as college students, and L.J. offered advice. His reflective classroom community was also fostered via weekly engagement with Yellow Dig, an educational discussion board platform modeled like a social media page. Though

L.J. used discussion boards in the past, he told me that he started using Yellow Dig so students could communicate in ways that were similar to the ways they already do outside of class. Yellow Dig was required weekly for students as low-stakes class participation and meant to be a kind of daily reflective activity for students.

His more "formal assignments" also functioned as an opportunity to practice reflection. They included a short story about a life-changing moment in their lives, a letter to a character from that story, and a letter to their future, present, or past selves. All the assignments were extensions of the kinds of reflection he required of students in their interactive discussions in person and online. As he told his students, reflection can be an opportunity to "knock your own hustle": L.J.'s colloquial way of explaining that reflection can help people address the experiences and feelings they tend to ignore, and thus dismantle the false identities they perform. Because L.J. did so much work disclosing personal stories about himself, neither the students nor L.J. saw his reflective assignments as out of the bounds of what could be welcomed in the academy. Especially as a graduate of Southern HBCU, L.J. felt like these assignments were important ways of recognizing the personal within a safe space.

Reflection, therefore, was an important aspect of L.J.'s pedagogy. Though he did not assign traditional reflective genres of writer's memos, freewrites, and cover letters, L.J. very purposefully incorporated personal writing in his course as a way of doing reflection differently. L.J's understanding of reflection differed from other instructors because he saw reflection as a way of working on the "interior" and "addressing blind spots." This, to me, seemed to be a more introspective rhetorical effect for reflection. It was almost as if his goal for reflection was an exploration of self to better the self, rather than to bring an awareness to thoughts and choices simply because it could help with rhetorical awareness in the writing process. Though his own definition of reflection was aligned with a reflection-for-introspection, L.J. was careful to give space for students to take up reflection in different ways. His insistence that students engage in reflective conversation to scaffold toward reflective writing gave ample space for students to match their own practices of reflection onto the myriad of genres that were ripe for reflective activity. L.J.'s culturally aware approach both made space for the emancipatory potential of reflection and left open whether or not students would feel comfortable taking it up for that purpose.

Conclusion: Reflective Pedagogy, Teacher Intentions, and Adapting to Institutional Contexts

In reviewing the five focal teachers' pedagogical choices for incorporating reflection, I hope I have made it clear how the definitions of reflection that the instructors themselves hold are instrumental in what kinds of reflection is made available to students. Throughout all the courses in all the contexts, writing was an available modality of reflection. This makes sense: writing classrooms often use traditional, alphabetic communication as a primary source of communication (see, for example, Shipka, 2009; Selfe, 2009; Yancey, 2004). Rhetorical rationales of students' own work (e.g., portfolio cover letters, writer's memos, artist statements) were the most common form of written reflection, with four of the five assigning them. Many of the course assignments themselves were deemed reflective, as was the case in Grace's, Jess's, Heather's, and L.J.'s classes. Kevin's students did not comment on his course assignments as reflective, but instead focused on the pre-writing that he emphasized—often discussing freewrites as reflection, which were common in his class. Yet instructors also hoped that dynamic moments of their pedagogy could be a way of practicing reflection. (Or, in Heather's and Jess's case, they lamented their inability to incorporate those kinds of reflective interactions given their course structure). Grace, for example, did weekly conferences, and her students commonly talked about her weekly student-teacher conferences as examples of reflection. L.J. used Yellow Dig, a social media–like interface that he used in lieu of a discussion board for community-building and responding to readings, and students often brought that up—as well as the whole-group discussions that he often hosted to help students work through their stresses about being 1st-year students. Kevin often included pre-writing exercises like freewrites, peer review, technology demonstrations, revision, and group work—all of which were mentioned by students. Jess often did pre-writing scaffolding, so students were constantly getting feedback from her, and students mentioned their interpretation of feedback as part of their reflective practice in her course, as well as applying the weekly meeting to the weekly assignments.

All teachers suggested that reflection is something they do in their daily lives—and they agreed that reflection is integral to the writing process. All teachers reported being indoctrinated into reflection in the ways most adopted by the field today: They were taught that reflection is a way of thinking about writerly choices (often retroactively, through writing) to foster rhetorical awareness and knowledge transfer. They were encouraged (even occasionally mandated) to include some sort of rhetorical rationale reflective assignments when they were teaching FYW courses. Whether they did take up these traditional genres of reflection or encouraged other kinds of reflective activity in their pedagogy was influenced by *so many* different rhetorical factors. In each of their cases, their teacher persona, institutional contexts, classroom contexts, student population, teaching philosophies, programmatic constraints, materials, technologies, affect, perceived power relationships, available means of communication, and more all contributed to how teachers tried to incorporate reflection in the writing classroom.

I hope this chapter demonstrates that reflection is *so much more* than reflective writer's memos and portfolio cover letters. It is conversational and dynamic; concurrent, retroactive, preemptive, and forward-thinking; and always collaborative. Teachers *very purposefully* structure moments that can be picked up as reflection in the most mundane of everyday writing classroom genres: whole-group discussion, analysis of sample tests, and classroom community-building conversations; student-teacher conferences that help with pre-writing, feedback interpretation; group work, peer review, and freewrites; personal narrative course assignments, multimodal course assignments, and traditional rhetorical rationale assignments; discussion boards, social media posts, and other online communication. Every one of those genres is carefully selected, curated, and designed to be a potential reflective activity. It is time that we, as a field, start to think about how reflection is just as commonly done in all these innovative and culturally responsive ways, for all sorts of rhetorical effects. Additionally, it is important that we, as teachers, continue to remind ourselves of all the many tools at our disposal to incorporate potential reflective moments in our classrooms—moments that are context-responsive and thoughtfully designed.

In this chapter, we have discussed how teachers adapt their definitions of reflection—and then translate it into pedagogical activities that serve as pedagogical invitations for students to do reflective work. We started our chapter reading a story about Jess, a teacher who "breaks all the rules" to try to meet the needs of her students. Though she does incorporate a relatively traditional definition of reflection—reflection is a way of practicing and articulating rhetorical awareness for writers—she made room for her students within her pedagogy. Jess was careful to respond to Covid-19; she did not assign work that made students feel like their reflection is performative and thus a waste of time. The next chapter will serve as insight into how students' own definitions of reflection help them identify and practice reflection that is both made available by teachers and made available through their own means.

When I talked to Jess's students, for example, they agreed with me: Jess offers lots of different spaces for reflection—and reflection was helpful for them to see the connections between what they are doing. One student, Francis, explained,

> Those weekly meetings are super helpful. Jess is always like, "Here's what we're doing this week, here's why we're doing it, here's how I see it building from last week, here's how I see it building towards the next." It gives me a sense of what's happening and why—and I can reflect on my progress in the course.

However, it's not just those weekly meetings that give Francis a chance to reflect on his progress. "I've never had a teacher who so clearly explains how each thing connects to each other," he told me in his last interview.

> Especially now, like looking back at the class in this self-assessment, I realize in her prompts, it's so clear: Everything we're doing helps connect to something else. I think that's why the smaller assignments never really felt like busy work. We knew why it was connected.

This kind of sentiment was exactly what Jess was going for: Reflection is an integral, important part of the writing process—not something that was assigned just for the sake of creating work for students. One of the reasons why Jess's offerings of reflection were named, identified, and practiced as reflection by Francis is because Francis's definition of reflection mapped on to Jess's—and that was not just because Jess gave him her definition and he adopted it as his own. In fact, Francis gave me the following definition of reflection the first week of the semester, even before Jess and I met: "Reflection is a kind of looking inward at your own thoughts and actions and considering them and analyzing what has been done and all that." Like Jess, Francis saw reflection as an intentional introspection. Additionally, Francis (like Jess) was apt to see reflection as central to the writing process, citing his definition of reflection as being most influenced by past reflective assignments that required him to explain his writerly choices. In Jess's class, these assignments were called "rhetorical rationales," and Francis saw those as the kind of reflection he did often in high school.

When I talked to Francis at the end of Jess's class, for our final interview, I asked about examples of his definition of reflection—and whether his definition has shifted. It had remained largely the same; Francis this time said it was a "time of introspection to figure out why I do what I do." For him, reflection is a pausing—and though he often describes reflection as having the rhetorical effect of self-awareness and growth, he never explicitly named that as part of his definition in this iteration (or the other two times that I asked him). Though the music presentation and peer response were very strategically pitched as non–peer review, he specifically named both the "peer review" and the "rhetorical rationale that the [peer review] helped us write" as examples of reflection happening in his class then. To me, it was not necessarily surprising that Francis saw the rhetorical rationale as reflection. He had named that kind of writing as reflective in his very first meeting with me, and it was his foundational experience for understanding what reflection was. It is important to note that I am not arguing that definitions are the sole factor in naming, defining, and practicing reflection. Contextual factors play a large role, as I discussed in this chapter and will continue to demonstrate in the next. Francis did acknowledge in this interview that he often "reflected on other people and world events outside of school," and reflection at school often relied on "looking inward." Additionally, even the contextual factors seemed to be important within the academic setting. He spent so much time reflecting on this project because "it was a really big cool project (for myself and for the grading)." In this instance, having time, energy, and excitement played a role in his ability to use reflection (and acknowledge its use).

Thus, the definition and the context work together for reflective activity to emerge. Francis explained that "for this music project, I had to reflect a lot, especially with me and my own language—and then be really clear about those reflections on my own actions and statements when I tried to describe my choices to Jess." When asked how he was reflecting in the course when we talked during our second meeting, he named the "rhetorical rationale" required of the music project as a type of reflection, as well as the "draft-in-progress presentation," "the peer review," and his interpretation of peers' comments. The experience of doing not just the rhetorical rationale but also the music presentation and peer response preceding it taught Francis that he "needed to get better about time management" and that it's "difficult to mix outside-of-school interests in academic spaces" because his "video review" was much more time intensive than "anything [he] had written in college." As Francis explained to me in the interview, the experience taught him that "in the future my own personal creative hobbies should be completely separate from school, I guess—as fun as it was to combine the two."

Both Jess and Francis had similar definitions of reflection—and they saw similar activities as examples of reflection in their classroom in this example. However, that was not always the case in Jess's classes, nor in any of the other teachers' classes. Students responded to teachers' well-intentioned pedagogies in a variety of ways. They sometimes latched onto moments that teachers designed as reflection, practicing reflection in ways that were intended. However, they also subverted and queered these moments. At times, they adopted them differently. They often pushed back against moments designed to be reflective by saying not only did they not see it as an example of reflection but also it could never be an opportunity for reflection. They so often found new moments of reflection—moments not designed to be reflection, per se, but taken up and practiced as it anyway. Additionally, they often included reflection in ways not required of them, taking up reflection outside of class to aid them in their reflective process (even when these moments were not required or accounted for by their instructors).

As Jess and Francis demonstrated, students naming, identifying, and practicing reflection was never as easy as an instructor finding an opportunity for reflection and hoping that it worked. Instead, students' and teachers' definitions, past experiences, goals, and contextual factors bumped against one another. It was only when they worked together in synergistic, communal, and distributed agency that reflection came to be in the ways that teachers intended it. Even still, students made plenty of opportunities to subvert, queer, and invent reflection outside of what was originally proposed. In the next chapter, then, we will explore this complicated phenomenon, considering: What causes reflection to be taken up and morphed into a different practice than what we were expecting? What causes reflection to be invented in new and innovative ways? What causes reflection to fail?

4
Practicing Reflection in the Everyday Moments of the Composition Classroom

March 2017—Urban State University

Mia, a focal student from Kevin's class, sits across from me in the computer science building's atrium, face animated and bright from the natural sunlight streaming in from the skylights on this unusually sunny day. It is no surprise that we struggled to find a table; students can enjoy the sunlight while still having table space, coffee, and internet: an undergraduate's dream. The atrium is so grand and modern—loft-like ceilings and all hard finishes—that the voices in the common area echo loudly, creating a raucous backdrop for our first meeting. Mia had selected our meeting place, and she chose the location because she just finished teaching in the building. Despite being a 1st-year student, Mia already serves as a teaching assistant in the Introduction to Computer Studies class; she is excelling in her area of study.

I start our interview by overviewing the focal student process, and Mia agrees to it. Then I tell her:

> The first thing that I'd like to do today is hear a little bit more about you. It's important that you get to share what you think the audience of my research should know about you. I'll give you an example of

https://doi.org/10.7330/9781646426942.c004

what would be important for me, if the situation was reversed and I was giving information about myself. I'd say something like I'm a 4th-year graduate student in rhetoric and composition, working on my dissertation. I'm originally from Michigan, and I still feel like a Midwesterner at heart, even though I've been living and working [here] for the last four years. In fact, I still cheer for the University of Michigan more than I'd ever watch a [local university] sports game—and that's even with the fact that I work directly with a lot of student athletes as part of SAAS—our student athletic academic services program. I'm really hoping to be a professor one day. I'm beyond over the financial insecurity of being a graduate student, but I do love my job as a teacher at UW, where I teach first-year writing and help a bit with training other TAs.

I pause, then say, "So that's me. How about you?"

Mia talks excitedly about her intended trajectory, gesturing largely throughout an animated, 2-minute-long monologue. Mia plans to finish her undergraduate degree in "no more than three years" so she can join "the industry" sooner because "financial stability" is on her mind. Although money is important to her, Mia wants to be careful to join an ethical company because she really "cares about the environment." Mia hopes she can find an entry-level job like the company that she is working at now: a start-up involved with renewable energy. "In a perfect world," she concludes, "I want to figure out how to combine my love for music and computer-coding together and then use that knowledge to benefit a social cause."

As Mia wraps up her long-winded response, she chuckles to herself and says to me, "So you caught me at just the right flavor of tired when I talk for way too long about stuff."

We both full-belly laugh, and I think to myself, How on earth is this student in her first year of college? Sure, Urban is on the quarter system, and, because it is the second day of spring quarter, Mia has been a university student for 6 months. All the same, I am struck by her self-awareness, and I'm interested to see if the topic of my research study—reflection—has anything to do with it.

We move next to questions asking her views about writing and composition requirements more specifically, and she tells me that she has "always been a writer for processing things," but she's "not a super fan of academic writing." Mia enrolled in Kevin's multimodal-themed first-year-writing course because she heard it was the "easiest" course that satisfied the first-year-writing requirement—and "figured the multimodal composition would make it more interesting." We share a brief laugh, and I tell her I appreciate her candor.

"I get it," I say. "I actually teach writing because it's so hard for me. I want to help other people understand it because it doesn't come naturally to me. Don't worry, I read trashy novels from the drugstore and pull all-nighters to finish term papers like the rest of us."

We laugh again, and I bring us back to the next set of questions.

"What does reflection mean to you, Mia?" I ask.

She begins, "Reflection . . . okay. Well, for me that has a very specific meaning."

She pauses again and looks upward, above our heads. I note the time in my notebook, telling myself to circle back to the movement; it seems like potential glimpse of what Sharon Pianko (1979) calls a "pregnant pause." "Pregnant pause?" I write, and when I review later, I see how Mia seems to be momentarily reflecting as she prepares to answer my question about her definition of reflection.

"Ok," she says after a moment, gazing once again at me, "So I went to grade school and my school is very secular. I wasn't really exposed to the church at all so walking in, you know, was a bit of a culture shock."

I nod along in agreement. Mia, with her unbuttoned flannel shirt hanging loosely over her fitted black dress, black tights, and black combat boots might be a bit uncomfortable with the sudden lack of personal expression as she shifted from a secular to religious schooling from grade school to high school.

Meanwhile, she elaborates,

> They were good at, you know, not forcing religion down your throat but one thing we did was kind of religious reflections, like, you know, kind of thinking about—and it wasn't always "think of how this deepens your relationship with God" kind of thing—but "think about how this really connects to overall, the good ideas of religion." By good ideas I mean care for your neighbors and that part, the secular part of theology.

I note the interesting choice of phrasing in my notebook: "The secular part of theology" and put down a time stamp to review this portion of the interview later too. When I journal about it later, I think about how reflection is often connected to civic engagement—a way of creating empathy for others, understanding the stakes of social activism, and even considering alternative perspectives.

As I do, she concludes, "So, that's what reflection means to me: more thinking about service reflection, reflecting on service I've done or when I think about a spiritual thing. Reflection tends to make me think really about the universe and really consider things."

I can relate to Mia's experience, so I tell her, trying to build rapport, "I went to an all-women's Catholic school, similarly liberal as far as religious schooling can go, where we wrote service reflections each year."

She nods and says, "So you get it."

I push on, asking clarifying questions about exactly how this definition of reflection shapes her current practice.

Mia tends to do "reflections for [herself]," mostly "in writing." Before her religious high school experience, her grade school was inquiry-based and taught her "to question the nature of things" and "understand how things worked." She applied that type of thinking to her high school's required reflective writing. Because of this, she had a "positive relationship" with the practice of considering complex issues through reflective writing that was required in high school—so much so that now reflection has become a daily habit for Mia.

"Interesting," I say. "What started as a required practice at school has transitioned into a daily practice." She nods, and I ask her, "Can you give me an example of what you mean?"

Mia quickly responds:

> Yeah cool, so, actually just came from teaching my [computer science] section, and I usually try to make a quick little reflection after I teach because in that moment, right after, that's when stuff is freshest and I try to say this is what overall I was feeling as I walked out, what feeling and maybe why, what were some things that went badly, or some things that went well and based off of those what do I need to do maybe tonight if I need to send everyone an email for the next section, what I may keep in mind to cover, etc.

What she says is interesting to me, and in my journal later I write about it. There is something about the past, the present, the self-motivation, the ephemeral, the affectual, the timing, and the materials that all work together to make these reflections have meaning for Mia. I pause, thinking, and reposition my pen from the note-taking column in my notebook to the analysis column in my notebook—a common practice for ethnographers. Perhaps we have looked at reflection only in the writing classroom in genres where we think it lives: the written reflections that teachers assign. But, what about all the other innovative ways that students use reflection that they come up with all on their own? How can we account for those? And does the affinity for one thing (in this case, journaling) translate well to related classroom genres (in this case, freewriting)? Why or why not?

May 2017—Urban State University

We're about two-thirds of the way through the quarter, and we're in the traditional classroom today. There's a bit of "I wish it was summer" energy in the room today among students. The sunshiny day makes its way inside via the wall of windows. Students tend to gravitate toward that side of the room, making small talk with each other as they sit down.

Then, Kevin arrives and says, "Good morning! Would you all mind helping me with something? I'm trying to make this room into a kind of a circle this morning, so we can have a round table discussion."

Present students quickly oblige, and newly arrived students help too immediately upon entering. It is unusual for Kevin to adjust the physical space for pedagogical purposes; he's only done this one other time in the semester (also in this room). Given the length of the desks and the size of the room, it ends up more as an oblong rectangular shape, but the students are careful to make the chairs all face interiorly so they can see each other's faces today, as they would in a circle formation. All students are present today, and once done with the rearranging, they all sit in the newly arranged classroom with a few seconds to spare before class starts.

Kevin begins class as he always does: the projector switches from a black screen to share the white-and-blue-themed Google slide presentation for the day. He begins class with what I refer to as a "cue for transfer," or an explicit attempt to connect learning across contexts. For Kevin, this happens daily in opening and closing statements that range from 5 to 7 minutes.

Kevin begins:

> Alright, so today we're going to continue learning about podcasts by doing a rhetorical analysis of a podcast on narrative medicine today. Yesterday you brought in samples of your favorite podcasts, and we worked in groups to come up with general genre conventions for podcasts. We even distinguished a bit across different kinds of podcasts—true crime podcasts seemed to have different genre moves

than news podcasts, right? So today I want to build from that. I want us to see how design and content choices get us to *react* to podcasts. Our goal today is to relisten to the podcast that you listened to for homework. I was hoping that listening to it last night would orient you to the content, narrative medicine. Today, we're doing a rhetorical analysis of it. I'm hoping to get into how rhetorically effective this podcast is for you. I chose a narrative medicine podcast because I know a lot of you are pre-med, so you're the author's intended audience for this episode. But, even if you aren't, I feel like you can try to put yourself in that position by pretending to be someone interested in being a doctor. We'll be thinking about how you feel when listening to the podcast. What do you feel? And what are the podcast creators doing with design and content choices that make you feel that way? I'm hoping this rhetorical analysis will make it easier to figure out your own design and content choices for your podcast, which is due this Sunday at midnight.

As Kevin talks, he paces across the front of the room, with a backdrop that only says, "rhetorical analysis of podcasts." Though their bodies are facing away from him because Kevin has requested that they sit facing each other, only two students bother to crane their necks or rotate to see him. Instead, students use this time to settle in, getting comfortable in their seats, rearranging coats and bags, sending out one more text or email. They eventually settle, and still by the end of his monologue but no one shows any outward form of engagement (e.g., following Kevin with their eyes, writing notes, or nodding along).

If I didn't know better, I'd think this time was entirely useless to students. But as focal students have told me during interviews (and as the surveys echo from their peers later), these cues for transfer are important moments of reflection for many. "When Kevin does that thing where he talks about what we're doing and why," one writes, "I just feel like I have this moment of clarity. Like this is why yesterday was helpful. This is what I need to pay attention to today." Another focal student says, "The way he opens and closes class is like the connective tissue I need for me to reflect across what I'm learning in his class. I wish all my teachers did that."

Then, Kevin switches from the title slide to a slide entitled "Freewrite." As soon as he does this, there's a flurry of movement; students reach toward their bags to get out notebooks, pens, paper, or computers.

He ignores the movement, saying,

But narrative medicine really troubles that bifurcation between subject and object as two different things. So that's what we're going to talk about, well, first you're going to write about in your freewrite. And then you're going to discuss. So, here's the freewrite. For the next five minutes—I'll go ahead and start a timer.

Kevin quickly reads the prompt from the slide (a hearty paragraph requesting that students do a reader response of the podcast they listened to last night). As he does, all students but three have turned their bodies to watch him and read the slide. Many seem to have a "thinking face" that indicates they're starting to ruminate on the prompt. Then, the students begin their freewrite. They never wait for (nor does he give) additional information about how to do the freewrite, how to use their bodies, or how to select materials. Once he's done reading, all the students face their desks and begin writing (presumably in response to Kevin's questions), almost all with a pen and paper.

May 2017—Urban State University

One week later, I am sitting in an interview with Mia. This time we're cramped in my light blue office, fluorescent light glaring above us. We're meeting here out of convenience; it is near where Mia is heading next. Mia sits alongside my desk, chair pulled to the right-hand side of my desk. In my office, there is no room for her to sit across from me, lest she block the door or the path to the desk of one of my two colleagues' with whom I share the space, so I rotate my graying office chair to face her at a 90° angle. We know each other by now, our familiarity making it comfortable for Mia to start talking about the course that she is TAing as soon as she plops down, coffee in hand. I ask her if I can start the recording and she agrees, but rather than getting right into the interview, we chitchat about her teaching for 10 minutes before the conversation dies down enough for me to gently transition us into our formal interview. I say, "I'm so glad that you care so much about teaching, and I'm sure that your students are benefiting from your constant self-reflexivity of your teaching practice."

"Thank you," Mia says. "And thanks for listening. Teaching has been taking up a lot of brain space lately."

"Totally. Are you ready to start our interview? Or do you want to talk more?"

"I'm ready."

Mia nods, and I continue.

"We will begin, as usual, with checking in about your definitions of reflection and moments where you identify potential moments of it and practice it in and outside your writing class lately," I say.

> Then, I want to conclude with a quick activity, so I can hear your opinions about the way scholars in my field discuss reflection. I'll give you three definitions of reflection and ask your thoughts about them—and whether you can think of any examples of them. You ready?

Her energetic mood is deflated; Mia lets out a tired sigh. I look at her concerned, with my eyebrows raised, as if to ask "Are you okay?" "Does that not work for you?"

She lets out a little a laugh. "I'm sorry. It's almost the end of the quarter, I'm tired, and confession time: I have not been to class much lately. I missed two days [of the four scheduled] last week and I missed yesterday. I just didn't want to go."

It's true; Mia's dependable attendance of the first half of the quarter has become unreliable in the latter half of the quarter.

With a comforting smile, I say, "Yeah. I noticed. What's going on?"

She grimaces. "I'm just getting really sick of Kevin talking at us all the time. He treats us like we're in high school."

I'm a bit surprised by her reasoning. No other focal students have mentioned feeling this way. Despite the familiar "I wish it was summer" vibe that seems to be everywhere on campus, students are generally happy and engaged in Kevin's class. So, I ask, genuinely curious, "Do you mind giving me an example?"

> I just feel like he's always just talking. Like our computer classroom is a space that demands interactivity, and since he's talking so much at the beginning and end of each class, we just don't get the opportunity to do enough interacting with each other.

I try to be objective. It's true that Kevin does incorporate moments that I consider a "cue for transfer" at the beginning or end of class; we just saw an example in the last story. Kevin describes what students have learned or will learn and how that connects to past learning/future learning goals.

I say, "It sounds like you're really frustrated."

Mia nods vehemently. "Yeah, his class isn't something I have the patience for right now, but honestly, it's probably me. I'm just over this semester."

"I hear that," I say. "You should talk to Kevin about how you're feeling. I bet he'd be receptive. Are you still up for our interview?"

She nods half-heartedly, and I'd push further, but it feels like, with us recording, this isn't the time or place. I'll loop back with her after the official interview.

"Mia, how have you been defining reflection lately?" I ask.

> You know. It feels the same. I've been thinking about it as a way of doing that kind of deep consideration that I talk about. But to be honest, I'm having trouble finding examples for you, at least in our class, because we're not really asked to think big like that. I guess we kind of do get to talk about our choices and stuff in the writer's memos, and I guess if an assignment got me to change my perspective or like see something differently, I might, I don't know it's possible I could get into that. But mostly, it just feels a bit performative to me because I know it'll influence my grade.

"Tell me more," I say.

> I don't know. It's like, well. Really, we just do these simple assignments almost every week, like I can mail it in. I don't really have to think too hard about it. And I can write these big writer's memos that talk about my project and "oh I learned *so* much" but I don't have to do that much learning, really.

As Mia talks, I make some notes in my analysis section of my notebook. There's something about the intellectual rigor of the assignments that is important to Mia. It seems to be related to her level of investment and her ability to do reflective work alongside it. Based on my immediate observations, I decide to encourage a follow-up.

"So, you think the writer's memos might be an example of reflection, but it really depends on if you feel like you're being honest in them," I say, trying to repeat back.

"Yeah, it's like sometimes, yes. Sometimes, no. Depends on if I'm being truthful or just saying what he wants to hear," Mia says.

"Reflection can be performative," I write in my notebook.

"Okay, is there anything that you can think of that's a more consistent example of reflective activity lately related to this class? Or is it just not happening?" I ask.

Mia pauses for a few seconds, and her face scrunches a bit as she thinks. "You know, actually, let me show you something. I didn't think of it at first because it wasn't something Kevin made us do. But I got really invested in our MP1, and I did a lot of reflective work for it."

"MP1" is the shorthand for the first major project in Kevin's class. Students had to create their own course description, course goals, and sample reading schedule for an interdisciplinary course of their creation. Mia is busy shuffling things in her bag; she finds a notebook and flips pages until she finds a handwritten page with lots of questions, arrows, and some circled declarative statements. As she pulls it out, she's telling me the context.

"I just got super into MP1," she says. "I really wanted to get this one right, so I did a lot of reflection on it. Like on my own. Outside of class."

I nod, encouraging her to continue.

"Here. Take a look," she says, giving me her notebook.

> So, like. I don't—well, it's kind of like the journaling I showed you in the first interview. But it's not the whole after something happens like I do with teaching. Well, I guess I also did some of that in my revision freewrites after peer review too, but this one here is more like a freewrite that helps with the ideation. The drafting. I did it in a way where I kind of open my mind and like let all my thoughts spill out. Like all my questions and ideas about something I'm working on just [hand taps on the page]. They just go on the page as I think of them. And I might try to show relationships between ideas if I have a sense of how they fit. But the real point is to just to think it out.

I switch again to the analysis side of my notebook: there's something about Mia's investment, her choice to do it, the way that she borrows from her journaling practice to do something more proactive, that's all at play here. I quickly jot notes down as Mia starts talking through her freewrite, unprompted. Mia is back to sounding like her typical energetic, cheerful self. She is clearly excited to show me the reflection she has done, pointing out what she hopes that I note.

"So, you see, here. Yeah?" I nod.

She responds:

> Right, so I started the page with a statement—"turning these questions into an argument for music education"—to remind me that I need to use these questions as a jumping off point when I get going on the work. Then, I've got all these questions, right? You can see them kind of building off each other as one thought leads to another. Like, I say, "what is music education," which leads to "what happens

as a result of music ed [sic]," and then "why should we care about enhancing music education." That leads to this question ("what values as humans and society are called into play") and another ("what should we do") and another ("how to contribute") and another ("what types of design exist"). I end with the questions "what is the goal of an interface," "how do design goals change when the audience changes," and "what is the best way to educate." I don't really ask these questions to answer them, but to show the thoughts I need to brainstorm and then address in my assignment.

I'm looking at the notebook entry and following her train of thought. There are a couple of arrows on the page to show relationships between questions that she posed, and three scattered declarative sentences that are circled, almost functioning as starting points for conclusions she wants to take up in the assignment. "This class is about contributing to music ed [sic]" sits near the first clump of questions she pointed out to me. "Moves into design" is near the second. And "we will use technology" is near the last.

I can see why Mia is so excited about this project: it's combining music and technology, her top interests that she noted in her first interview. I also see elements of what Mia described as reflection in the first interview. The freewrite that she shows me seems to employ the kind of inquiry-based thinking that she practiced in K–8 but takes on the written form that she adopted in 9–12. I'd talk to her more about it, but with the 10 minutes of our time spent on teaching-talk, I need to move us along.

"Thank you for sharing this," I say. "You ready for the activity? I'm really looking to hear your thoughts about how the field describes reflection."

I close out the rest of the interview as quickly as possible. I share a paraphrased definition of reflection-in-presentation and learn that Mia sees writer's memos, student-teacher conferences, and the end-of-class ePortfolio as examples of reflection in presentation. Then, I share a paraphrased definition of reflection-in-action and learn that the self-prompted drafting freewrites like the one she just showed me (in addition to the ones she creates for revision ideas) are examples of reflection-in-action. And I share a paraphrased definition of constructive reflection and learn that the design and writing skills that Kevin tends to teach in the computer classroom are examples of constructive reflection.

In my notebook, I write down a note to go back and review what she does not identify as reflection: in-class freewrites. Kevin has included more freewrites throughout the quarter than any other focal teacher. (Kevin asks students to do five freewrites, which means at least 25% of the days of class, students are asked to engage in that activity. Jess and Heather do not incorporate them, L.J. does one, Grace does two.) I know too that Mia journals often as her primary form of reflection, and she has adopted a kind of loose journaling/freewriting practice to brainstorm for her assignments—and I know that she has included those outside-of-class journaling and freewrites as reflection-in-action. So, does she purposely miss freewrites in class? Or is it something that she just forgets to mention? I ask.

> I so appreciate your examples, Mia. I noticed, though, that you started our interview with an example of reflection that you loosely related to freewrites. But, then in this activity, you didn't mention in class "freewrites" as an example of reflection-in-presentation, reflection-in-action, or constructive reflection. You haven't mentioned the in-class ones as examples of reflection, either. Is there a reason for that?

"Oh, like the ones where Kevin tells us to answer a specific question in class?" she asks.

I nod.

"Well, those aren't any kind of reflection for me. They don't allow me to reflect. They're too rigid. It's just not a reflection when it's a directive like that."

I nod, encouraging her to continue. In my notebook, I write, "Sees a disconnect between self-prompted reflective writing and Kevin's prompted writing." Mia rejects Kevin's encouragement for reflection—despite her own practices of self-prompted journaling, brainstorming freewrites, and revision freewrites, as being similar to what Kevin was requiring students to do. It seems like the different materials, timing, structure, investment (or lack thereof)—and her resulting affect—makes it impossible for Mia to take up reflection in the way that Kevin imagined that she would. Of course, this is not the case for all students. All the focal students besides Mia and about half of the surveyed students pinpoint in-class freewrites as an example of reflection in their writing classroom.

After our meeting, I journal in my notebook, asking myself questions: Can Mia's refusal to view in-class freewrites as an opportunity for reflection help us understand the complicated ways that students decide to take up, subvert, queer, or ignore potential moments of reflective activity in the classroom? And how can we take that knowledge to do reflection successfully (or at least with realistic expectations) in our classroom spaces?

*****

In chapter 3, I demonstrated how instructor definitions of reflection, along with the surrounding context of an activity, shape what kinds of reflection teachers try to make available for students. This chapter discusses the complex nature of how reflection is defined, identified, and practiced by students. We opened with a series of stories to try to tease out the messiness of how reflection is understood as a rhetorical activity bound by definitional descriptors; identified or located in potential activities or moment; and practiced or taken up and experienced as reflective activity as potential. It is never as simple as teacher plans for reflection and student reflects; nor is it teacher plans reflection and student refuses to reflect. Sometimes students reflect when the teacher hopes they will and other times they do not. But that success of reflection relies on *so much more* than teacher directive. Students and teachers have definitions of reflection. These definitions of reflection are built from past experiences, and they work as terministic screens to understand what might count as reflective activity. Then, reflectors associate reflection as occurring within certain activities, especially with certain times, feelings, goals, emotions, affects, relationships, materials, and spaces. And, finally, all those contextual factors need to come together in a complicated synergy, working together in a distributed agency to bring reflection into being.

In the above story, Mia, a focal student in Kevin's class, had a different definition of reflection than Kevin did. Mia seemed to associate reflection with a shift in perspective, while Kevin sees reflection as moving knowledge across contexts. Mia's definition of reflection was shaped by her past experiences: she had done inquiry-based reflection and civically minded reflection in her past educational experiences. Her experiences with service reflections had the potential to taint her relationship with reflection; she could have labeled it as something associated with religious ideologies (and thus not something she practices, since she doesn't identify as religious). Mia's rationalization that these reflections were the "secular part" of religion allowed her to engage in reflective activity—albeit subverted from its intention of developing spiritual growth. This experience influenced her capacity to define reflection as a cognitive process that results in perspective-shifting work.

Mia's ability to define reflection and its rhetorical effects influenced the ways she identifies reflection in her daily life (e.g., through journaling, self-prompted freewrites that happen outside of class, and the occasional reflection assignment, in which she was tasked with explaining the rhetorical choices she made about an assignment she was invested in) and then go on to practice it. Mia was able to take these experiences and translate reflection into other genres, ones that she created on her own time. We saw this in Mia's story of adapting her journaling practice to a kind of self-prompted freewriting for writing that she is invested in within Kevin's classes.

Mia subverted in-class freewrites as a potential reflective activity, instead seeing them as moments to simply answer questions. She practiced reflection through something entirely new, something that Kevin never actually saw: her self-prompted pre-writing outside of class. The pre-writing was a mix of journaling and freewriting that Mia already did on her own time to learn from experiences, plan out assignments, and think through revisions. There were places of alignment, where what Kevin put in the curriculum as potential reflective activity and what Mia acknowledged as moments of reflection were in sync. Mia sometimes gravitated toward writer's memos as places where she could do reflection. At times, they could help account for shifts in her perspective—and thus reminded her of the work that she did in high school with service-learning reflections. But writer's memos were not consistent for her because other things get in the way: the power relationship between her and Kevin, the inherent understanding that the honesty in this reflection may result in a higher or lower grade, and the way that the genre tends to push students to talk about their rhetorical choices rather than the effect that the assignment had on them.

When asked to try on different definitions of reflection, though, Mia could consider classroom moments that she might not otherwise consider as reflection: things like portfolio cover letters, student-teacher conferences, or technology overviews. Likewise, when doing the same activity as Mia when given other definitions of reflection, Kevin saw reflection in his daily cues for transfer, analysis of sample texts, peer review, and conferences as new potential moments for transfer. Mia's and Kevin's ability to both identify reflection based on their own definitions and experiences, and to do so with those of other people, makes it clear that reflection is in part rhetorical because naming, identifying, and practicing an activity as reflection is what makes it reflection.

The actual practice of Mia's reflection happened because of the distributed agency of contextual factors. For example, with her post-teaching journal entries, the "thing power" (Bennett, 2010) of Mia's reflective tools—her notebook and black pen—made it possible for her to do the reflective work; using other tools like a tablet or computer would not work for her. The timeliness—both the fact she had time along with the kairotic nature of the reflective activity—played a role. Her memories, her special notebook, having time after class, the feelings she holds, and much more worked together to make reflection possible. Forgetting her notebook, misplacing her black pen, being preoccupied by an upcoming exam, running into a friend after class, or having a headache could reshape her reflective activity or even derail it. This sense of distributed agency of contextual factors explains why freewrites were reflective to Mia in one context but not in another. Kevin designed these freewrites to be taken up as reflection based on his own definition of it, his teaching philosophy, his writing experiences, his view of the available materials, his writing program's requirements, and his own teaching experiences. For Mia, though, these freewrites did not have enough flexibility or stakes for her to feel like they could fall within the bounds of her definition of reflection—and thus she could not identify or practice freewrites as reflection.

Other students in Kevin's class did take up these freewrites as reflective—and they took up other things to be reflective that Kevin didn't even intend to be, particularly Kevin's cues for transfer. Even though Kevin disrupted the typical pattern of physical arrangement in the traditional classroom by asking the early arrival students to rearrange the room so there could be "a large circle"—something he had done only once before during this quarter—students still reacted to and practiced reflection in the slightly rearranged space. His students had developed patterns of arranging their bodies and materials to take up reflection (or not) in the classroom space. In fact, the rearrangement just made the embodiment of reflective practices a bit more obvious to me as the researcher.

Students typically did not follow Kevin with their eyes or bodies during his cue for transfer. They tended to face their bodies away from him (and still did not take notes during the framing statement). Yet, when he mentioned the word freewrite, they engaged with their rhetorical context differently, rearranging their bodies and materials to be how they would typically be: turning to face the person giving instructions momentarily during the explanation and gathering the materials they felt like they needed. Without being prompted by Kevin on how to move their bodies to begin the freewrite or what materials to gather, students began shuffling things in their bags, grabbing paper, pens, pencils. Only a few used computers. In this space, with the materials being used left up to them, students gravitated toward the paper medium, seemingly in response to the rhetorical context they were in for the day: a traditional classroom. Overall, many things play a role in whether the classroom activities will be defined, identified, and practiced as reflection.

Though Mia did not identify this moment as reflective, three of the four focal students and nearly half of the surveyed students mention in-class freewrites as examples of reflection.

Throughout the chapter, then, I am careful to list these three verbs separately—"define," "identify," and "practice"—because they were, in fact, distinct moments to participants. Participants could describe how they think about reflection, locate moments that have reflective potential, and choose to enact reflection (or not) in those moments. Sometimes what teachers planned mapped onto what students did. But for those moments that did not, there were reasons behind that—reasons that often fell outside of the teacher's control. Mia's high school requiring reflections influenced how she reflected through "writing done on [her] own time" about topics she "cares about." Her definition of reflection functioned as a terministic screen, helping her identify and practice reflective activity. Given her affect about the course and the parameters around freewriting in class, she did not practice reflection in the moments Kevin hoped she would.

To be clear, I did not share the opening story as a way of seeing how we could do freewrites differently, nor am I critiquing Kevin's practice. Yes, Kevin could have he altered how he framed freewrites, giving more space for open-ended thinking that might have helped Mia latch onto these moments as potential spaces for reflection. Yet, doing so might have affected the ways other students (who did see freewrites as reflection) were able to practice reflection; perhaps they succeeded in reflection because of the concrete direction. Instead, I shared this story to explain how important it is for a teacher to be aware of students' wide-ranging experiences with reflection and thus their varied needs for finding reflection in their classroom spaces. I share this story to give insight into how students define, identify, and practice reflection more broadly. I share this story to demonstrate how materials, timing, past experiences, emotions, relationships, spatial layout, and affect work together, via a distributed agency, to make students identify reflection in one context and not another.

In the next sections, then, I discuss the role that defining, identifying, and practicing reflection call reflection into being—at times aligning with, disrupting, or rejecting available moments of potential reflection. In doing so, I hope to illuminate why reflection is so complicated; why it's not as simple as setting up and being aware of the rhetorical context, the different definitions of reflection, and then asking students to do it. I explore how reflection is sometimes taken up in the way that the teachers intended but also subverts teacherly expectations. In fact, students were just as apt to engage with planned moments of reflection as they were to ignore those moments as potentialities for reflective work, take up unintentional reflective activities and practice them as reflection, or incorporate unprompted reflection in their day-to-day life outside of class. What was especially important to students' identification and practice of reflection was seeing connections between definitions of reflection and the potential activities available to practice it. The next section begins, then, with an overview of the power of students' definitions.

Defining Reflection: How Definitions of Reflection Can Locate Potential Reflective Moments

In this project, I had 20 focal students: eight students at Urban State U, three students at Rural CC, and nine students at Southern HBCU (see Table 2.1 for each individual participant's unique demographics)—and each of these students had their own definition of reflection. Definitions of reflection do important work in helping students decide whether an activity has the potential to be reflective or not. In *Language as Symbolic Action*, Kenneth Burke uses the term "terministic screens" to describe the ways that language can help select, emphasize, and differentiate meaning. Especially because reflection is an abstract concept, language plays an important role in helping students determine where reflection might live (and rule out places it might not). Definitions of reflection are based on past experiences, and all focal participants could point to a specific moment where they learned what reflection meant to them.

In each interview, I asked students to give me examples of reflection that they practiced both within and outside of class. In our first interview, I asked each focal student to tell me what the audience of this research project might find important about their identity, what their definition of reflection was, and where that definition came from. I then asked students about their definitions of reflection in each interview thereafter, for a total of three times. I was struck by the diversity of activities that focal participants offered as examples of reflection: listening to music, practicing yoga, praying, meditating, walking, brainstorming, freewriting, doodling, engaging with discussion boards, participating in online class forums, trying to use new technologies, participating in group work, responding to readings, doing peer review, conferencing, listening to scaffolding explanations, considering applications to other contexts, using information in new contexts, talking with others, engaging in social media, doing rhetorical rationale assignments, and answering teacher questions. I then coded these examples in the same way as Table 4.1. The general categories are conferences, cue for transfer, extracurricular writing, external processing, feedback, group work, internal processing, online communication, personal reflective assignment, processing time, revision on assignments, rhetorical rationale reflection assignments, transfer of knowledge, and whole group discussion. In Table 4.1, I present an overview of focal participants, their definitions of reflection, the foundational experience they associate with reflection, and the examples of reflection they associate with those definitions.

Throughout our interviews together, I learned how students had a mixed relationship with writing: about a third of students reported enjoying writing and being excited and/or happily willing to engage in their course, a third reported being indifferent about the writing requirement, and a third were frustrated with and/or worried about the course. Their relationship with writing—and whether they thought reflection should be a part of writing at all—played a role in how they defined, identified, and practiced reflection. This was also true of their linguistic repertoires. More than half of the students identified as multilingual or multidialectal—and nearly all those students talked about how they tended to reflect about certain things in one language more often than the other (or just generally reflected in one more often than another).

Likewise, students shared how reflection was inspired by personal events or shaped through interpersonal relationships. Some family members had been instrumental in how they viewed reflection: a loved one introducing them to journaling, nightly conversations with parental caregivers, and girls' nights were readily explored as avenues for reflection. Personal happenings too seemed to trigger reflective action: students shared how the transition to college triggered a kind of uncertainty or lack of familiarity that inspired a more reflective stance. For example, a participant from the West Coast to whom I talked at Southern HBCU experienced extreme culture shock—and this prompted them to be in a "more reflective headspace" than they usually would. Participants with access to cars or gyms, for example, often talked about these spaces as reflective spaces. Participants with different family dynamics and relationships at times pointed to mental health therapy as instrumental to how they reflected and why. Students talked about how tragedies like a loved one's death, a falling out with friends, or a hardship made them realize they should be more present and reflective in their stance.

TABLE 4.1. Focal and surveyed participants' definitions, foundational experiences, and exemplary moments for reflection

Name	School	Definition of reflection	Foundational reflection experience	Examples of reflection
REFLECTION-FOR-AWARENESS				
Angel	Southern HBCU (L.J.)	"I feel like it's a time for considering how do we think we're doing and what do we still need help on."	Using journaling as a coping strategy	1. Extracurricular writing 2. Personal reflection assignments 3. Whole group discussion
Colby	Southern HBCU (L.J.)	"Reflection is that process where you think back or understand the actions that you've taken."	Experiencing change	1. Personal reflective assignments 2. External processing 3. Online communication 4. Whole class discussion
Francis	Rural CC (Jess)	"Well, it's kind of like looking inward at your own thoughts and actions and considering them and analyzing what has been done and all that."	Explaining his writing process to teachers	1. Personal reflective assignments 2. Rhetorical rational assignments
Jennifer	Rural CC (Heather)	"Reflection is the time to take and make sure you're coming across how you want to. Kind of like looking at your work and seeing if that's correct or what's going well."	Experiencing a mental health day in middle school	1. Internal processing 2. Feedback 3. Pre-writing 4. Personal reflective assignments 5. Rhetorical rationale reflective assignments 6. Revision
King	Southern HBCU (L.J.)	"It's a way of looking back at a certain moment in time. When you use your senses to evaluate a situation that's already happened."	Thinking through how tough experiences could have happened differently	1. Personal reflective assignments 2. Internal practice

continued on next page

TABLE 4.1.—continued

Name	School	Definition of reflection	Foundational reflection experience	Examples of reflection
REFLECTION-FOR-INTROSPECTION				
June	Urban State U (Grace)	"I feel like reflection is more like I have done something and how do I feel about it kind of thing. Like how did I get there and how do I feel about it kind of thing. I guess that's what came to my mind when I think of reflection."	Creating scrapbooks through her teenage years to document her experiences	1. Conferences 2. External processing 3. Feedback 4. Internal practice 5. Rhetorical rationale reflective assignments
Tracy	Southern HBCU (L.J.)	"It's like looking inside yourself and digging deep and owning feelings so you can really take the time to consider why you feel that way."	Experiencing grief and loss—and using writing to cope with that	1. Extracurricular writing 2. Personal reflective assignments 3. Whole group discussion
Vanessa	Southern HBCU (L.J.)	"Reflection is when there is stuff in my heart, and I'm trying to get it out. When things hurt me, writing it out gets it out."	Experiencing grief, loss, and regret	1. Extracurricular writing 2. Online communication 3. Personal reflective assignments
REFLECTION-FOR-LEARNING				
Alan	Urban State U (Grace)	"In general, for me reflection is kind of the same thing as metacognition. Thinking about how you do certain things, kind of like how you can do, how you can better yourself in certain ways in situations, I mean they could be different from in different contexts, being introspective about how you do something so you can take that knowledge elsewhere."	Producing reflective texts to practice "metacognition" in a high school class	1. Conferences 2. Internal practice 3. Personal reflective assignments 4. Processing time 5. Rhetorical rationale reflective assignments

continued on next page

TABLE 4.1.—continued

Name	School	Definition of reflection	Foundational reflection experience	Examples of reflection
Conan	Urban State U (Kevin)	"When I think of reflection I guess I think of looking back into the past or like what you've done, your progress and then take from it, take what you've learned from it. I guess if you haven't, if you don't learn anything from your prior action then it's really not a reflection. You need to have something to build upon."	Writing metacognitive rhetorical rationales required in his high school AP classes	1. Processing time 2. Rhetorical rationale reflective assignments 3. Whole group discussion
Maya	Southern HBCU (LJ.)	"To me, reflection is looking back and figuring out what you could have done differently—like what you did wrong and right—so you can do it differently or do it again."	Considering interpersonal dynamics within relationships	1. Internal practice 2. Personal reflective assignments
Paris	Southern HBCU (LJ.)	"Reflection is when you look back on like previous actions or what you've done previously and gather intel and learn from what you gathered."	Identifying as reflective because of being a writer	1. Extracurricular writing 2. Personal reflective assignments
Serena	Urban State U (Kevin)	"Kind of like evaluating what's happened and maybe thinking about different things and why they happened or like I am also seeing where some things maybe went wrong or could have gone better or like being able to be like self-aware of your progress and like your performance. Feel like it's pretty important to growing, learning from failure."	Participating in mandatory conversations with her cross-country coach during high school	1. Conferences 2. Processing time

continued on next page

TABLE 4.1.—continued

Name	School	Definition of reflection	Foundational reflection experience	Examples of reflection
REFLECTION-FOR-MINDFULNESS				
Julie	Urban State U (Grace)	"Well when light passes a mirror or reflecting surface it like bounces off and creates an image of you at a particular angle which is equal to the incident angle so that's the physics meaning but I know you don't mean that, you mean like a reflection of myself or something like that, which is more of like how you can be present."	Taking advanced physics courses in high school taught her the scientific definition, but creating a scrapbook for a going-away gift is how she understands it practically	1. Conferences 2. Feedback 3. Internal practice 4. Personal reflective assignments
REFLECTION-FOR-PERSPECTIVE				
Autumn	Urban State U (Grace)	"I think reflection is like taking the time to be honest with yourself. A lot of the time, you kind of get caught up in whatever you're doing and like I have this, this, and this to accomplish today and so I want to get it all done and you don't take the time to sit back and say where am I going, how did I get here, or maybe even how can I get there."	Going through a difficult time in high school and using journal to work through feelings	1. Conferences 2. External processing 3. Extracurricular writing 4. Internal practice 5. Personal reflective assignments
JoAnn	Southern HBCU (L.J.)	"I just see this as, well, like you think about the actions and something you said and how you did it. Like, how that affects you today and how that affects the world."	Experiencing grief and loss	1. Internal practice 2. Extracurricular writing 3. Online communication 4. Personal reflective assignments

continued on next page

TABLE 4.1.—continued

Name	School	Definition of reflection	Foundational reflection experience	Examples of reflection
Mia	Urban State U (Kevin)	"It tends to make me think really about the universe and to really consider things."	Producing reflective texts about the effects of service on the world and on her personhood at her Catholic high school	1. Extracurricular writing 2. Rhetorical rationale reflective assignments
Miles	Southern HBCU (L.J.)	"It's when I take a step back and evaluate my life, everything I'm doing and want to do and where I'm at, etc."	Experiencing a falling out with friends that changed his perspective on his daily life and future plans	1. Internal process 2. Personal reflective assignments
Rachel	Urban State U (Kevin)	"Reflection is like how does what I'm doing right now connect to everything else that I want to do in my life and even further than that. Kind of like, who am I? Who do I want to be? And how will I get there?"	Taking a psychology class in high school	1. External processing 2. Extracurricular writing 3. Internal practice 4. Processing time
Ryann	Rural CC (Jess)	"When you take the time to see things and apply it to yourself and it just, like, I don't know, totally shifts your world view."	Writing, performing, and listening to spoken-word poetry	1. Extracurricular writing 2. Feedback 3. Personal reflective assignments 3. Rhetorical rationale reflective assignments
Tracy	Southern HBCU (L.J.)	"Looking inside yourself. Sort of like digging deep to own your feelings and thinking about how they might shift your life today and your life in the future."	Experiencing a death in the family	1. Extracurricular writing 2. Personal reflective assignments 3. Online communication 4. Whole group discussion

These fundamental, definition-forming moments of reflection varied in time, location, and affect. Scholarly settings were instrumental in focal students' understanding of reflection. Six focal students pointed to school experiences as integral to their understanding of reflection: two associated reflection with learning about metacognition in their psychology courses, one generally associated reflection with doing reflective assignments in high school classes, another associated reflection with a mental health day program in middle school that explained its importance, one associated reflection with a scientific understanding of the term used in her physics course, and another associated reflection with the service-learning reflective writing required at their high school. Eight other focal students associated reflection with something they learned as a practice associated with an extracurricular activity, six from a creative hobby (e.g., writing, journaling, poetry, and scrapbooking) and one from embodied practices (e.g., running). Emotions also seemed integral to focal participants' practices of reflection; seven focal students mentioned a challenging time in their lives as being instrumental to how they understood reflection. They reported taking up reflection as a means of coping during a time of uncertainty, grief, or difficulty. In the next section, I discuss how students used these definitions to identify moments of reflection.

Identifying Reflection: How Students Identify Possible Reflective Activity

The two most common rhetorical effects for reflection—awareness and learning—totaled 11 of the 20 focal students. These students found their definitions from a variety of sources, but the most common of which happened in the school setting. The rhetorical effects of awareness and learning seemed to be closely related, with all six of the reflection-for-learning having elements of an awareness-based rhetorical effect for reflection—with an additive quality that their resultant awareness should lead to moving knowledge across contexts. When I was talking to these focal students, and again in reviewing the transcripts, I noticed slippage between the terms "metacognition" and "reflection." Students often brought up the term "metacognition" explicitly, especially at Urban State U, where the programmatic outcomes used that term in lieu of "reflection" for the required course goals. Even students not at Urban State sometimes mentioned the term "metacognition" as something they learned in high school or in another college course.

A student at Urban State, Alan, explained,

> In general, for me reflection is kind of the same thing as metacognition. Like, thinking about how you do certain things, kind of like how you can better yourself in certain ways in situations, I mean they could be different from in different contexts, being introspective about how you do something so you can take that knowledge elsewhere.

In his definition of reflection, Alan saw the desired effect of reflection as being able to articulate choices—something he associated as being synonymous with his understanding of metacognition. He then made an added quality for reflection—that this metacognitive awareness needed to result in learning so that it could be counted as reflection. Alan was a student who learned about metacognition in high school, so when his teacher, Grace, talked about how metacognition and reflection were similar, likening it to how a yogi is aware of their breath, Grace's definition felt familiar and safe to him. He easily and readily mapped reflection in ways that Grace would expect, discussing how her weekly conferences, processing time, freewrites, and reflective course assignments were all examples of his daily reflective practice in her course.

Likewise, another student at Urban State, Serena, explained reflection as

> kind of like evaluating what's happened and maybe thinking about different things and why they happened or like I am also seeing where some things maybe went wrong or could have gone better or like being able to be like self-aware of your progress and like your performance. Feel like it's pretty important to growing learning from failure.

Serena's definition did not quite map onto Kevin's definition of reflection (which he saw as the "space between thinking and doing"), but her understanding of reflection mapped onto the programmatic goals for her FYW course; Urban State students were encouraged to engage in metacognitive work to aid in knowledge transfer. Because Kevin adopted the word "metacognition" and explained reflection in accordance with the school's definition often, Serena was frequently able to find reflection in the activities he purposefully offered for students to engage in reflective activity; she just subverted those activities to better align with her reflection-for-learning definition.

The Urban State program required portfolios and cover letters—and encouraged instructors to do smaller assignments throughout their curriculum to scaffold for the metacognitive rhetorical rationales required at the end of the course. In her definition, Serena explained a rhetorical effect that results in reflection-for-awareness but then went on to explain that this meta-awareness must propel her to make different choices for a more successful future. For Serena, reflection was a dynamic process; she reported that her understanding of reflection stemmed from repeated conversations with coaches about her performance. Serena was an athlete, a cross-country runner whose middle school and high school coaches always required that she debrief after each practice and race so she could "do better on the next one." Serena took that embodied knowledge of reflection—that it be a dynamic, conversational approach to be aware of choices so she might improve—as being a means for improvement into a similar context in the writing classroom. She readily reported reflection as occurring in the two student-teacher writing conferences that Kevin required of students, which was most like her foundational experiences for reflection. She also found moments when she could reflect in places where she could "kind of do that conversation, but just with myself." Thus, Serena took up reflection in ways that Kevin did not necessarily plan for reflection to happen (the conferences) but also in ways that he did (the freewrites). As a student, Serena was able to find moments in his curriculum when she could practice reflection, even when their definitions (and expectations for modalities) did not quite match up.

Many students, like Alan and Serena, talked about how they used reflection to learn from past mistakes. Others reported reflection's resulting rhetorical awareness as an opportunity to both capitalize on strengths and remediate weaknesses. Another student, Jennifer (a student of Heather's), sees reflection as a way of slowing down to learn from both successes and failures. As she explained, "Reflection is the time to take and make sure you're coming across how you want to. Kind of like looking at your work and seeing if that's correct or what's going well." Even the way that Jennifer framed learning from failures is explained as positive; Jennifer focused on seeing whether something was "correct" rather than if it was "wrong." The difference in what can count as reflective (failures-only versus both successes and failures) perhaps stemmed from her past experiences with reflection.

Jennifer associated reflection with a mental health day that she had in middle school; in her public school, the administration invited a guest speaker to talk about mental health. The speaker was memorable to Jennifer:

> He didn't just shove it down our throats. Reflection was just this thing you could do so you could see what you were doing well and keep doing

it. And, maybe what you could do differently. He was like, "just because you realize you're doing something wrong, doesn't mean that you have to keep doing it." And, I don't know, it stuck with me. Teachers brought up that speaker too from time to time, even in high school.

Jennifer saw herself as a reflective person, just like her teacher, Heather; the two both commented upon doing reflection internally constantly throughout the time. Jennifer took advantage of the multitude of class assignments and explicitly reflective assignments that Heather includes in her curriculum for reflection, as well as locating reflection in other moments too: peer review, pre-writing, and revision. Like Serena, Jennifer readily found the moments of reflection where her instructor hoped that she would—but also was innovative in finding them in other everyday writing classroom activities.

A student of L.J.'s at Southern, Maya, also saw reflection as a place for successes and failures. As she explained to me in her first interview: "To me, reflection is looking back and figuring out what you could have done differently—like what you did wrong and right—so you can do it differently or do it again." Maya's teacher, L.J., defined reflection differently; he saw it as a means for introspection, of doing deeply personal identity work. Though he had been trained at a large R1 school with a strong rhetoric and composition program that encouraged reflection for metacognition and transfer, L.J. purposefully adapted his reflective pedagogy to be more in line with his own experiences of reflection and what he saw as valuable reflective work: examining thoughts, feelings, and emotions to consider personal areas of struggle that might otherwise be ignored. Especially because Maya, like Jennifer, hoped to recognize what was going well too so she could capitalize on that, Maya was resistant to L.J.'s definition of reflection and resultant offerings for it. She did not want to engage in her "dark spaces." Maya had to subvert L.J.'s curriculum to make it work for her.

L.J. had designed reflection through personal narrative assignments: students were tasked to create a story of a life-changing moment, a letter to a character in that story, and a letter to themselves. Maya pushed back against what most students opted to do: discuss a hardship in their life, write to one of the people involved in that hardship, and then write about how they might improve (or even cope with past trauma). L.J. scaffolded those assignments with incredibly robust readings from Black authors that modeled the kinds of writing that he hoped they would do. Though Maya loved the readings in the course—like Alice Walker's "The Flowers," James Baldwin's "A Letter to My

Nephew," and Kiese Laymon's "Dear Uncle Jimmy"—she was hesitant to write something similar of her own. As Maya explained,

> The stuff we read is so different than what I read in high school. He picks from Black writers, which is rad. But what they talk about is a little depressing, and when I write, I just kind of want to escape from it. Most of what we talk about in class is still recent and relevant, and I'm down to do it there. But, when I get to my own reflective work, I really focus on writing the positive. What changed my life for the better. How can I keep doing what I'm doing well at now. That kind of thing.

Maya's definition of reflection, her view of what it could invite in, really shifted how she took up reflective work in L.J.'s class.

Though L.J. invited in discussions of heavy topics with the readings he chose and his own disclosures during class discussions, L.J. also made it clear to students that they did not need to do that kind of work to do well. Before each assignment, he always reminded students that they could take up an identity investigation about anything. Their work could invite an exploration of love and joy. Out of all the focal students in her class, Maya purposefully did that with every assignment. In our last interview, we talked about how she struggled with the last assignment, a letter to her past, present, or future self. Maya explained,

> I had to go back to my understanding of reflection. It helped me shift what I was writing about so I could find my groove. I was writing to my future self, and I realized I needed to look more at what has been going right lately. Basically, I wasn't giving myself enough props at the things I've been doing. That first draft was really depressing at first. And, I was like, nah. Gotta switch it up. Needed to say I'm proud of me and stuff like that. It doesn't really do nothing for me to beat myself up.

Maya's resilience to take up reflection in her own way, even pushing back against the published and powerful authors that were doing reflection differently, demonstrates how incredibly strong definitions of reflection can be for students. And it also shows how important flexible and adaptable reflective pedagogy can be. Had L.J. only allowed students to define reflection as he did—a way of looking at things that students were resistant to review (and thus perhaps hesitant to partake in)—then Maya might have struggled through the assignments and perhaps not gotten any benefit from them, failing to identify these course assignments as a moment in which she could practice them as reflection. By giving space within his pedagogy for students to take up reflection in ways that made sense to them, students (like Maya) were able to subvert the assignments enough for their own practices of reflection to shine through.

For many students, the reflection-for-awareness or reflection-for-learning were not quite the kind of rhetorical activity that they thought reflection should do. As one of L.J.'s students, Vanessa, told me, "Reflection is when there is stuff in my heart, and I'm trying to get it out. When things hurt me, writing it out gets it out." Vanessa, a shy student who filled pages upon pages of her notebook with commentary on class happenings but very rarely offered a verbal contribution to class, quietly thrived in L.J.'s class. Vanessa identified as extremely reflective. Her reflective practice helped her through her first crisis of identity in college: switching from pre-law to music. As Vanessa explained,

> I write in my journal every day. My grandma gave me this journal, and I took it up after she died. The more I prayed on it and wrote on it, I realized that God was like "nah, sis, do what you love." So, I'm switching to music. I hope to be a preacher and worship singer one day I think.

Vanessa loved the way she could explore her identity, work through challenging memories, and consider her future goals in L.J.'s class. Each assignment was "a lot of fun" and "nothing like [she'd] done before in English class."

Three other focal students saw reflection as resulting in introspection, like Vanessa did, or an exploration of self, while six saw reflection as building from an exploration of ideologies and beliefs and resulting in a perspective-shifting moment. Most of these students located reflection definitions from their creative practices of using reflection in scrapbooking, poetry, and journaling—and/or as a way of processing difficult moments. Miles, another student in L.J.'s class, saw reflection as not just introspective but perspective shifting. Miles was an outlier in his class: he was a 3rd-year student. His first 2 years of college were filled with what Miles simply said were "the wrong people and the wrong choices," and he hoped that this year would be a fresh start at Southern. Though Miles did not often process his reflection extracurricular writing, he leaned into reflection after the previous year's rather dramatic ending. He had a falling-out with his friends; Miles told them that he would like to focus more on school so he could go home and run the family business, but they were not supportive of his change in behavior. Miles leaned into an introspective, internal processing to shift his perspective on what his life could be like as a college student. He even followed the advice of his dad: after the fight with his friends, Miles wrote a letter to himself about the experience and how he wanted to change his life outlook. His definition of reflection and consequent uptake of it was much more similar to what L.J. intended, and Miles thrived in the course.

Shifts in definitions of reflection changed how students in the same class, with the same reflective writing prompt, tackle a task differently. When talking about the self-addressed letter, Miles tells me:

> Writing is therapeutic. A lot of people don't take time to write about themselves, often. Like I told you, I've written to myself like this before because my dad suggested it after I had an experience that I don't really want to talk about again. I wrote that letter to tell myself how I felt at that moment. To kind of just put out the feelings so I could just get them out of me. But also, to like figure out how I wanted to approach everything going forward.

Miles used his past experiences with reflection, which were very similar (writing a letter to himself), to use L.J.'s letter-writing assignment as an opportunity to take stock of where he was again. Vanessa used her letter to imagine what her future might be like. Maya felt like the letter was an opportunity to capitalize on her strengths. The resultant rhetorical actions vary, and so does the timeliness of when students associate reflective activity. Students had the option to write to past, future, or present selves, and their definitions and views of reflection lent themselves to each of the different options.

The one student who saw reflection as an opportunity to result in mindfulness, Julie (a student in Grace's class), stuck out to me because her definition was unique from those of the other focal students (as well as the numerous surveyed students). Julie was an international student from India who experienced a "traditional Indian education." In Julie's experience, Indian education systems were different from American ones because Indian high schoolers pick a specialty; "I specialized in physics in high school, which is a difference between American and Indian education," she explained. Her physics education, along with her extracurricular interests and personal affect, influenced how she thought about reflection. She explained: "Besides school, I really enjoy meditation and scrapbooking. All too often, we just go from one thing to the next without being present with and grateful for our now." Julie used reflection as a kind of philosophical approach to life; she was a deeply reflective student who brought reflection into all she did, especially when she was invested in projects.

When I asked her about her definition of reflection, her immediate reaction was to reach for the physics explanation of the reflection of light. She said, "Well when light passes a mirror or reflecting surface it like bounces off and creates an image of you at a particular angle which is equal to the incident angle so that's the physics meaning." Then, she paused, reconsidering, before continuing: "But, I know you don't mean that, you mean like a reflection of myself or something like that, which is more of like how you can be present." Her response shows her initial response as trying to translate the scientific definition of reflection she used so often—trying to connect to what it might mean in the writing classroom before giving up on that connection. Interestingly, when Julie paused and gave me a second definition of reflection, it was still built from her experiences: this time her scrapbooking and meditation practices. Her definition of reflection helped her find reflection in her course; she saw course assignments—along with Grace's prompting for internal processing, student-teacher conferencing, and peer reviews about them—all examples of reflective practice.

Some students, like Julie, saw themselves as reflective, while others did not, but they all reported using reflection in the classroom. June, for example, refers to herself as an "open book" who would "talk to anyone" and even "talk to [herself] in the mirror" to reflect. Conan, on the other hand, struggled in the first interview to identify where these types of reflective activities occurred. It was not something habitual in his life that he practiced; Conan joked with me that he would be "doing a lot better if [he] did," but it is still something he does in class. Yet, for all students, definitions then work to function like terministic screens, shaping the participants' view of reality and what they might identify as reflection within a context. In the next section, I discuss how students move from defining and identifying to the actual practice of reflection.

Practicing Reflection: The Rhetorics of Reflection

Definitions of reflection helped shape students' identification practices of where reflection might emerge, but the practice of reflection did not always emerge because a student saw the possibility for reflection's practice. Reflection is rhetorical; it emerges through the entanglements within a rhetorical context. The interactions between the various factors of a rhetorical context must coordinate with one another. The time, materials, affect, technologies, and more play a role in every rhetorical context—and only in synergy can the rhetorical context become a catalyst for potential rhetorical activity. Even within an activity that students saw as potentially becoming reflective, reflection was slippery, only sometimes emerging as reflective practice—and if practiced, likely for brief glimmers. It is this in-and-out-ness of reflection, the way that it can start and stop and start once more—all the while within the same activity—that makes reflection rhetorical. This first subsection reviews the patterns of potential reflective activity that students reported in each rhetorical context, along with their ability to find reflection in new and unexpected places.

PATTERNS OF POTENTIAL REFLECTIVE ACTIVITY

In each of the classes I observed, there were what I call moments of "potential" reflective activity, or moments where students may notice an opportunity for reflection and practice it as such. I identified these moments based on what students reported to me as examples of reflection. These examples were gathered in two ways: focal student interviews and whole-class surveys. In each focal student interview, I asked participants to recount moments of reflection they practiced both inside and outside of class related to their writing class's work. At the end of each course, I also asked all students to anonymously complete a survey about their reflective practices as well. Using both examples from interviews and survey responses, I located examples of reflection that were provided by at least two or more participants and then noted them as potential moments of reflection. My list of potential reflective moments included many different types of activities: listening to music, practicing yoga, praying, meditating, walking, brainstorming, freewrites, doodling, engaging with discussion boards, using online class forums, trying a new technology, participating in group work, considering reactions to course readings, participating in peer review, listening to teachers' explanations about scaffolding, doing pre-writing work, considering applications of something to a future or concurrent context, considering how a past experience might help them in a current project, using information in new contexts, talking with others about their writing, writing rhetorical rationale assignments, answering teacher questions in class about their perspectives, writing in response to personal narrative assignments, doing multimodal writing work, writing for courses, writing for themselves via journaling or poetry, and so much more.

Upon gathering the list, I then used grounded theory to create categories of reflective activity. A code like "extracurricular writing" might include personal writing in journals, self-prompted pre-writing, or poetry. "Cue for transfer," for example, could include opening or closing class statements, explanations for assignments, writing a memo to themselves about how this assignment might help future goals, or asking students to talk with another about how a classroom activity might help their own project. "Processing time," a term I borrowed from Grace, included activities designed for students to think, write, or talk with others about their reactions to college experiences, course materials, perspectives on current events, and more. I included things like L.J.'s class community-building conversations, Kevin's freewrites, and Grace's time set aside to "metabolize thoughts" in this category. Since Heather and Jess taught online asynchronous courses, these kinds of activities were absent. "Group work" included any activities where students worked together in collaboration to reconsider perspectives, recount writing processes, or connect learning across contexts. These, again, were not used in Jess and Heather's course due to their asynchronous nature (though both noted they would have done activities like this, had their courses been synchronous). "Feedback activities" included formal and low-stakes peer-review assignments, including peer-review worksheets, discussing drafts, and responding to instructor feedback. "Reflective" assignments included traditional written rhetorical rationales, as well as non-traditional genre activities like screencast videos that explained a multimodal project, a Spotify playlist that explained their course experience, letters to instructors about their view of themselves as writers, and more. I loosely split these reflective assignments into two categories: reflection-for-awareness and/or learning kinds of assignments (which I called "rhetorical rationale assignments") and activities oriented toward reflection-for-introspection, reflection-for-perspective, and reflection-for-mindfulness (which I called "personal reflection assignments"). Online discussion included both traditional "discussion boards" included in many CMS (content management system) platforms, but also other kinds of online conversations like L.J.'s use of the social media platform, Yellow Dig, and his class's WhatsApp group messaging. Pre-writing included any brainstorming and ideation assignments that were assigned or self-reported. Revision included any drafting or re-drafting assignments that helped students rethink ideas. Reflective course assignments included assignments that included introspective elements—often incorporating personal narrative or encouraging an exploration of personal experience. Whole-group discussion involved communication between students and the teacher about new ideas and concepts that inspired new awareness or perspectives. Students located all these activities as examples of where they found

TABLE 4.2. Patterns of potential reflective activity identified by focal and surveyed participants

	Cue for transfer	Feedback activities	Group work	Processing time	Whole-group discussion	Personal reflection assignments	Revision assignments	Rhetorical rationale reflection assignments
Grace's synchronous in-person class (computer classroom)	5	2	2	18	9	0	2	6
Heather's asynchronous online class	10	1	1	N/A	N/A	1	3	4
Jess's asynchronous online class	10	4	N/A	N/A	10	5	3	1
Kevin's synchronous in-person class (traditional | computer)	13 | 13	3 | 0	5 | 9	0 | 5	6 | 6	0	2	6
L.J.'s synchronous in-person class (traditional classroom)	5	0	3	5	20	3	0	0

reflection in the daily happenings of their writing classes. I was struck by the diversity of examples that students gave but also the very clear patterns that I saw emerge from each class. Students could find reflection in a myriad of genres, regardless of their definitions of reflection (and reflection's consequent rhetorical effects). See Table 4.2 for more details on the patterns of potential reflective activity in each course.

Table 4.2 represents focal participants' self-reported examples of reflection. Again, this table presents pedagogical opportunities that students *may* pick up and practice as reflection. The table does not represent how many times students reported reflecting in each class, nor does it indicate that students find potential reflective activity each time these activities occurred. It is important to note that this table does not account for the robust and incredible amounts of self-prompted reflection that students reported, either, like

Mia mentioned in our chapter opening and I will discuss later in the chapter. The point in sharing the patterns of potential moments of reflection is to demonstrate the wide-ranging opportunities for reflection, as I identified by students in these case studies. Students were always looking for moments of pedagogical activity that mapped onto their definitions of reflection—and found those moments even when what was intended for reflection did not work for them.

Many of the reported moments of reflection happened within the classroom contexts, with some being done outside of the classroom at the request of a teacher (e.g., homework). Classroom contexts, as we know, are so brilliantly complex—with different emotions, affects, people, technologies, experiences, materials, and more swirling in their ecologies. Because reflection is rhetorical, it was dependent on all those things within the context. It did not emerge simply from a reflector's desire to reflect, nor a teacher's instruction to do so. The contextual factors needed to align in a sort of beautiful synergy for reflectors to do the hard work of reflection. The timing, the feelings, the music, the temperature, the interlocutor(s), the journal pages, and/or the energy were just right. Reflection's rhetoricity was distributed across all sorts of contextual factors, only to be taken up by some students and not others. When the contextual factors all worked together—and reflection was defined, identified, and then actually taken up and practiced—reflection produced various rhetorical effects.

In the six observed classes, students were not typically unanimous in their agreement to select a certain assignment as reflection. As we discussed earlier, freewrites for Kevin's class were seen as reflective by three of the four of his focal students. An exception to this was the three course assignments in L.J.'s class; all his focal students mentioned that these personal reflective assignments were examples of how they practiced reflection in his course. The first assignment was a short story about an instrumental experience, the second was a letter to a character in that story, and the third was a letter to themselves. As King, one of L.J.'s students, explained succinctly, "I think I reflect all the time in L.J.'s class. Like every single assignment for his class. Only because his class asks us to do personal writing. I just have to do reflection to do that." L.J. spent a lot of time ensuring the climate was safe for personal reflective writing. He held in-class writing days where students could share drafts in progress on four occasions. And he spent five full class periods talking with students about their transitions to college and the emotions and concerns that came with that.

Students also reported enjoying dynamic reflection via online communication and collaborative communication with their peers. One innovative example was Yellow Dig, an assignment that students were told to engage with throughout the semester in L.J.'s course. It was an online platform made to look like a social media platform, assigned as a way for students to make connections between readings and current events, brainstorm ideas for their personal reflective writing, and build class community. As Vanessa explained,

> Yellow Dig was kind of the backdrop to what was a really great class. This specific class was geared toward self-expression and yourself. It's all reflection. We've done so much research and writing about yourself. So Yellow Dig helped us do that work, weekly, all the time. It made it come more naturally during the assignments.

Another shared her weekly post to me, laughing about how comfortable she had become with her classmates in the space. Her post wrote,

> Am I the only one thinking about next semester already? I've come up with goals and things I want to improve and do better on already. I feel like I started off so good but then I fell off and I really want to prevent that next semester. I know my own potential and I know I could've met that, but I didn't, so next semester I'm coming for that neck. #word2mm.

She used the space to reflect on her progress in the course, make goals for next semester, and put a public declaration of those goals to classmates that could keep her accountable. Students reported that this genre felt natural to them because they use it regularly. In fact, some already used those platforms for reflective work. Tracy explained,

> Outside of class, I do a lot of tweeting, but my tweets aren't funny. They're more introspective. Sometimes about school. So Yellow Dig just feels like I get credit for something I already like doing. Something that I already do.

Students from asynchronous classes noted examples that fell outside online writing too, locating course assignments that welcomed personal reflective writing as examples of reflection. Heather assigned a "hero" essay where students could pick any hero, even one they knew personally, to investigate the hero arc in their story. Jess incorporated many low stakes as well, the most popular of which was her "mixtape" assignment—a two-part assignment that asked students to introduce themselves via a self-curated mixtape and then create a second mixtape for her to listen to that accounted for their course progress. Jess used both to get to know her students, and even played the second while reading their final projects. Both Heather and Jess noted that they typically did more personal reflective writing, along with activities to scaffold for that writing, when the courses were done synchronously. Even still, their students repeatedly mentioned their courses as safe and welcoming spaces for reflective activity about their identities. Establishing a sense of community, then, seems to be an integral step in creating spaces for reflection that ask students to engage in reflection—especially when it is reflection that requires more than a recounting of writerly choices.

In Urban State's two multimodal composition classrooms, students reported that working in new technologies helped encourage them to engage in reflection. Grace amplified that pressure to engage in reflective activity by doing weekly conferences; students were discussing their projects with her throughout the drafting process. Therefore, they were apt to brainstorm ways of trying out new technologies within their conferences, even though her assignments never mandated a specific technology to be taken up. Kevin's students were instead explicitly taught a new technology that was required of them for each assignment. For example, students learned Audacity as a class and then created podcasts. They also learned to use PowerPoint to create printable research posters, and then created them according to the standards listed for an upcoming university research symposium. Because of this, Kevin's focal students consistently named whole-group discussions as examples of various types of reflection. Kevin often used whole-group discussion to think about the affordances and limitations of a new program or analyze sample work. This suggests that unfamiliar technologies and writerly situations may indeed prime students for reflection in important ways.

Students appreciated a range of modalities, technologies, and materials for their reflection. Student-teacher conferencing, pre-writing, revising, free-writing, or other teacher-audience reflective texts were much more successful when done habitually and with flexibility. Grace's students were so into student-teacher conferencing as reflection because it occurred weekly; they got to practice it often. L.J.'s students were so into personal reflective assignments as well because he very clearly scaffolded for it and provided three opportunities to do it. Jess's students loved pre-writing because she gave them so many opportunities for it, along with clear descriptions about the stakes of doing such work. Kevin's students and Heather's students did pick up written rhetorical rationales as reflective because they were associated with each project. Across all these examples, students were constantly willing and able to find reflection, even in unlikely spaces. In the next section, I discuss how students were able to invent new ways of doing reflection that were unprompted and unplanned.

IMAGINING REFLECTION IN NEW PLACES

In the previous subsection, I focused on the kinds of reflection that happened within the classroom spaces, both through purposefully designed pedagogical moments of reflection (perhaps taken up differently) and in new ways that teachers did not expect. Yet, as we saw in the opening story, students often reported and shared examples of self-prompted, personal reflection outside of class. In Mia's case, for example, this consisted of both journaling and pre-writing practices. This last section celebrates the beautiful and profound ways that students did reflection outside the bounds of classrooms, all on their own. In our weekly interviews, focal participants consistently shared stories of doing reflection in their daily lives: a specific Spotify playlist on their commute home, a walk between classes that they used to call a best friend, or a daily journaling practice. Sometimes students took up these personal reflective practices because they are habitual; students often reported doing weekly journaling, conversations with loved ones to cope with difficult situations, a meditation practice to inspire mindfulness, conversations with mentors to assess progress toward goals, or incorporating reflective hobbies in their daily lives as ways of being present (e.g., spoken poetry, yoga, running). At times these individual reflective practices were done in favor of what teachers hoped they might pick up (as was the case with Mia). Other times, though, students' individual reflective practices helped students find classroom activities that aligned with available reflective moments in their classroom contexts (or in related contexts due to homework).

The students in this chapter teach us a great deal about why reflection works, works differently, or doesn't work in our classrooms. They show us all the ways we fail to see the amazing things students do as reflection outside our purview. We can see how their teachers were largely unaware of the ways that their students were practicing reflection outside of class requirements. This was not a fault of their instructors, but it is something that we can learn from; we can know that it could be helpful to ask. In asking, we can learn important insight about both how students reflect and how to capitalize on what students already do. We can be less concerned about students picking up reflection in ways we imagine it. We can avoid getting frustrated when students do not produce reflection in the genres we hoped would produce rich and thoughtful reflective activity, and instead lean into the ways students are doing that rich and thoughtful reflection in the genres that feel natural and exciting to them.

When I pitched my project, at each MSI, I always told students the reason I hoped they would become focal students: they would influence future pedagogy; their insights and experiences could help other students like them (maybe their younger siblings or friends) benefit from their generosity of time and spirit. I hope this chapter has worked to serve this goal and will inspire future researchers to listen to and hear our students, especially our minoritized students. Their lived experiences of how reflection works has the power to make our reflective pedagogy more equitable, inclusive, and culturally responsive. Students reported that reflection happened through all sorts of activities and in all sorts of contexts: in classrooms with student-teacher conferences, peer review, genre analysis, and writer's memos, but also through introspection and conversations in contexts outside the classroom: in cafeterias, on bus rides, or even watching Netflix. They teach us that reflection is rhetorical because definitions of reflection shape the naming, identifying, and practice of reflection. Therefore, reflection does not always occur every time a moment is identified as potentially reflective. The contextual factors must align for reflection to be taken up and practiced. Instead, what makes an activity do reflective work is what is happening within that activity: the timing; the conversation content; the power relationships about the topic; the affect, emotions, and people around them; the temperature; the surrounding global context; and so on. This is one of the reasons why reflection is rhetorical; identifying and naming something "reflection" is not the only thing that makes an activity do the work of reflection. Instead, that identification and naming must work with the overall contextual factors for that activity to emerge, through distributed agency as reflection. Across all three schools, participants were always able to (a) describe reflection and explain how their understanding of the definition is built from prior experiences, (b) provide examples of when reflection worked and what it resulted in as well as explain moments of failed reflection and explore the reasonings for that, and (c) hear other definitions of reflection and locate examples of that kind of reflection in their daily practices.

Table 4.3 shows another reason for reflection's rhetoricity: students were able to imagine reflection in new activities with definitions other than their own. The table shows the things students identified as potential moments of reflective activity (indicated with an "X") along with new ideas they had about where reflection could live ("A" after hearing about Yancey's definition of reflection-in-action, "C" after hearing about Yancey's definition of constructive reflection, and "P" after hearing about Yancey's definition of reflection-in-presentation). For clarity, I use the same categories as before: cue for transfer, conferences, embodied processing, external processing, feedback, internal processing, online communication, personal reflective assignments, revision on assignments, rhetorical rationale reflection assignments, and whole-group discussion.

Definitions of reflection largely stayed the same for my focal students throughout the course duration. I asked focal participants within all three interviews—paced at the beginning, middle, and end of their course—to discuss their definitions of reflection and examples of it happening in their daily lives. Though they were able to build upon examples, often adding new and timely examples, their definitions were all reworded versions of what they told me in their first interview. In other words, despite their lived experiences affirming, contesting, or complicating their definitions, students' understandings of what reflection could be remained relatively static. As educators, we might find this pattern among my focal students—that students tend to define, identify, and practice reflection in the situations in which reflection maps onto their definition—to be disheartening: what if we, as instructors, are hoping that they can practice reflection for a different rhetorical purpose, in a different context, or at a different time than what they tend to associate with reflective activity? Is it possible for students to consider something as reflection that falls outside their definition scope?

In Table 4.3 we can see that students were already adept at updating the purpose of everyday pedagogical activities to be reflective. This tells us that students can and will find activities to practice reflection that we, as teachers, did not expect to be practiced in that way and new ways to do reflection that we, as teachers, did not expect to meet their needs for reflection or taking up a new, unplanned moment as reflective. Julie, for example, saw peer review as reflective when her teacher, Grace, did not necessarily see her peer reviews as a practice of reflection. Conan, a student in Kevin's class, saw using new technologies for his course assignments as something that inspired reflection; Kevin mandated using these new technologies because he designed a multimodal-themed course. As we instructors know, students are smart and savvy. They will find reflection where they need to; students want to do the work of reflection. They find it important to their writing, their learning, their identities, and their relationship to the world.

TABLE 4.3. Identified moments of potential reflective activity identified by focal students

	Whole-group discussion	Transferring knowledge	Rhetorical rationale "reflection" assignments	Revision	Reflective course assignments	Processing time	Online communication	Internal processing	Group work	Feedback	Extracurricular writing	External processing	Embodied processing	Conferences
KEVIN'S CLASS														
Conan	C	C	X, P			X								A
Mia		C	X, C								X, A			P
Rachel	A	C				X, P		X			C	X		
Serena	C					X	A						A	X
GRACE'S CLASS														
Alan		C	X		A	X, P, A		X						X, P
Autumn	P	C	P		X, A			X			X	X		X
Julie		C			A					A				A
June		C	P		X			X		X, A		X		X, A

JESS'S CLASS

Student							
Francis			A	C	X	X,P	P
Ryann	X				X	X	

HEATHER'S CLASS

Student							
Jennifer		X,C		X	X,A	A	

L.J.'S CLASS

Student							
Angel	X		A	X,P			X,A
Colby	X	X	X,P	X,C			X,A
Joann	X	X	X	X			
King	X	X		X			
Maya	X	X		X			
Miles	X	A	(A)	X,C,P			
Paris	X	C		X		C	
Tracy	X			X,C,P			X
Vanessa			X	X,A,C			

A: reflection-in-action; C: constructive reflection; P: reflection-in-presentation; X: potential moments of reflective activity

Further, students can also try on new definitions of reflection and imagine new opportunities for reflective activity. In the third interview, I provided each participant with new definitions of reflection, asking them to identify examples of that kind of reflection within their lived experiences. Each participant heard definitions of traditional understandings of reflection—Kathleen Yancey's reflection-in-action, constructive reflection, and reflection-in-presentation—and they could all identify new moments as reflective when they "tried on" these new definitions. Throughout this activity, participants were able to see something as reflective that previously did not fall into their understanding of what reflection could be. As students who reported engaging in reflective activity both within and outside the writing classroom, they sometimes did reflection in ways that were like the intent of their teachers, but other times they subverted the intent or came up with new ideas entirely. Paris, for example, initially gave me examples of reflection happening through her extracurricular writing (poetry and creative writing), internal cognitive process, and the personal narrative assignments in her class. When presented with other definitions of reflection, Paris also saw the way she used her internal rumination to transfer knowledge across contexts as an example of reflection. Likewise, Conan saw freewrites, working with new technologies, and rhetorical rationale assignments as reflective—and then selected conferencing as a potential place for reflective activity after hearing other definitions. This pattern was true of the pool of focal students; every single focal student was able to add at least one new potential place for reflection upon hearing the definitions. This finding is exciting for instructors: students have the capacity to try on new definitions of reflection—definitions that might better align to our pedagogical goals and values.

Even though they were able, some students were resistant to practicing new ideas about reflection. After hearing a reflection-in-presentation definition, one student laughed and said, "I've never had to do anything like that, and I'd really have a problem if I had to." They were not the only student to feel that way. Others said comments like, "That doesn't really feel like reflection to me," or "I just feel like this would be really hard to think of as reflection." Responses like these remind us that definitions of reflection are strong; students may be able to stretch their selection to include new activities as potential moments as reflection, but they also can and will resist doing so when it falls outside their values of what reflection can be. We ought to be prepared for this reality in our classrooms.

Conclusion: Applications for Reflective Practitioners

This chapter has showcased how definitions of reflection are built upon foundational memories or moments in which focal participants reflect about something important happening in their lives. I hope it demonstrates that just because teachers define reflection one way doesn't mean that students will. Reflection is an abstract term. There is no right or wrong way to do it. When we open our minds to this possibility, we can acknowledge the capaciousness of what reflection can entail—perhaps even broader than what my participants have shared here—and then make opportunities for various kinds of reflection: different modalities, different timing, different materials, and different potential rhetorical effects. Students need to find stakes in reflection and apply it to their own personal reflective practices. Further, we can and should learn from students: how do they define reflection? How do they practice it? How do they want to do reflection in this instance? What might help them do that work? Sometimes students think about reflection as part of what they do for school and for learning. Other times students use reflection as part of their own personal growth and goals. They might use it as a form for rhetorical awareness, for learning, for introspection, for perspective, for mindfulness—or maybe even something different. Reflection is, and must be, bigger than writerly choices being made about a paper. Because student definitions are wider than what reflection assignments tend to offer, students latch on to other moments in class where reflective thought and practice can live, subvert well-intentioned moments of hopeful reflection, and reject others. As teachers, we so often assume reflection is for awareness or for learning, but when a student is coming in with an identity that is reflective, they often feel that reflection for awareness or for learning are performative and don't offer space for deep thinking and find it a waste of time. I want us, as teachers, to know that reflection can live in a lot of places different than what we consider to be reflective assignments and for a lot of other rhetorical purposes. It is imperative, especially as those who identify with feminist pedagogies, that we approach reflection with openness and flexibility.

As a researcher who got into this project with a heart for my students and my interest in becoming a better teacher, I will spend the concluding chapter with what I'd hope for: some practical ideas of doing reflection differently along with ways to account for the diversity of reflective definitions and practices that I was inadvertently ignoring in my classroom. In the next chapter, I will share innovative ways that teachers and students have done reflection in the writing classroom (or perhaps outside the classroom, but still related to work in the classroom). I will also use my research as inspiration to suggest new activities for reflection. Finally, I will conclude with ideas for future research and teacherly interventions.

5
Reflection Research, Reflective Pedagogy

Where Do We Go From Here?

September 2021, Southern HBCU

It's hot. Like really hot. September means the crisp entrance of autumn in so many places, but here at Southern HBCU, the air is so humid that it feels like we would be better off drinking it through a straw. When I arrive at the classroom, I'm grateful for the air conditioning, humming loudly, to help cool us off. Sunlight still pours in from the wall of windows to remind us of the heat we just escaped, and the students are lined up in straight rows, gossiping about their upcoming homecoming plans. I've settled into a desk at the back left corner of the room so I can both view the space in its entirety and give students 6 feet of space, should they want it. There are more seats than students and most have opted to be closer to the front.

One particularly gregarious student, Hayden, leaves his seat and struts confidently to the front of the room. As he reaches the front, L.J. opens the door. Hayden enthusiastically says, "Hey, Dr. J!" to L.J., but Hayden doesn't return to his seat. Instead, he sits in L.J.'s seat at the front of the room. L.J. pauses at the doorway, an amused look on his face, while students giggle in anticipation.

"Alright y'all," Hayden says in his best imitation of L.J.'s voice. "Let's talk about descriptive language. You know there's a lot going on in 'The Flowers.' What did you notice?"

Everyone laughs, full belly laughs—even L.J. Students play along; Hayden calls on willing students, all while making overexaggerated gestures and comments to emulate L.J. Two minutes later, Hayden bows deeply to signal the end of the show. L.J. and the students cheer, and Hayden makes his way back to his seat.

L.J. thanks Hayden and sits down at the front of the room, occupying his usual location: the long teacher desk at the front of the room, facing the students. Students face him, sitting in long rows. L.J. wears crisp dark jeans, a flat-brimmed Southern HBCU hat, a plain black T-shirt, a sparkling clean pair of on-trend Jordans, round "hipster" glasses, and a KN95 mask. He simultaneously looks like a professor and looks like someone students could imagine being one day.

"So, the thing is, we're not talking about descriptive language today," says L.J. with a laugh.

Hayden yells out, "C'mon man, how you gonna do me like that?"

Students laugh heartily, and we can see the smile wrinkles crinkling by L.J.'s eyes. L.J. seems relaxed and in control; he is not bothered by Hayden's gentle ribbing. He is enjoying this as much as the students are.

"So, um yeah, I thought we'd be going another way," L.J. says with a smile in his voice. Students, still in a jovial mood, smile and let out a few more laughs. "Yeah," he continues, sounding a bit softer. "So today we're going to take a break from our regularly scheduled programming," he says, winking at Hayden. "I feel like I'm killing the vibe, but I already had this planned today. I'm really going through it. And I know I ain't the only one. Students be coming to me like, L.J., I'm stressed."

Students lean in curiously. A few visibly nod their heads in agreement. L.J. goes on, "So I know it's only a couple weeks into the semester, but it feels just so hard already. I just feel like we could use class today to just open up about it all. I'll get us started." He pauses and takes a deep breath.

"I don't know about y'all, but I cried today," he admits. And, to my surprise, no one looks uncomfortable; those that haven't rotated to face him yet do. Many students look at L.J. encouragingly to continue, and he obliges.

Students settle into listening to his monologue about his morning. L.J. talks about his stresses: he's feeling lethargic and overwhelmed by the pandemic, he's struggling with juggling his many commitments (teaching, applying for jobs, finishing his dissertation, making time for family and friends), and his rheumatoid arthritis has been flaring up.

He concludes, "Um so I was telling my students in my morning section, every day I drive up and then I kind of park and then I sit in my car until the absolute last minute until I gotta get out. And, when I say the last minute, I mean sitting in my car at 9:05 and my class starts at 9:05."

A few students laugh in a kind of empathetic way, others snap, and one proclaims, "I feel that, fam."

"Yeah," he continues, nodding at the student. "And, like I love being with y'all. Truly. Teaching brings me the greatest joy. But I'm stressed. I park and all of the weight of everything that I have to do just kind of caves in on me, right?"

I hear a few audible mm-hmms and snaps, and I notice at least five students enthusiastically nodding. Nearly all of the 15 students here today are paying attention, staring at him as he continues on:

> And it's really hard to kind of get up here every day and talk about writing or books or whatever. It's kind of hard to perform that every day. And, I was thinking, if I feel that way, you might too. So yeah. I just kind of wanted to take the day for y'all to have a space. And, yeah, I know it's really early in the semester—it's only like week three or four or whatever—but I hear so many people saying like "I'm stressed." And so, um school comes with that of course, having a lot of things to do, having a lot of outside pressure and all of that kind of stuff, but having Covid as a backdrop is another level of that.

He pauses, and again, the class responds with murmurs of affirmation. L.J. goes on,

> And, even if it's not like you're thinking about Covid day to day, it's still in your unconscious mind. It's still something you have to think about in the background. So, um yeah, you have the floor to kind of express yourself. I know that you don't get the opportunity that often to talk about how you're stressed and what are some ways that we can start to manage that. So, I'm gonna give you that opportunity. And I'll probably do that a couple times throughout the semester. If I can help, I'll try to help. But a lot of it is me preaching to myself too. Because I'm in it with y'all.

Four students immediately raise their hands. L.J. indicates the order he'd like them to share, saying, "Here and here then here and then here," gesturing to each person to signal who is first, second, third, and fourth.

Turning his gaze to the first, he says, "Alright, so how you doin'?"

The first student announces, "Hey y'all! I'm Mikaela!"

Students, without prompting, collectively respond back in a chorus of "Hi, Mikaela!" in a call and response.

"Okay, so," she starts, "I kind of got accepted into Southern like really late so I was kind of last minute. I'm stressed like financially because my mom had surgery three times in the last six months so like it's been really hard." She pauses, seeming to wait for L.J. to weigh in.

L.J. says, "Yeah finances are one of the easiest ways for stress to kind of creep in." Mikaela nods, and L.J. continues,

> I know people were talking about refunds. Unfortunately, I can't help with that. But I know that these things are kind of always in our minds. Causing stress. But I do think that we can try to help with self-care. And, I think we have a romanticized view of what self-care is because a lot of times we think of it as a way to spend money but that's not necessarily the best thing. I like retail therapy like anybody else—

He pauses for a beat, smiling as students laugh. "But it adds stress. Especially when your stress is financial. So, yeah, I feel you on that."

"Yeah, it's really hard," she responds. "Financial stress is just a lot. My mother cannot give me any money. I feel like I'm going broke. I need a job. I'll be like by myself listening to rap music and then I just start cryin'."

As Mikaela finishes her sentence, a classmate turns around to face Mikaela and says, "Girl, yes. I cried on the way here."

Another rotates their body sidewise to see Mikaela and the classmate and says, "Yo, me too! It's just one of those years."

As Mikaela, L.J., and the classmates talk, the class participates in an active listening space. Her peers let out snaps, enthusiastic nods, and vocalizations throughout her narrative, just as they did for L.J. I'm continuously writing notes about how shocked I am about students' openness and their support for one another in sharing. And, though there are a few students studying their phones lying on their laps under their desks, L.J. and the rest of the engaged students ignore them. In doing so, the attention is on those that are bringing energy to the space. The vast majority of students are paying attention and the community, overall, feels invested and engaged in each student's story.

L.J. waits for the conversation between peers to die down and then gestures to the second student who raised their hand. "Hi, I'm Audrey." Once again, the students engage in a call and response, saying back "Hi, Audrey" to greet her.

Then, Audrey says, "I'm just so stressed. Like I'm a first gen[eration] college student and it just feels like everyone's hopes and dreams are pinned on me. Like if I don't do well, then I'm letting everyone down. And, the thing is, like I don't really know what I want to do. I'm just so tired. It feels like I'm doing business and I don't even like business, but I should do business to get a job and make everyone proud." Students watch her as she talks, many turning to face her. Again, many let out vocalizations and nods to make her feel heard.

L.J. responds empathetically:

> I feel that. I've been in this area for ten years—first as an undergrad at Southern and then a grad student at [another local school], but in terms of like, the physical manifestation of stress and anxiety, I didn't really, really feel it until I was studying for prelims. It's like this big qualifying exam to get your PhD. And I was still TAing at the time. And, at this point I sorta feel like I have a good grasp on what's goin' on. I'm in the middle of this PhD program. But, this exam, man. It's just eating at me. And, one day, I pulled into my parking spot and just burst into tears. I just kinda cry all day long because everything kinda caved in at the same time like, right?

Students nod, empathetically like they can imagine this feeling.

He continues:

> So, I understand, now, like you have to rest. I have to take some of those days where you get up and eat and sleep and watch TV and that's it. And I know from talking to a lot of y'all that you don't sleep enough. Like I know you have a lot of pressure from yourself and your goals and your families. The pressure of being involved, keeping scholarships. It's a lot, a lot of pressure. And a lot of times we aren't kind to ourselves. And, unfortunately, it doesn't really stop. Um but we have to be better at managing how we feel. Because we don't want our bodies to tell us to sit down. We don't want to get to that point. If you've never experienced that, I hope you don't. It's always inopportune, there's always a lot going on and your body is just like 'nope you gotta sit down.' You don't want to have that happen during finals or on a week with three tests. But, if we never slow down, we never sleep enough or eat right, we keep going and going, our bodies *will* tell us to stop. And they'll do it at the worst time. You need to manage time. For me, I make a lot of lists. I make either daily or weekly lists, depending on how busy I am. And I scratch those things out, and it feels so good. It helps me from, like, feeling like I have to do everything.

"Yeah, you're right," Audrey smiles. "I hear you. I need to slow it down. Give my body a break. I can't keep going at this speed. I got to pace myself."

With a nod, L.J. calls on the next student, Tamara.

She continues the conversation: "So I feel kinda like the opposite of what you were talking about, Audrey." Audrey nods, looking at Tamara with curiosity. "So, I'm Haitian."

A few students give a knowing look. Audrey even enthusiastically says, "Girl!" as she widened her eyes in faux fear.

"Right?" Tamara says.

> So yeah, I got all this pressure from my family. But it's actually 'cause all my siblings have kinda done well for themselves and now I'm like in the final stretch of what to do with my life, and I don't know what to do with myself. And I feel like I just have no friends here that get it. I really miss my old friends. I have no one to talk to about it.

One student, sitting by Tamara, pats her arm and says, "Yo, let's exchange numbers. I got you, girl." They quickly and quietly do; Tamara hands her phone to input her number. L.J. waits for the exchange to happen before responding.

L.J. says,

> Like I'm not Haitian so I don't know how that is, culturally, but I feel you. I'm the youngest in an over-achieving family too. My sister was IB and graduated with her BA in three years. And, then I came and I'm the social butterfly.

Students share a bout of laughter.

> School came easier for me—she always worked harder than I did. Even though my dad and sister never told me I had to do a master's degree, they both did, so I felt like I can't be the one who doesn't.

Sensing his self-deprecating humor, the students laugh again.

> Um so I put all this pressure on myself. And then eventually I decided I wanted to be a professor, so now I'm like dammit, I need a doctorate. But the idea of being a first-generation doc student was fine at first. I didn't understand that pressure of being first gen until I was going to take those prelims, like I said. And then my family was like trying to help but really couldn't relate. My dad was like either you're gonna pass or not, not the end of the world. And I was like I'm 30, and I've been in school for like my whole life, so it effectively *is* the end of the world if I do not pass this test.

Students let out some laughter, and L.J. smiles before going on:

> Yeah, he just didn't understand it. My dad could help me with my thesis because he wrote one. My sister could talk to me about coursework because she did it. Right but these other steps: the exams and the dissertation. They were like "we're rooting for you." But that didn't feel like enough. I didn't understand the pressure of *not* having my main support system really get it. And so, I just really empathize with y'all when you're the first or the last to come along and do it. You might be feeling pressure that isn't even really there. Like be kind to yourself. You will be successful in whatever you do, whenever that is supposed to happen. For a lot of you, you were excited about a certain major when you came to college. And it might change and that's okay. I told y'all that I came in thinking I wanted to be a band director. And then I got here, and I realized, like, "I don't want to audition." So, I did sociology. Let's get in, get the degree, and get out. And then I was like wait, that ain't gonna work if I don't care about it. And then I was like I'm interested in education but realized quickly that I can't do little kids.

Students laugh along with L.J. after his last line.

Then, he says:

> That's not me. I can't do this little kid thing. And then I was like let's do secondary. That was my new plan, and then I finally got in an English class, and I was like okay this is the thing I'm supposed to do. Right? It just finally felt right at that moment. You know? Look, y'all are so young and there's so much time to figure it out. And, with social media out there, and you see people with the perfect life and the perfect relationship, y'all those are pictures and reels. And in real life, there are tears and anxiety and depression and feelings of failure. Do not feel like you have to live up to that expectation. That false sense of reality. College is really a time to figure it out. That's all to say, move towards something. And be okay with going towards it, even if it veers unexpectedly. It's better to have an open mind to that.

Tamara nods. "I gotta work on not letting the pressure get to me. Figure out what it is that I want to do. I'm not there yet, but I hear you."

L.J. nods, and says, "Okay, Jeremiah, you're up. What's happening?"

The conversation continues fluidly, with L.J. moving from one student to the next, for the whole class period. Reviewing my notes and writing my reflective memo later, I notice the sense of community that L.J. is building through this class-long conversation. Though L.J. very clearly takes the longest turns and provides the most advice for students, classmates actively listen to students' stressors, along with L.J.'s advice, with vocalizations and embodied responses. At times, some even offer their own advice (unprompted) by just verbally responding without raising their hands. L.J. encourages these student-to-student conversations by pausing for the exchange, nodding along during student advice, and then acknowledging their contribution with an anecdote of his own that builds from them or thanking them before moving to the next student. Throughout the class period nine students have an opportunity to discuss the difficulties they have encountered with their new start as 1st-year college students adjusting to life at Southern. At the end of the hour, L.J. is still giving advice to the last student, and the two continue chatting after class, walking out together. It seems to signal that L.J. is truly interested in the hardships of his students; it wasn't just a way to spend the hour, but a continuing conversation he hopes to have with them.

November 2021, Southern HBCU

The air has finally turned cool enough for long-sleeve shirts, but it's not quite cool enough for a jacket; L.J. says it will be more toward the end of November. Since the class's first whole-group discussion about their transition to college, L.J. has opted to use full class sessions for whole-group discussion about students' mental, social, and emotional well-being three more times, the latest of which was yesterday.

L.J. starts class today by telling students how excited he is to talk to them about their latest course reading: "Dear Uncle Jimmy, We Will Never Ever Know I Love You" by Kiese Laymon.

He's introducing the text to the class, saying,

> Y'all, I'm so excited to hear what you thought about Laymon's letter. In graduate school, I got really into writers who talked about Black masculinity, and Laymon's work was some of my favorite. It just really resonates with my own experiences as a Black man.

In framing this text as something that he is interested in, as a scholar and a person, students seem to lean in a bit more than is typical. I write a note in my notebook: "Does [students'] respect for L.J. give them a sense of connection to the text?"

L.J. starts the discussion of the reading the way he usually does: just asking for general reactions to what they read. As they talk, I take notes; each called-upon student shares their reactions, listening students angle toward the speaker, doing active listening techniques. Each speaker also tries to connect to a previous point from another student. Even though students are engaged and interested in the reading, the affect is kind of mellow today. It just seems like most students would rather listen and let the more talkative students take the lead today.

L.J. stays seated at the front desk, quietly reacting to each takeaway with a simple "yes" or "okay" before going to the next student. Once the five or so students with their hands raised have been called upon, he calmly encourages more interaction from other students, ready to ask more specific questions.

L.J.'s gaze settles on Miles, and he asks, "So as you make the choices that you be makin'... how do I want to phrase this question? Hmm. Okay, let's try it this way. Have you ever talked to anybody about the choices that you were making?"

Miles, begrudgingly, says, "Choices? Nah."

"Nah," L.J. repeats. "And did their choices affect yours?" His tone is inquisitive. There is no judgment present in the question.

"Yeah," Miles says, a bit warmer now. "It was like just a lot of friends doing stuff and then me doing it."

"Got it," L.J. says, like he really does relate to that experience, with a kind nod and a hand to his heart. "So, yours was a peer pressure experience."

Miles nods, and L.J. gives him a soft smile before he continues, "And so your experience might be a little different than the letter. Like the way he writes makes it seem like he was genetically set up to act this way, kind of, right?"

Miles agrees with L.J. "Mm-hmm. Yeah. He almost makes it seem like his choices were connected. Like he was meant to do it."

"Hmm. Yeah. Have you ever felt like you were making choices, but you almost weren't responsible for those choices?" L.J. asks.

When Miles doesn't immediately respond, L.J. looks away from Miles for a moment, turning his body more center again, gaze resting now on the whole class. "Have y'all ever felt that?" About two-thirds of the class nods, a few of which murmur "yeah" (one of whom is Miles).

L.J. then turns his gaze back to Miles and asks, "Why do you feel like you're not responsible for those choices?"

Miles clarifies, "Are you asking me?" L.J. nods, and Miles answers. "Yeah. It makes me uncomfortable to, like, tell people that I want to do something different."

L.J. nods and asks, "So when is the time that you take responsibility for it?"

Miles responds, "Like I do take responsibility, but it takes a minute. Like I need to make sure I have time to think about it."

"Okay, okay," L.J. says, nodding. L.J.'s voice gets softer, somehow making him seem even more approachable.

> Um, so let's think about those moments when you realize "this is a choice I made, and this isn't the best choice." Does that realization happen in the moment or is it when you kinda reflect on that? Once you got through it?

"Yeah, more like, for me, it's like after a bit and I think about what I did, why I did."

"Okay, so that's how you're, like, talking about reflection. How often do y'all reflect on the choices that you make?"

Another student, Jasmine, speaks up: "Every day." The student next to her, Ciara, gives her a snap and a "mm-hmm" in agreement.

L.J. turns to the left, nods at them. "Yeah. Do you change the ways that you make choices every day?" he says, looking at Jasmine.

Jasmine nods. "I try. Yeah."

L.J. nods again, and shifts his gaze back central, body rotating so it's open toward the class again. "Aight. So, we are reflecting. I'm like, 'I know that this thing wasn't the best thing to do.' Let's say I bought clothes for homecoming, but now I don't have money for food to eat." He pauses to laugh along with students at this relatable example. "And, I'm only saying this because I have been this person."

The laughter grows louder, and one student even hoots an "oooh!"

"And I didn't live in a dorm, so I had like rent and utilities to pay."

A couple other students echoed the first hoot with some more hoots of "oooh!" L.J. looks at them with a grin.

"Mm-hmm. Things happen but you gotta look fly for homecoming."

Students laugh and nod knowingly. I hear multiple mm-hmm agreement sounds and one loud "you know that's right!"

L.J. continues, "You reflect. Like, 'Okay um I really have gotten myself into a tight bind you know like I don't have any money. My flex bucks are gone. And now I gotta go eat in the caf and I really don't wanna eat in the caf.'" Students are nodding in agreement. A student yells out, "I hear that!" L.J. goes on, "But you gotta do what you gotta do. The next time you are faced with that, what is that process?"

Ciara says,

> You gotta, like, think about it. Like, you know what's going to happen if you do that again. You gotta be like, "Is this the moment we gonna do that again? Or is this the moment when we remember what happened and don't do that again?"

L.J. smiles. "Exactly. Like, I may do it again." Students cackle with laughter, and L.J. chuckles, continuing, "I may do it again like a month later too. And, then a month after that. But eventually when it happens again, I'm going to look at myself be like, '*What are you doin'?!*'"

He shares another knowing laugh with his students.

> But, for real, Ciara, I'm glad you said that. Like, for me is that look at yourself, that look at what you don't want to see. And sometimes I might have to be like, "What's wrong with you?" This is what, remember I told you about this letter and I was talking about how um he almost steps into his uncle's shoes, and has this conversation with himself. Like he does this in the letter y'all read. Did y'all catch that part?

Students affirm, many audibly saying "yeah" or "mm-hmm." He nods at Ciara, eyebrows raised as if to ask, "How about you?"

She immediately responds, "Yeah!"

L.J. asks her, "Where's this moment where he steps into his uncle's shoes? What was this moment in this letter?"

Ciara pauses for a beat too long. "Wait, nah. I don't know. I think I missed it."

L.J. jokes back. "Well, this is open note, open book."

Ciara smiles and scans the text while L.J. patiently waits. "Oh, I found it!" Ciara says excitedly. L.J. nods at her to read it, and she does.

"That's right," affirms L.J.

> I love that bit about "knocking someone's hustle." What he means by that is we need to love each other enough to tell those we love that what they're doing isn't the best thing for them. Or maybe isn't the best thing for us.

He pauses, then says,

> And though this is true for everyone, this author is making the argument that this is especially true for Black men. He says that what

Black men need is another Black man knocking our hustle. So, Black men, how do we do that?

Miles offers, "We need to keep each other straight."
"Yes," nods L.J.

> You can get caught in a spiral. And sometimes it's very difficult to find your way out. You can get to a point that it's too much and it can overtake you. It doesn't mean you don't get out; it just means that it's very difficult. Love is so important. This is kinda what Baldwin was talking about in his letter too, when we read that last week. So often Black men are not taught to be gentle, to be kind, to be patient, to be understanding, to be vulnerable. And, like that doesn't just affect Black men, does it? What do we think, Black women? Does this affect y'all?

Many call out, "yes" and the remainder nod.

> And that's why we need to do this kinda critical reflection. Like in this case, the author is like, "Yo, I was so caught up in not knocking another man's hustle because that's how I thought you love Black men." And so why does he think this is a problem? What is the only emotion we say that Black men can let out?

A student yells out, "Anger."
L.J. says:

> Yes. But we know that crying helps. It lets out a lot of stuff. When I let it out, I'm a lot happier. There are stigmas in Black families to talk about emotions, especially emotions other than anger. I feel like we don't talk about this. And this letter does a good job of pushing back on those ideas. We have ideas about how Black men and Black women act. We need to be able to open up and talk about our feelings. And we need to love our people enough to tell them what they're doing is wrong or hurtful. This is often so hard, especially in the Black community.

Casey speaks up,

> Yeah. I feel like this is true for a lot of Black kids. Like there's this emotional ignorance thing. My dad was always like hold it in until you get to the court. I was raised so much by my father that that's how I learned to handle situations. Growing up, I'd be like, "I'm gangsta. I

don't cry." It wasn't until recently that I learned how to cry. I'm trying to be okay to let myself break down. It's really necessary.

"Exactly, yes." L.J. agrees. "Yeah, like if we don't let it out—and also see where we're coming from, where those emotions are coming from, like we won't realize that the people around us are affecting the ways we live our lives and like how we handle our emotions. We need to be around people that knock our hustle. And we need to be able to knock our own." He pauses, takes a breath. "So, what are some qualities that you like about people who are close to you?"

"Loyalty," Casey immediately responds.

"What does that mean, like?"

"They got you. They gotta be able to tell you stuff and trust they not going to tell nobody. So, you know, yeah."

Alexis, a student a few rows over, chimes in: "And, like if they not in the room, they still stand up for you."

"Okay, and what does that look like to the rest of y'all?" L.J. asks.

Alexis says, "Like if you not gonna tell me I'm wrong, like you ain't my friend." Jasmine, who has turned to face Alexis says, "For real," in agreement. Alexis continues, "And, I think that a lot of this letter like hits that."

L.J. agrees,

> Yeah like this is his blood. His blood. And still these kinds of social norms and stigmas stop them from having these kinds of open conversation. This kind of open critical reflection. It stops 'em both. And y'know if you start making changes to yourself based on those reflections, what you learn here, your family and friends might instead be givin' you crap. You come home for Thanksgiving, and you say, like, I been thinkin' about it, and I want to eat differently. Want to really take care of my body. And they like, yo, you vegan now?

Students laugh, knowingly.

L.J. continues, "Like if you be knocking hustles, then you best believe they gonna be knocking yours too. Fact. This is why this kind of stuff don't happen often." Students laugh again, in agreement.

L.J. continues:

> I'm not telling y'all to come home to Thanksgiving and be like *an' another thing*. But, yeah, these kinds of conversations are important. Super, super important. So, like, your letter is really important too.

> Like it's just the one side right now. It's your letter. This is your time to let someone else hear about what you have to say. About your experience. But I think why this letter is so dynamic is because it can, if you want, allow some space for reflection. It can be a way of thinking about your relationships. It can be a way of looking at yourself too. You might have a lot going on that's hurting you. You can have your own family or friend that's kind of calling you out. It's your chance to have a voice in it all. I mean, how often did you have a voice about anything? We never really listen to children en masse. People are insecure about their voices because they ain't ever had one. You been told that your voice didn't matter. Now, we get to college, and everything is your choice. We need to get out of our own way to have these conversations with ourselves. Confront things that don't feel good.

Throughout this long explanation about the stakes of the letter, students are following along. They're nodding and adding along words of agreement. The energy in the room has shifted from that of a slow Tuesday morning way too close to Thanksgiving break to a productive and energetic "I can't wait to get to work" kind of buzzing energy.

L.J. glances at the clock, seeing that students have about 2 more minutes. He concludes:

> Aight. I'ma let you go. Tomorrow we'll go over the genre conventions of letters and the assignment prompt. If we have time, we'll have some work time on our letters so you can draft them in a place where you can ask me questions as they come up. And, Thursday, we'll use the whole class period to draft. So, make sure you bring whatever you need to start writing tomorrow. I think we'll at least have a bit of time to get to it. See you tomorrow!

November 2021, Southern HBCU

For only the second time this semester, L.J. has a PowerPoint up. It's finally cold enough for a jacket. L.J. sits in the front of the room, his jacket (a Southern fraternity letterman jacket) is slung over the back of his chair, revealing a sweater and jeans, that again coordinate with his hat and shoes. Students notice the jacket and compliment him on it as they walk in, talking to him a bit about his fraternity experience. Behind him, the projector displays a PowerPoint titled Genre Conventions of a Letter.

Once the clock indicates class has begun, L.J. gets to work.

> Like I said, we're going over how to write a formal letter. Please jot down notes or take photos of slides as I talk you through this because for the next assignment, I'm going to expect that you make your letter formatted like a letter, using the information I give you today.

L.J. goes through the conventions (e.g., block formatting, salutations, addresses). When he's done, L.J. closes out the PowerPoint and pulls up the prompt for the assignment. They go over the requirements (e.g., one to two pages single spaced, to a specific person that was present in the short story that they turned in for their assignment one and following the genre conventions they just went over).

"Alright." L.J. says, glancing at the clock.

With his attention back on the students, he continues:

> So, we have plenty of time to work. Like I said, I really want to give you space to draft in class, so I'm right here if you have a question. I know this might be a new kind of writing for you, and I know it can kind of break the flow of writing when you have to stop and wait for an email response each time you have a question. So, I hope you can kind of use this time to start drafting and ask questions as you need, live and in-person. You can of course email me over the weekend too. As a reminder, this assignment is due a week from today. Any questions before I let y'all get to work?

Alexis raises her hand, and L.J. nods at her to signal that she can ask her question. "So, I know we've talked a bit about this, but once again we can be honest or blunt in our letter, and I won't be graded on that?"

L.J.'s voice softens, and he asks, "What do you mean?"

Alexis tries again, "Not like graded on it, I guess, but like. Um."

Ciara, seeing Alexis's struggle, chimes in. "Like if I'm talking to my future self to my present self so like um there are certain things that I do that like well maybe I'm not proud of. Can that be said?"

"Sure, yeah." L.J. says softly, talking still from a place of curiosity and openness.

> This is as much about you looking at yourself and kind of understanding like where you're trying to go, how you're trying to mature. 'Cause a lot of times, we rely on what other people say about us and we don't rely on what we say about ourselves. And a lot of this journey over college, over college and how we grow is about us learning, like, about ourselves. Like you don't always want to rely on what

> other people say about you. You want to be in control of your own narrative, right?

Alexis says, "Right," and L.J. continues.

> Mm-hmm. Like other people will tell your story for you if you don't tell your story for yourself. Like what kind of person do you want to be? What type of person do you want to become? What kind of person do you wish you would've been? Right?

Alexis is nodding along, so L.J. continues, "How can we get to the things that I wish I'd become as a child? Right?" "Yeah," Alexis says. "Right, those are the kinds of things that we want to talk about in this letter." Seeing she looks satisfied, L.J. says, "Any other questions?" Vanessa raises her hand, and L.J. nods to her to give her permission to ask her question.

Vanessa says,

> Is there a certain way that we format dialogue in the story, I mean the letter? Like I know we had to do it a certain way in the first assignment. If we have a story in our letter, does our dialogue have to be a certain way?

L.J. thinks for a moment, then says,

> Not necessarily. It doesn't have to be like the short story assignment, unless you kind of do that back-and-forth dialogue. But even then, it can be like in the paragraph. It just needs to be discernible who's talking, and how you do that is up to you.

Vanessa, satisfied, smiles and says, "Okay. Yeah."

JoAnn speaks up. "So, hold up. Why would we have dialogue? I know it's a letter to someone else, but why would we have a back-and-forth conversation?"

L.J. answers,

> Sure. Like you're writing to a person from your story. And you're talking to them about whatever you want to or need to talk about. But there might be a moment in the letter where we have dialogue. Like where that other person that you're writing to talks back to you.

"Ohhhh okay. Yes." JoAnn says.

L.J. continues, trying to make sure that he has made his point clear: "So depending on what's going on will change what they say. Okay?" JoAnn nods.

But you can talk about whatever you need to talk about, but it is kind of like this deeply kind of deeply reflective, introspective conversation with yourself. Like I want you to pause and think, "What will I miss if I don't reflect? What will you miss if you don't define success for yourself? What will I miss if I don't allow my brain the space to roam?" That's what this letter is supposed to be.

"So, you're saying that whatever our kind of reflection work is, that work is integral to this letter?" asks JoAnn.

"Correct. Correct." L.J. nods. Assured they're on the same page, he says to the class: "Any other questions?" After a 5-second pause and no students move or talk, he nods. "Alright, let's get drafting!" Students get to work, working diligently and occasionally asking questions until the bell rings.

December 2021, Southern HBCU

It's the Monday following Thanksgiving, and students are quickly transitioning to the last assignment. They turned in their short stories in October, their letter to a person in their short story in November, and now they're turning to the last assignment: they need to write a letter to their past, present, or future self. L.J. has the projector up again. First, he pulls up the prompt to review the specifications of this letter, and then he pulls up the genre conventions of a letter PowerPoint again that they reviewed in November. L.J. is just finishing up his explanation of what makes this assignment unique. Students, though heavy with that restlessness that so many have in the quick time between the return from the Thanksgiving holiday and the release for finals, are paying attention. They've been taking photos of slides and writing down notes. L.J. then asks them to get out something to write with.

"We're going to write a profile today," he says.

> I want you to write the things you know about the character that you'll be writing to. Like, your present, past, or future self. She might be 5 years old with a nickname that she likes to be called. Her favorite color is orange, and she loves to play with rocket ships. Every day, she wants Fruit Loops for breakfast. She might also really not enjoy her kindergarten teacher, or she might be scared of eating lunch at school because her food looks different than the other kids. That kind of thing. So, think about favorite names, favorite activities, favorite friends, favorite colors, all the things that bring the character joy. And get into all the fears and the frustrations and the hardships too. I

want you to start by picking who your character is: what's their name, age, interests. And then get into the details. Any questions?"

He pauses to wait.

"Alright, let's start."

Ten minutes later, L.J. calls the class's attention to the front. "Okay, you have notes now on who you're writing to." L.J. is standing at the front, the prompt once again illuminated. "So, we're writing to ourselves, and we have an idea of who that person is like. We're using the same formatting stuff as last time, so you know how to do that. And we have questions to answer in the letter." He gestures to the bulleted list on the prompt. "So, if you're writing to your past self, what's the question?" he asks.

A student reads off the question, "What have I missed?"

L.J. nods. "Yes!" he confirms enthusiastically. "And what about when we're writing to your present self?"

Another student calls out the next question, "What am I missing?"

L.J. nods his head in agreement again. "Exactly! And what about writing to your future self?"

Another student calls out, "What will I be missing?" "You got it," L.J. exclaims.

"Do we know what I mean by these questions?" he asks. Though many students nod, L.J. elaborates to assure those that don't understand.

> What things have I missed in your past? Did I grow up too fast? Do I regret not telling someone how I feel? And, if now, writing to your present, be honest: am I missing true friendships? To be healthy? To have relationships with family? And, to your future: am I going to miss out on true happiness? My goals? Does that make sense?

He pauses for questions, and after 5 seconds continues: "Yeah, um, so it's deep. Yeah, it's deep. But, if you're not thinking about these things, which as a freshman, and let's be honest, I was *not* thinking about them—." He interrupts himself with a loud laugh that some students echo.

> And yeah, I should have been thinking about the stuff that I missed. Because it's the random stuff that I missed over time, right? Like it's the opportunities that I didn't take, right, to maybe study abroad or whatever. Not going on this trip, not talking to this person, not saying the things I need to say, not getting the information that I could, I missed out on certain things. This assignment is like, going forward,

> L.J. isn't going to miss out on these things. Because this is the time to do it. If you ever want to study abroad, you need to be in the office of international education right now, college is that time to really find yourself, but you can only really find yourself if you're doing this kind of work. And writing is therapeutic. Sometimes you don't get it until you reflect and write it out. And you save this letter and you read it as a grown up and you're like, "Okay, I see where you were trying to go. I see the person you were trying to be. Right? That will help you out. Does that help tryna frame what we're talking about?"

A few students say, "Yeah," and most nod.
L.J. asks, "Are there other questions?"
King hesitantly raises his hand.
"Yes," L.J. says, calling on him.
"Um, so is it like internal?" King asks.
"Yeah, like an internal look at yourself. I'm not asking you to think about if you're going to miss getting pizza at 2 am." Students laugh. L.J. reconsiders for a moment, realizing he might seem a bit more prescriptive than he wants; he had put space on the prompt for students to talk about anything: positive or negative.

> Well, I mean. Not necessarily like that because it's shallow. Instead, we should be thinking about the things that made you who you are, think the way you do, make choices the way you do. The deeper stuff. Does that make sense?

King nods, "Yeah."
Paris asks, "Can you talk more about how you'd do this if you were writing to your present self?"
"Sure," L.J. says.

> I'd think about the ways that you're limiting yourself. And, again, this is just how I'd approach it. You could do it differently based on how you define reflection. Like, for me, I'd be thinking about what I will miss if I don't take the opportunity now. I'd be like, "How am I right now and based on that and my future goals, do those line up?" If I'm not happy now, I'd ask, "What choices am I making to make sure that I'm happy in the future." Does that make sense?

Paris says, "Yes."
L.J. continues:

> Mm-hmm. So y'all might be like what's the point of doing that now? Yeah so, it's kind of looking in the mirror. It's kind of like these are my majors and my friends but like a lot of times we don't critically assess the place that I'm in. I want you to be thinking like, "Am I happy? Do I rely on other people to make me happy? Is this the person I want to be right now? Am I a good friend?" I want you to think about the totality of who you are. You may want to think about like, "Yeah, I'm one of the only people that made it out from home. I'm proud of myself." And, like, yeah, you might still look at it all and be like, "Am I really happy, though? Did you really plan on this? You know you can't survive if you want this life. If you keep making the choices that you're doing." I'm hoping this letter will help you have that conversation with yourself. It's almost like your conscience, right? Like, you can talk to yourself: "What are we doing right now? Because you seem to be spiraling to me. You're not happy, not eating good. You're sleeping all the time." You got me? It's like having those honest conversations with yourself.

"Okay," Paris nods. "So just kind of put it all out there?"

"Yes," nods L.J. "Like there's no limit or cap on length on this assignment. Just write. Critically engage who you are, where you come from, all these things. That's the assignment."

He pauses, then asks, "Other questions?"

Ciara asks, "Now, what about Grammarly?"

L.J. thinks and then says,

> I mean I guess, if you want. It's gonna give you some ideas about sentence-level stuff, but this is a letter to you, so write how you would write to yourself. And Grammarly is not going to tell you formatting for that. So, follow what I showed you for that.

"So, can we talk informally?" Ciara asks.

L.J. nods enthusiastically.

> Yes. Like, for me, at my core I'm "Scooter." That's who I am at the core. And I'd be talking to Scooter in my kinda way. You gotta think about how you're speaking to yourself depending on the time frame. That's why we just wrote that profile. You gotta know your audience and your grammar and tone should be for that audience. Does that make sense? You don't have to announce "past Ciara" or whatever. Like, I should be able to tell that from context clues and your audience appeals that you're writing to past Ciara.

Tracy raises her hand, and L.J. calls on her. "So, can we model these after the letters that we read?"

"Yeah, absolutely," L.J. answers.

> We've read a couple letters, right? Like "A Letter to My Nephew" and "Dear Uncle Jimmy." But I could even see you doing like the stream of consciousness kind of writing that we saw in "Girl," too. I assigned that as a reading because I thought that would be cool to take up that style of writing. And I've seen that done really well in letter format for this assignment in past classes. I am here for you to be as creative as possible.

"Okay," Tracy says. "I might try that."

> Go back to the samples, go back to your profiles. That's why I told everyone to make a profile of who you were writing to—favorite snacks, close friends, age, where they're at, how they sound, and all that. Aight, y'all ready? We're going to use the rest of this week to draft this letter out. You can get started.

Students shuffle around in their bags, getting what's necessary. They get to work, occasionally raising their hands for L.J. to help them through a specific spot, but mostly using the time to get their thoughts on the page when they have dedicated time to do so. L.J. has a Spotify station playing in the background, inspired by the favorite songs that his students gave him on their first day of class. Students bop to the beat as they stop and stare, visibly reflecting in between bouts of written work throughout the class writing session. They ask questions as they need, and again work nonstop until the bell rings.

*****

My goal in this chapter is to summarize the findings of the preceding chapters, but also to provide sample activities inspired by those findings. The goal of this book was not to prescribe reflection in any way but, instead, to hear from reflective practitioners on how, where, and why they practiced reflection in the ways they did. Overall, my data demonstrates that reflection is a rhetorical activity, emerging from a rhetorical context to result in a participant-identified rhetorical effect. Definitions of reflection vary among teachers and students, but all participants use these definitions to help them locate potential moments of reflection. The actual practice of reflection is dependent upon the distributed agency among contextual factors, both human and nonhuman, working together to bring reflection into being. My data suggests that:

1. Reflection is rhetorical because it is embedded within classroom activities that make up the fabric of the course.
2. Reflection is rhetorical because it is entangled with various contextual factors.
3. Reflection is rhetorical because its emergence is subject to the distributed agency across those contextual factors.
4. Reflection is rhetorical because it is ongoing—always linked to past, present, and future reflective moments.

Though teachers may specifically incorporate an activity in the hopes that it becomes an opportunity for reflection, students are creative and resourceful. They often practice reflection through those genres specifically incorporated for reflection (e.g., the portfolio cover letter, writer's memo, freewrite, or student-teacher conferences), but they just as readily associate reflection with and practice reflection by other classroom genres (e.g., peer review, whole-group discussion, and online communication), as well as self-prompted reflective activity (e.g., transferring knowledge across contexts, external or internal processing, and extracurricular writing). Because reflection can be defined in so many ways, it can be located and then taken up in a variety of activities. This might prompt reflection to be done at different times throughout the writing process (before, during, or after) as well as through different modalities. Students and teachers report designing and practicing reflection through dynamic and interpersonal ways, as well as more individualistic and internal ways. Regardless of form or timing, reflection is always subject to so many contextual factors: both immediately (e.g., emotions, relationships, timing, materials, spatial arrangements) and globally (e.g., cultural, socioeconomic, racial, and other identifiers). They are haunted by past happenings, steeped in genre expectations, and layered with sedimented ideas of what can and should occur. In this way, reflection is simultaneously influenced by past happenings, current realities, and future possibilities. Everything must work in synergy to result in reflection.

One particularly important contextual factor that influences the way that reflection is taken up and practiced is the way that it has been taken up and practiced in the past. Definitions of reflection play a powerful role in identifying and practicing reflection. Reflection is an abstract term, and there is no agreed-upon definition of what it entails among my research participants. There is consensus, though, on how the definitions are formed: reflection definitions are built upon past experiences that have been identified and practiced as reflection. In other words, past experiences with reflection help shape future experiences of reflection. Definitions of reflection vary, but they always result in some sort of rhetorical effect. So far, I have identified the following potential effects: awareness, introspection, learning, mindfulness, and perspective. I am confident that a broader research base would elicit even more possible rhetorical effects, and I encourage researchers to find them.

Reflective practitioners, at least in this study, did not often change their definitions of reflection; their definitions are formed through an important happening that leaves a firm foundation. Some participants, though, could hear new definitions of reflection and consider the extent to which those definitions might help them imagine new vehicles for the kinds of reflection they do. When participants saw these new definitions as too far afield from their own definitions of reflection, though, they were resistant to these new definitions and consequent considerations of what these new activities could be. This seems to indicate that reflection is subject to past understandings of reflection but also has the potential for malleability, if the right circumstances arise. In the next section, we will consider how these findings can be illuminated once more, by the opening series of stories.

A Final Look at Reflection-in-Motion and the Rhetorics of Reflection

From reading Chapter 4, we know that students in L.J.'s class see reflection as having various rhetorical effects: awareness, learning, perspective, and introspection. We know from reading Chapter 3 that L.J. himself sees reflection as resulting in introspection, a kind of investigation of self. This kind of reflection can lend itself well to critical pedagogies and antiracist teaching practices. We also know that L.J. does make plenty of room for this kind of reflective activity in his class: all three of his course assignments are personal reflective assignments. In the above stories, though, we can see firsthand how careful he is in making room for others' definitions of reflection within those assignments. Students can use those assignments to practice mindfulness, document a change in perspective, account for awareness they have about choices they made, or suggest ways they might learn from that rhetorical awareness. They can also opt to take up reflection for its emancipatory potential, as L.J. does in his own practice. In keeping the options open for students, we can see that students were more apt to be able to find a way into the assignment than if he had kept the bounds of the assignment so tight that it only applied to how he practiced reflection.

One of the things that helped students acknowledge and practice that flexibility within his classroom is the relationship that he had with students. Even by September, students knew L.J. well as a teacher and mentor. Throughout the semester, students knew, wholeheartedly, that L.J. wanted them to take up assignments in ways that felt authentic to them. L.J. repeatedly made clear that students had options for what their first short stories could be about. And, later in the class, he made it clear that they had choices about their purpose in writing the letter to a character within the story and the letter to themselves. The kinds of rich and deep reflective work that L.J. asked for required disclosure, and so he was careful to curate a culture of respect among students. He encouraged communication between students as they shared about their struggles with transitioning to college. L.J. also emphasized the importance of doing this kind of work by curating a culture of respect around reflection, talking explicitly about the importance of reflection in both his discussion of course readings and his explanation of coursework. He explicitly acknowledged reflection as a deeply personal act—an act that required trust in him and trust in the overall class community—and he practiced it often through whole-group discussion, online communication, and classroom assignments.

In my years as a writing researcher, teacher, and administrator, I have not seen many teachers so explicitly and so frequently address students' mental, emotional, and social well-being as I did in L.J.'s class. In the above stories, we can see that L.J. repeatedly invited students to talk about their identities, their positionalities, their hardships, their goals, and their emotions in his course. It was integrated into the fabric of his course through the selected course readings and conversations about them, the required online communication on Yellow Dig and the resultant community-building, and the ongoing conversations L.J. made space for in which students explicitly talked about hardships associated with their transition to college and he shared his own. L.J. taught, modeled, and insisted upon reflection as being related to writing. Reflection was always something valued and integral to writing. It was never a separate afterthought tacked onto a final draft to satisfy a programmatic requirement. L.J. took the risk to be honest and his students responded in kind. This helped L.J. build community; it helped students develop as whole people. And it created the level of trust necessary for reflective writing to be used in this way.

L.J. built this trust by purposefully and thoughtfully making his classroom context hospitable to the practice of reflection. The readings that L.J. selected for the course were themselves examples of (published) reflective writing. Authors enacted personal writing, narrative writing, and counter storytelling in their short stories, performative letters, and poems. Engaging with these public-facing reflective texts broadened the audience of who reflection could be for—along with why it might be done. If reflection was part of writing itself, and this kind of reflection was something that students could read as public-facing work worthy of publication by people who looked like them, whose experiences they could relate to, then perhaps this reflection thing might be worthwhile. It might be important. It might be worth trying. In L.J.'s class, reflection was never positioned to be shallow or performative. Instead, it was something we could use to result in students' desired rhetorical action, and it could also do something more: it might inspire and influence others. L.J. also worked toward deeper, reflective discussions about the readings themselves.

For example, in the conversation with Miles that I document above, I was struck by the intimate conversation that L.J. and Miles have in front of the class. Through gentle prodding, L.J. encourages a reflection-in-action kind of conversation between himself and Miles, just with a classroom of students happening to look in on it. Linguists typically see a pattern of initiate, respond, and evaluate, where a teacher asks a question, a student is called upon and responds to the question, and the teacher evaluates the appropriateness of that response. L.J. started class that way, in fact. (L.J. asked students about their responses to the reading, students responded, and then he evaluated with a simple "okay" or "good.") Yet, with Miles, L.J. initiates with a question and Miles responds, but L.J. evaluates and asks another question of Miles.

The kind of conversational pattern that we witnessed between L.J. and Miles was more like L.J. initiated, Miles responded, L.J. responded and asked another question (much like the kind of speech pattern we saw in Grace's school). Then, the two remained in that loop. It was still very clearly a student-teacher dynamic because Miles was not asking L.J. questions; he was not in a place to initiate topics or contributions from L.J. In this way, L.J. and Miles's conversation was more like what we might see in a one-on-one conversation between a student and a teacher. L.J. used whole-group discussion, then, as practice in reflective thinking with both the student being questioned and the students that were present. For many students that were external processors of reflection, or folks who liked to talk aloud to do reflective work, this practice was very helpful. Even for those that were more likely to engage with a more internal practice, or a way of thinking through alone, it might illuminate how reflection could be more dynamic or outwardly spoken, if necessary or helpful.

L.J. also asked about his students' reflective practices, assigning reflective writing—and giving them time in class to look at, react to, and practice that written reflection since he assumed it might be an unfamiliar and therefore uncomfortable genre to write in. Through in-depth conversations with students like Miles and Alexis, he learned about how students reflect, and he made it clear that students can take up assignments in ways that work for their reflective practice. When talking to students about their reflective practice, he kept his tone and body language neutral and inviting, so students were more likely to be honest and realistic in their responses. Assigning reflective texts as course readings, along with discussing them in class, helped scaffold; L.J. was modeling how to do their letter by offering them a published letter as an example and helping them work through it, mapping on their own experiences to see how they might build from their reader response to make their own letter contribution. If L.J. had offered his students a published letter to read but had not taken time to work through their reactions or offered time for them to consider how their own experiences might differ from what was modeled, students might have struggled to find their way into the assignment (especially because, as we know, L.J.'s students had a wide variety of reflection definitions). And in creating this space to talk about their own reflective practices as something that are not set but unique to them, an individual student (like Miles or Alexis) and their classmates are able to think about reflection as an individual practice.

In the next section, we will explore what the opening stories, along with the stories that we've read throughout the book, might help us understand about how to thoughtfully and purposefully prime students for locating reflection in the everyday fabric of our writing courses—along with how to learn about and celebrate the kinds of reflection that students do outside of the writing classroom, self-prompted, that play a role in their writing and identity-building processes.

ADVICE FOR WRITING TEACHERS HOPING FOR REFLECTIVE CLASSROOM COMMUNITIES

Before we get into advice for writing teachers who hope to curate reflective classroom communities, I want to pause for a general disclaimer about my suggestions. In *Teaching to Transgress*, bell hooks write about how an exciting classroom cannot be made so just by the actions of the teacher. hooks writes, "It is rare that any professor, no matter how eloquent a lecturer, can generate through his or her actions enough excitement to create an exciting classroom. Excitement is generated through collective effort." As a teacher, I have found this to be true. And as a researcher of reflection, I have found this to also be true about creating a reflective community. Teachers should not assume that we are solely responsible for encouraging, fostering, and creating a reflective community. We are an integral piece, to be sure, but a reflective community is also built largely from the labor and willingness of students. Their reflective definitions—and the ways that contextual factors interact with those definitions of reflection—help reflection emerge. In other words, teachers should not and cannot set up the perfect context for reflection to happen. Instructors can, though, be aware of the various definitions of reflection, the contextual variables that play a role in reflection, and the ways they can account for reflection that fall outside their own definitions of reflection and/or the immediate classroom context.

Throughout this project, focal teachers and students inspired me to give specific advice for those hoping to integrate reflection in the writing classroom:

1. Make reflection habitual. Provide opportunities for reflection daily in various forms and modalities, scaffold for it often, and be willing to share your own reflections.
2. Acknowledge that reflection definitions and practices vary among students. Therefore, purposefully learn about students' definitions of reflection, give space for questions, and create flexibility in course happenings to allow for individualized uptake of reflection.
3. Recognize that reflection is dependent upon the context. Thoughtfully and responsibly curate a community that is a safe space for students to do the deep and thoughtful work of reflection.
4. Incorporate published or personal texts of reflection, especially those that are multimodal or translingual. Students need to see the prevalence of reflective writing and consider how and why they might use reflection as a rhetorical tool.

We know that reflection is rhetorical. It emerges from a rhetorical context and is thus subject to distributed agency across teachers, materials, students, emotions, past experiences, technologies, spaces, identities, and more. It results in various rhetorical effects. Data demonstrates that reflection might be identified and practiced in activities that result in rhetorical awareness, identity introspection, a mindful awareness, and/or a change of opinion. In doing so, reflection can also have a kind of emancipatory potential that does the important work of making space for students to develop a chronic self-reflexive approach to their positionality. This could help white students identify and understand their deep-rooted ideologies so they can work across difference and be a better ally for those who have different life experiences to them. And it could help students of color work through the trauma of recognizing that the academy is so often a whitewashed, discriminatory space not designed for them. Either way, that kind of work requires a reflective community—and we will turn to L.J.'s class to review how we can emulate that.

Fostering a Reflective Community

In the excerpts of L.J.'s class above, we see plenty of opportunities for building a reflective community. The class readings model reflective writing, the class assignments that encourage reflective writing, and the reflective conversations about both the readings and their own writing work to make a safe and welcoming space for students to bring in their own knowledge and expertise. L.J. consistently scheduled readings that were examples of the kinds of reflective work that he hoped students would produce, and then he made space for analyzing those readings through extended, reflective conversations. He also created flexible opportunities for reflective writing, and he gave in-class time for them to practice in these new genres with support. And, to scaffold for all of this, L.J. incorporated classwide discussions about students' college experiences often. L.J. was able to foster a reflective community and establish community trust for personal disclosure.

Spending so much time looking at and practicing reflection helped model what dynamic, external processing of reflection might look like. By dedicating multiple class periods to talking to students about their transition to college, assigning reflective readings, and requiring reflective writing, L.J. signaled that reflection was worthy of time on the class syllabus. Focal participants reported that generally students were engaged in these pedagogical choices. When students were talking about their transition to college, for instance, they purposefully gave each other advice and built off one another's responses. Only two students in one class and three in another repeatedly disengaged. Even then, they weren't disruptive in doing so. They quietly fiddled with their phones under their desk, watching TikTok on mute, reading tweets, or texting friends. But, even then, their disengagement might have been from more of an emotional guarding (e.g., "this is too difficult to discuss in this setting") than a lack of interest (e.g., "this is not happening to me, so I have nothing to contribute").

This kind of intentional distancing makes sense; it was a lot of emotional labor for the students and L.J. to participate in this kind of conversation.

Whether students participated or not, though, the dedicated class periods on whole-group discussion about students' social, emotional, and mental health normalizes personal disclosure in L.J.'s classroom space, encourages students to reflect internally about what they are feeling, and builds trust in both L.J. and the overall class community. Though I'm sure that some classes might be resistant to this kind of challenging emotional labor (and in fact some students did use the time to check out), most leaned into the opportunity to build community and empathize with one another's successes and struggles. The relative "success" of students identifying and practicing whole-group discussion and course writing assignments as reflective as likely because it was habitual, which both scaffolded for reflection and made space for it. L.J. regularly and often transgressed the typical boundaries of teacher disclosure in the classroom, sharing with students past and current struggles. In doing so, L.J. made a safe space for students too; he set the stage for it to be okay to talk about the uncomfortable. He also made the space even safer by encouraging a classroom community where students got to know and supported one another. They had started the first class not with a syllabus day but with introductions that took the whole hour—each person talking about their identities, what brought them to Southern, their favorite music, and more. Their syllabus required them to engage on the class's social media–like platform, Yellow Dig, a classroom media platform that is reminiscent of Twitter. Students use Yellow Dig to share connections that they see in current events to class concepts as well as process their emotions and experiences as 1st-year students. L.J. also encourages students to create a class WhatsApp (without L.J.) so they can communicate with each other informally outside of class.

Throughout the semester, they got to know him and each other well through in-class conversations and online conversations too. As a graduate of Southern, L.J. knew of their college experience and could relate to it—and students knew that. Students felt comfortable joking with him, and he could tell them jokes they could relate to as well (e.g., spending too much money on homecoming clothes or not loving the cafeteria food). L.J. tried to empathize and relate to their experiences as college students. He often gave advice by sharing his own experiences, and he tended to wear Southern clothing to share his own pride in being an alumnus. This was especially important at an HBCU, where students are particularly prideful of their university and celebrate university culture with schoolwide events. When he wore his fraternity letter jacket, for example, students were quick to ask about his experiences in his fraternity on campus and whether he stepped. L.J. tells me that he does so much work on class community-building because "it is necessary for the kind of work in our class. I also find that it helps with the kinds of writing [he asks] students to do." Since "reflection and writing are so tightly interwoven in [his] practice," it felt "necessary to model that relationship" in the way he "designed [his] course." All of their assignments in the course are personal reflective writing assignments: a short story about an instrumental experience in their life; a letter to a person within that short story; and a letter to their future, past, or present self. L.J. himself sees writing as a way to "engage in the dark spots"—a deep and honest investigation of the self. He hopes these assignments can help students do that.

Sample Reflective Activities: Inspiration From Our Focal Participants

From L.J., we can learn about ways of developing a classroom community that welcomes and celebrates reflective writing. We could do this by assigning reflective texts, analyzing them, and then creating a classroom community that honors reflective discussion through reciprocal teacher-student disclosure. When L.J. was teaching at a PWI as a graduate student, he learned that reflective writing should incorporate metacognitive writing that resulted in awareness of writerly choices, learning, and transfer of knowledge across contexts. His scholarly interests in Black literature and literacy studies, though, exposed him to such beautiful and powerful reflective writing from Black authors. These published pieces that incorporated personal narrative and storytelling methodologies seemed to better map onto his own experiences of reflection and his own ideas about what good writing was: writing was a way of looking at the self.

Watching L.J.'s pedagogy firsthand gave me so many ideas about using different public-facing reflective texts to expose students to ways that reflection does important self-reflexive work but also can serve as commentary about commonly held beliefs, critique for different ideologies, or promote social justice aims. L.J.'s texts, for example, commented upon institutionalized racism, domestic violence, and sexism. All of the authors that L.J. selected are Black, and all used elements of personal narrative. As Frankie Condon explains, "Personal narrative is necessary and integral to the creation and sustenance of community and solidarity among and between peoples of color" (2012, p. 31–32). Since he asked students to write short stories and letters, L.J.'s course texts included readings that took up those genres, like Alice Walker's "The Flowers," Jamaica Kincaid's "Girl," James Baldwin's "A Letter to

My Nephew," and Keise Laymon's "Dear Uncle Jimmy." And, with these texts, L.J. was able to share how reflection worked in public-facing genres and model reflective thought within the whole-group discussions about them.

There are many other genres that do this kind of public-facing reflective work that students could read as examples of reflection. I could imagine students looking through reflective testimonials in popular social media responses to current events. For example, many people who have had abortions reflect publicly upon their experiences as a way of pushing against the stigma of the procedure, enumerating the multitude of reasons potential childbearing people might have for choosing abortion, and (hopefully, consequently) humanizing abortion to others who struggle to understand childbearing people's right to make decisions about their own bodies. We can see examples of this in the "Shout Your Abortion" campaign (a campaign that began as a hashtag movement, #shoutyourabortion, in 2015 as a response to politicians trying to defund Planned Parenthood), #youknowme (a social media campaign in 2019 that emerged in response to the most restrictive abortion ban signed to date [at the time] in Alabama), and #whateverthereason (another social media campaign that shared stories of abortions after the *Dobbs v. Jackson* decision that overturned abortion rights in the United States). Doing this kind of investigation of public-facing reflection on a platform that so many students use in their daily lives might help illuminate the motives behind public-facing reflection and the affordances and limitations of a tactic so often used by feminist activists to humanize social justice issues and advocate for human rights for all.

L.J. was not alone in having distinct and thoughtful patterns for encouraging reflective activity. Jess too worked to value reflection as something integral to the community. Like L.J., she assigned course texts that included public-facing reflective work. She also started her course off with a reflective activity and thoughtfully and strategically created low-stakes reflective activities in a variety of genres. Jess asked students to engage in a variety of modalities (e.g., videos, written responses, audio notes) at different points in their writing process (e.g., at the brainstorming, drafting, and revision stages of the writing process) and in the course itself (e.g., from the first to final day of the class). Though the medium had to remain somewhat the same—the class was asynchronous online and therefore run through the community college's course-management system—Jess typically engaged in a variety of mediums during her in-person, synchronous classes. Like L.J., she was apt to use class discussions and personal disclosure as a way of fostering trust in her classroom community. She did this in similar ways to L.J., offering snippets of her personal history while modeling reflective thought. When assigning personal reflective writing, this is a really helpful way to build trust with students. It is a lot to ask for students to share about themselves when they know nothing about their audience. Along with verbal anecdote sharing, which she did in her weekly meetings, Jess always gave her own samples of reflective work. She had her own draft of her mixtape assignment, her own multimodal reflection about her relationship to literacy, her own rhetorical analysis of a sample text, her own letter of assessment of her performance in the course. In engaging in this kind of writing herself, she made the reflection in her course reciprocal. Jess signaled the importance that she placed on reflection, and she also signaled the trust she had in her students.

Jess, then, inspires me to suggest that we consider the same when time and boundaries permit. She worked to create relationships with her students—and she worked to help them create relationships with each other. Even online, she set up classroom-facing, low-stakes discussion board posts that both fostered classroom community and encouraged reflection upon students' identities, goals, and writing processes. In doing so, Jess hoped to disrupt their ideas about their welcomeness to the academy by disrupting the rules and expectations for writing classroom pedagogy. Some teachers' positionalities make it uncomfortable and/or impossible to create these kinds of classroom moments. At times, there are actual legal regulations for what we can and cannot share with our students about our identities, beliefs, and experiences. We of course need to honor this and recognize it as a potential reason why some kinds of reflective pedagogies do not work in the writing classroom. But, for those willing and able, engaging in reciprocal reflective writing is a powerful way to establish trust and build rapport with students. It is important that we acknowledge that our students too might have reasons for not engaging in reflection that relays their trauma. We should not require that students engage in reflection that makes them unsafe. When designing personal reflective writing prompts, then, it is also important that what students are required to reflect about is open-ended and so are the modalities, genres, and mediums they can use to reflect. This can allow students to take up what they feel comfortable sharing and how they share it.

Perhaps one way of learning what reflection is appropriate to students is asking students themselves. Heather designed her reflective activities based on input from students. From talking to students, she realized that they wanted to develop an awareness of White Mainstream English and discourse conventions of the academy. She therefore integrated metacognitive writing so they could become rhetorically aware of the kinds of writing choices they made. Inspired by Heather's student-centered approach to designing reflective opportunities for students, then, we could perhaps consider surveying students about their definitions of reflection, where they tend to locate it, and why they tend to take it up. In this process, we might learn—as was the case in each of my case studies—that students differed in their definitions of reflection, the desired rhetorical effect of the practice, and thus located and practiced it in many different types of activities. Knowing this information could allow for a fruitful discussion with students about ways that they reported defining reflection, along with ways they like to practice it. Then, together, we could brainstorm how to honor those definitions and make space for the various timings, modalities, and genres they like to employ to do reflective work.

Another way to learn about students' reflective practices is to get to know them personally. Grace fostered personal relationships with each student in her class by requiring conferences in lieu of her fourth class during the week. In meeting with students individually and so frequently, students often shared their self-prompted reflective work with her, just as they did with me. They often brought self-prompted brainstorming materials, recounted reflective conversations that they had with other students or mentors, or discussed instrumental reflective breakthroughs that they had in class. In incorporating this one weekly reflective practice, then, Grace gained insight into many more reflective practices that her students did. She learned about the multitude of smart and thoughtful ways that students were doing reflection that fell outside of the ways that she had purposefully designed as reflection in our pedagogy.

Again, we can learn from this practice. Grace's weekly conferencing might be entirely too much of a time commitment to be feasible as a sustainable practice with our workload, but developing relationships with students, along with providing time and space for them to share what kinds of reflection they already do, is something that we can accomplish. I could imagine doing this in a few ways. Perhaps we ask students to turn in some sort of scrapbook for the course, where they include these kinds of reflective moments that were instrumental to their writing process, their goals for their course, or what they will remember from their time in the classroom community. Perhaps, like Jess, we ask them to create a playlist of the songs that represent their journey in our course. Perhaps, more simply, we could just ask students how they are doing reflective work and try to incorporate ways that account for that in our incorporation of reflection in our pedagogy or our assessment, should we use reflection in our assessment practices.

This could be especially important in multimodal projects, which often rely on reflective writing as a way of assessing students' rhetorical awareness rather than their actual production. In Kevin's course, for example, students were tasked to create new kinds of writing with various forms of technologies—often technologies they had never used before. As reported by other scholars (see, for example, DePalma & Alexander, 2015), students in this case study often saw multimodal composing, especially when using new technological platforms, as a catalyst for reflective work. Kevin and all his focal students reported that reflection played an integral role in how they took up the new kinds of writing that he required them to do in the course. And, though Kevin did require they create writer's memos and freewrites to document their writerly choices in the class, students were apt to find reflection in other genres as well.

Therefore, it is important to remember that traditional reflective genres often do not tell the whole story, and some students do not find them as even reflective activity. In fact, it might be helpful to talk to students about what kinds of modalities they naturally gravitate toward when analyzing their own writing. If they talk out their work, perhaps a screencast would be more appropriate than a writer's memo. If they tend to engage in mind mapping, perhaps that would be a better use of their time than a required freewrite. If they tend to do more reflection in the planning phases and less in the retrospective, perhaps they should create a journal or blog throughout the course. If they tend to learn a lot from looking back at a completed draft or even a completed course, perhaps they could write a letter to themselves. There are ways that we can be individually responsive to our students and their practices, all while meeting our pedagogical goals.

Throughout this research process, I learned so many robust and insightful ways of doing reflection. I was struck by the absolute bravery that all the teachers and students had in opening up their classrooms to me, and I am still in awe of the generosity in spirit. I have been absolutely honored to share their insights, and I feel privileged to be able to share the smart and innovative things they did with reflective pedagogy. I look forward to the thoughtful pedagogical contributions that practitioners come up with upon reading this book.

Conclusion: Future Scholarly Implications

Throughout this book, I have shared many observations about the rhetoricity of reflection. One area of future scholarly research could be about the building of reflection definitions. From my research, we know that: (a) definitions of reflection act as terministic screens that interpret available activity as reflective; (b) definitions of reflection are not universal but instead built from past experiences; (c) other definitions can be used to identify moments as "reflection"; and (d) definitions can be affirmed, contested, and malleable when confronted with new reflective definitions and practices, but most often reflection definitions remain static. We also know that focal participants varied in the rhetorical effects they saw as a result of reflective activity. Some commented upon reflection as resulting in awareness, using reflection as an opportunity to ask, Why did I do that? Some then took that question and added another one: What can I learn from it? Others saw reflection as commenting upon internal introspection, asking questions about their identities: Who am I? Who do I want to be? How does this make me feel? This critical evaluation of the self sometimes led to more worldly implications; participants used reflection to reconsider a deep-held belief or ideology by asking How does this new realization about myself make me want to interact with the world differently? I could imagine future research both exploring definition formation and documenting new rhetorical effects that reflectors associate with reflection.

I am particularly excited about future research thinking about how reflection has the power to help students work across difference; it has the power to change minds and hearts, which in turn changes policies and lives. In fact, as Beth Berila explains, "bringing a level of self-reflection and critical analysis to choices that many of us do unconsciously is partly what we are trying to do in diversity classrooms" (2015, p. 154). In future research, I'd love to see more attention paid to the ways that reflection is incorporated purposefully in self-proclaimed antiracist, culturally responsive, and feminist pedagogues' classrooms. I wonder if we could learn about the interesting ways that reflection is purposefully curated for political purposes in classrooms. I wonder if, like we saw in the examples within this case study, teachers and students purposefully play across modalities and genres in productive ways.

We also know that reflection emerges from distributed agency among contextual factors. Though I did try to diversify my contexts by working with three distinct institutional types that supported a variety of students, all of them were in the United States. I wonder what we could learn from exploring new ways of doing reflection in non-Western settings. So far, Asao Inoue and Tyler Richmond (2016) have done some incredible work thinking about how non-Western students reacted to reflection done in Westernized institutionalized spaces. In fact, I hoped to build on this research in this book. The two had drawn data from first-generation American students and international college students at a large state school to argue that their cultural experiences shaped their reflective practices. I found that to be the case with the one international focal participant, Julie, who talked about reflection as a kind of mindfulness. Julie drew on her educational background from another country to make the kind of assessment about what reflection is and could be. Though future researchers could work with students that were first-generation or international students, I think a far more promising strategy would be to explicitly look at reflective practices in institutions located in other countries.

Another way to consider new kinds of reflection might be to look at public-facing reflection, which is a global phenomenon. Reflection, as disseminated in personal narrative and storytelling, is such a powerful and underresearched practice for activists. As Frankie Condon (2012) writes,

> Critical race theorists have long used the practice of story-telling to trouble or destabilize claims to universality that continue to prevail in courts of law, in evaluations of the scholar and of scholarship, in political and economic discourses, within and across communities. (p. 141)

And, yet, to date, there is no sustained scholarly work that studies how these phenomena can tell us more about the rhetorical nature of reflection. In the future, I hope to see so much more scholarly work on public-facing reflection. Of course, some may argue that these kinds of testimonial, narrative, or storytelling writing are not reflection because they are performative. I'd argue that all reflection that we can view, listen to, or read is somewhat performative because reflection is often published—whether for a teacher, a classmate, or a more global audience. Therefore, it feels like, at least to me, that this public-facing reflection could be interesting to look at from a rhetorical perspective. Understanding this kind of public-facing reflection could be so important to us as educators because of its classroom implications. As Beth Berila (2015) writes, "Academic classrooms were fundamentally changed by contemporary feminist movement's insistence that 'the personal is political,' that experience is to be valued as much as factual information, and that there is indeed a place in the learning process for telling one's personal story" (p. 55).

At first glance, I'd say public-facing reflection is doing different work than the reflection that we've seen so far. This kind of reflection is for others just as much as it is a form of healing for oneself. It's an exploration of feelings—a form of perhaps that kind of reflection-for-introspection that we saw in some of the focal participants' definitions of reflection—but shared purposefully in the hopes of becoming a catalyst for reflection-for-perspective (or maybe even something a bit different that future research can illuminate). More research can and should be done about how reflection can help us sit with trauma—and then, in its performance, move others into empathy or understanding. I look forward to reading more about what other scholars must think about whether this kind of work is reflective, and if so, what we can learn from it.

Epilogue

My body stirs, my sleep is complete. Waking up without an alarm is my favorite. There's something about that cozy warmth. That knowing that I slept exactly how long the universe wanted me to. I pull the eye mask back over my eyes, and I let my mind wander. I need to finish my book today, and I'm not sure how to end it. I know I want to talk about my own reflective work, as a way of again giving a bit of myself as an acknowledgment of how much my focal participants gave me. As a way of giving some of that back. It just feels like we know so much about how everyone does reflection because of what everyone shared with me. And I know that their work was so generous, so brave. Reflection is so deeply personal. Their contributions have shifted and reshifted the way that I think about reflection, both as a writing practitioner and as just a reflector in my daily life. I've started thinking about it as so multifaceted, so multidirectional, that it seems like my own reflective practice can now take on and try out the different rhetorical effects my participants identified. It's almost like a game of dress-up.

"Reflection, for me," I think, "lives in so many places."

As a writer, I still see reflection as something so deeply connected to my writing practice. It's in the momentary pauses that I have between thoughts that I write down, the silence between typing keys, when my eyes glance upward or sideways. It's when I take a deep breath or let out a sigh before keys clatter once more. It might even be within the next clatter where I type "jksaL.J.dklajsL.J.," out of frustration because I can't figure out how to put into words what I wanted to put onto paper. It might be in the rereading or the reading aloud. It might be in the Zoom calls with my best friend, as we gossip about ways to revise this very book.

In the tough moments, it always seems to need to be embodied. It might require a walk on the beach or a trip to hike in the woods with my dad. We're always using walking to work through the tough parts. It might be curled up in the crook of my mom's arm, as I talk about what's been on my mind lately that I can't seem to put into words on the phone. It might even be with my dog, Bruce, when I call him over and we lie together, his body pressed against mine. I try to still my mind by taking deep inhales. Quieting it down enough that I can hear my thoughts again instead of just the anxiety loop. Bruce somehow always smells like just-popped popcorn.

As a working parent, I often find reflection in the stolen moments: a voice memo as I drive to pick my daughter up from school, a comment quickly left on a Google Doc when I hear Parker wake from a nap so I can come back to the writing later with a bit more ease; or an iPhone note written under her crib while I hold her hand so she can drift off to sleep. I often find reflection in the quiet moments that my family helps me carve out of the constant commotion of our lives.

Brett always takes Parker in the morning so I can do some form of self-care. As a retired athlete, I often gravitate toward exercise, using our stationary bike or rowing machine. I find reflection in the warmup, when the exercise is not too hard yet, and I can relax into the monotony. It's in the push and pull of my rowing machine, or it's in the up and down or the bike pedals. And, in days like today, it's in the slow Saturday morning of a quiet house: when I skip my workout, Brett takes Parker for donuts, and I get a chance to sleep in and have a moment to let my body find its rhythm. To work through the hard parts. The parts I'm too tired or too busy to see on the other days of the week.

Reflection, for me, has changed throughout the lifetime of this research project because of both what I've learned from my research participants—they've so clearly broadened the different places where I can see it in my writing and teaching practices, along with the different rhetorical effects it can have—and also because of a life-altering event that happened while I worked on this book: I became a parent. Parenthood has shifted every aspect of my life: my sleep patterns, my working hours, my eating, my emotional capacity, my hobbies . . . my life.

As a reflective person, I quickly and readily brought reflection into my parenting practice.

I started this book 2 years ago, writing about how reflection was found in the quiet moment, baking with my daughter asleep on my chest. And now, I could almost laugh thinking of the audacity of my energetic, all-too-helpful toddler sleeping through baking. It's all fishing out eggshells, over-pouring the cinnamon, and having a bit of flour in our hair. But my reflective practice has adapted; it's found its shape among the changes in my life.

As a parent, I do so much reflecting. It looks different than I thought it would, but it's there, ever present. I'm just coming to accept that I stopped writing my reflections out on pen and paper years ago. It stopped feeling right.

As a new mom, I was so excited about writing the reflections required of Parker's baby book. It started in utero and went all the way until she was a graduate from high school. I loved the idea of giving Parker these stories of her babyhood, childhood, and teen years that exemplified her character. I loved the idea of writing these stories out for her, powered by my reflections, triggered by the book's thoughtful questions and prompts like: What was her first bath like? Who makes her laugh the most? Tell the story of when she first said, "I love you." I loved the idea of the physical nature of it too. Being able to hand her a leather-bound book, filled with writing in different pen colors, some hurried and some languid. I wanted her to be able to read my reflections. To read about her life through my eyes.

But the physical nature of the journal just never worked. Whenever I tried to write, my hand would cramp, then my wrist would hurt, and eventually my whole forearm would ache so painfully that I'd relent and stop writing. I couldn't find reflection while my hand cramped.

Plus, I found handwriting so slow. It was almost like the thoughts that I had moved faster than my body would allow. Typing, since I did it so often, is where my hand strength and speed was. It could keep up with my cognitive practice of reflection. And the form wasn't quite right either. I wanted to write out that reflection in the first moments that I awoke, like I was doing today.

Though that planned reflection failed, I find reflection so often in my daily practice of parenting. I read constantly, voraciously about motherhood.

In fact, I decided to move all my "work" books to my school office so I could both create healthy boundaries of when to work and fill my bookshelf with my ever-growing book collection about parenthood. Every topic dots the shelves: encouraging healthy sleep habits, understanding the science of eating, spending time in nature, fostering a relationship with literacy, learning to set and maintain boundaries, welcoming all emotions, learning to share the parenting load with a partner, and so on. When I was pregnant, I would reflect upon my reading and then create carefully organized lists on a Google Doc about what was the most important about each topic.

Now, when I read the books, I remember what I remember (who has time for writing down my reflections when I have a toddler?!). Sometimes it comes up when my partner and I reflect on our parenting. This usually happens at night, after our daughter goes to bed. We often reminisce and look at goofy pictures that we took that day—or even months ago. Sometimes, this leads to us reflecting upon something that went well, simply relishing in that moment of parenthood perfection. Sometimes one of us might lament about how we wish we would have done something differently. We might use reflection to work through why it happened. Or we might use reflection to just acknowledge that it really was triggering to us. Occasionally, our reflection might lead us to consider how we could avoid the whole situation next time by taking care of ourselves and therefore our own emotional capacity. Or our reflection might help us think about how Parker might have been hungry or tired, and how we could better set her up for success. Sometimes, we think back to our own childhood, what we liked and didn't—to think of new strategies for our current realities. Other times, we think of an imaginary possible second child, and we imagine how we will do something differently.

Even outside of my conversations with my partner, I find reflection about parenting in my nightly ruminations. Reflection is in my nightly scrolling when I look at Instagram and see reels and posts that give me information about toddler emotional well-being, eating practices, gentle parenting, social development. I find reflection too in the Facebook scrolling when posts from my Facebook groups are filled with parents asking for advice. They always start their posts with "N_R" (with the "_" filled in with the first letter of the company's name), and they often ask parents for insights—for reflections on their lived experience to help them make a choice or get advice. Sometimes, I'll read a post that really hits home, and it inspires me to reflect, tell my story, and give a bit of comfort to new parents. And, sometimes, I take the time to post about the memories I have about my daughter, what I like to think of as "Parker lately" posts. It's been a lot more realistic for me to curate reflective writing about Parker's life in this medium. Motherhood, for me, is one big exercise in reflection.

Perhaps I want to end this book, then, with an encouragement to look broader, wider for reflection. It would be so exciting to start to consider how reflection is shaped and reshaped from our life-altering events, from our hobbies, from our relationships. How does the death of a loved one change our relationship to reflection? How does a new practice of meditation or yoga change our relationship to reflection? How does a new identity, like parenthood or marriage, change our relationship to reflection? Maybe future researchers should start thinking more about how reflection works in daily lives more broadly. Maybe some other smart and thoughtful researcher will think about that next. I cannot wait to find out.

Acknowledgments

This book took a decade to write—and it's been a lifetime in the making. There are a lot of people to thank. So much love and generosity of time and spirit and knowledge and support to be grateful for.

A heartfelt thank you to my dad, Terry Fiscus, who is my rock. I have never had to wonder if I should believe in myself because he has always, unwaveringly, believed in me. He taught me what it meant to work hard and believe in myself harder. His own hard work made my life so much easier, so filled with privilege. That privilege gave me the extra means I needed to finish my MA and PhD in five years, land my dream job, write this book, and find another dream job in a city that could support my family's needs. My dad always encouraged me to just "Be You." And I can be that *you* because you believed and supported that *me*, dude daddy.

A huge thank you to my mom, Linda (Vanderheyden) Fiscus. Mom, you have carried me through this book journey by taking care of me as a whole person. You have showered me with love, food, hikes, and childcare throughout this journey. There's never a call that's too late for you to answer, nor is there an ask of your time and energy that's been too big for you to give. You have enveloped me in your love for a lifetime, and I am forever grateful that your love buoyed me through some of the hardest times along the way of this book-writing process.

To my family, especially my brother, JD; my grandmas, Ruth and Gertrude; my cousins, Regina and Kristen; my Uncle Gary; and my Aunt Lynn. Thank you to the families that raised me—the Fiscus and the Vanderheyden families—and to my wonderful bonus family: the Cannaday family. You have always believed in me, and I am so grateful.

Thank you especially to my husband, Brett, who has given me two wonderful children: Parker and Quinn. Their pregnancies may have made this book just a bit more challenging to write, but our children made the victory of finishing it all the sweeter. Being a mom has been the best thing I've ever done. And, somehow, you've lifted me up enough, taken on enough, and just tried hard enough to support me in more than just my motherhood. No matter how full our days are, you have always and forever supported my career. You have rearranged your life to support my goals, whether that be Saturday morning donuts so I can get a few more hours of sleep after staying up late writing or working remotely so you could follow me wherever my professorship takes me. Thank you.

Because of my family, I always have the comfort in knowing that I had a safety net to fall back on. Gosh am I blessed to live with the certainty that if I ever just leap for my goals just a bit too far, they are always there to catch me.

And the most amount of gratitude to the so, so many that have helped along the way, as mentors, family, and friends.

A big thank you to the University of Michigan English and Linguistics Departments who shaped me as a teacher-scholar. I first met Anne Curzan in English 305, a prerequisite for English teachers, and it reshaped my entire trajectory. I dropped my dual-major in history, picked up linguistics, and decided to go to graduate school and teach college courses about sociolinguistics instead of teaching K–12. The next semester I met Robin Queen in the language and gender course she cotaught with Anne, and I went on to take every course that they offered. Anne and Robin, your courses lit a fire in me that still burns bright: in my courses, I work to try to help students see and re-see their language ideologies just like you did for me. I hope I do your legacies some justice.

A thank you, too, to the support that I found in those undergraduate years—that carries me still today. My skating girls from UMSST. My roommates, Aditi Hardikar and Laura Nobec. My soul sister who I met as a camp counselor in the Sierra National Forest: Mindy Honaker. You are my biggest cheerleaders, and I have needed all the cheering I could get. Thank you.

During my time at the University of Washington for my MA and PhD, I met some absolutely incredible people who have shaped me and this book to be what it is.

A huge thank you to Anis Bawarshi, my mentor. The person who helped me find the seed for this project. What started as a simple conversation in a genre theory grad class turned into a term paper, a PhD candidacy exam question, a dissertation, and now a book. Anis, you know how to foster brilliance. To sit and listen, asking all the right questions at all the right times.

Thank you to Colette Moore, my mentor. The person who called me when I first was accepted to the University of Washington and got me excited about the program, and then guided me through my next five years with grace and kindness.

Thank you to Gail Stygall, my mentor. The person who helped me find my place, a place where linguistics meets composition.

Thank you to Candice Rai, my mentor. The person who helped me find myself as a burgeoning teacher-scholar, and whose guidance helped me find a job that supported my whole family's needs.

And the biggest thank you to Olivia Hernández. The godmama to my baby. My girls' Nina. You excitedly listened to my ideas when the writing was flowing, and you patiently listened to my complaints when the process felt like a trash fire. Through it all, you gently coaxed out my best; always my first reader. (Yes, even the surprise of reading these acknowledgments in print form was spoiled because I needed your opinion.) This book evolved into something so much more than I could have ever imagined because of your careful prodding, your thoughtful questions, and your unmatched intellect. I am so grateful for you, for us. I am a better teacher and a better writer because of you—no question. But I am also a better friend, a better mother, a better wife, and a better person because I know you, and I love (and have been loved by) you. Thank you.

A thank you, too, to the Florida State University community. Thank you to Florida State's English Department, especially the Rhetoric and Composition program, for taking a chance on me: a brand-new junior professor. The love and support from all the faculty and graduate students there gave me the support and energy needed to move this project from a dissertation to a book.

Thank you especially to Michael Neal, Kathi Yancey, Rhea Lathan, Tarez Graban, and Kris Fleckenstein, who guided me in the publication process. I spent a lot of time in the Rhet/Comp Suite eating chocolate, talking through ideas, and listening to your wisdom on our well-worn couches. Thank you, too, to the graduate students, especially those in writing group, who sat with me to write week after week (especially on the weeks when I wanted to do anything but write). And a thank you to my Tallahassee family: Lindsey Eckert, Alexis Demeo, and Joel Smith.

I have so much gratitude for the University of Minnesota Writing Studies Department, who welcomed me to their community as I was finishing up this book and about to give birth to Quinn. They gave me the support I needed to finish *Reflection-in-Motion*, all while becoming a mom of two. Thank you especially to Amy Lee.

Thank you to the Utah State University Press team, who made this book a reality. I have so much appreciation and respect for the work you do. A special thank you to acquisitions editor Rachael Levay and the reviewers of this book. Your comments shaped it to be something so much smarter than I originally dared to imagine. Thank you, too, to the copyediting team, marketing team, and all the other folks who made this book become a real, printed book that I can actually hold in my hands. (It is still incredibly surreal to me.)

Thank you, readers, for reading this book. I hope just one teacher will read it and make space for even just one student to do reflection differently: in a way that honors their big, beautiful ideas of what reflection can do. Maybe, just maybe, with a little more reflection we can start getting people to rethink their ideologies and work across difference.

And, if that happens, it's really all thanks to the teachers and students who made this work possible. I asked such a big thing of you: to let me—a white woman—into your safe spaces. And you chose to trust me, to let me learn how minority-serving institutions were doing reflection. Thank you. From the bottom of my heart, thank you.

Works Cited

Ahmed, S. (2017). *Living a feminist life*. Duke University Press.
Ahmed, S. (2021). *Complaint!* Duke University Press.
Anson, C. (1994). Portfolios for writing teachers: Writing our way to reflective practice. In L. Black & D. A. Dalker (Eds.), *New directions in portfolio assessment: Reflective practice, critical theory, and large-scale scoring* (pp. 185–201). Boynton Cook.
Baca, I., Hinojosa, Y. I., & Murphy, S. W. (2019). Introduction. In I. Baca, Y. I. Hinojosa, & S. W. Murphy (Eds.), *Bordered writers: Latinx identities and literacy practices at Hispanic-serving institutions* (pp. 1–12). State University of New York Press.
Baker-Bell, A. (2017, October 9). For Loretta: A Black woman literacy scholar's journey to prioritizing self-preservation and Black feminist–womanist storytelling. *Journal of Literacy Research*, 49(4), 526–543. https://doi.org/10.1177/1086296X17733092
Baker-Bell, A. (2020). *Linguistic justice: Black language, literacy, identity, and pedagogy*. Routledge.
Ballenger, B., & Myers, K. (2019, June). The emotional work of revision. *College Composition and Communication*, 70(4), 590–614. https://www.jstor.org/stable/26772586
Banks, A. J. (2010). *Digital griots: African American rhetoric in a multimedia age*. Southern Illinois University Press.
Barad, K. M. (2007). *Meeting the universe halfway: Quantum physics and the entanglement of matter and meaning*. Duke University Press.
Barrios, B. (2023, January 1). The butterfly affect. *Pedagogy*, 23(1), 11–19. https://doi.org/10.1215/15314200-10081959

Baumgardner, J., & Richards, A. (2020). *Manifesta: Young women, feminism, and the future* (20th anniversary ed.). Picador USA.

Beaufort, A. (2007). *College writing and beyond: A new framework for university writing instruction.* Utah State University Press.

Beck, K. (2022). *White feminism: From the suffragettes to the influencers and who they leave behind.* Simon and Schuster.

Behm, N., Rankins-Robertson, S., & Roen, D. (2017). *The framework for success in postsecondary writing: Scholarship and applications.* Parlor Press.

Bennett, J. (2010). *Vibrant matter: A political ecology of things.* Duke University Press.

Berila, B. (2015). *Integrating mindfulness into anti-oppression pedagogy: Social justice in higher education.* Routledge.

Bishop, W., & Ostrom, H. A. (Eds.). (2003). *The subject is story: Essays for writers and readers.* Boynton/Cook Heinemann.

Blair, K. L., & Nickoson, L. (2018). *Composing feminist interventions: Activism, engagement, praxis.* The WAC Clearinghouse; University Press of Colorado. https://doi.org/10.37514/PER-B.2018.0056

Blankenship, L. (2019). *Changing the subject: A theory of rhetorical empathy.* Utah State University Press.

Brabeck, K. (2003, May). IV. Testimonio: A strategy for collective resistance, cultural survival, and building solidarity. *Feminism & Psychology, 13*(2), 252–258.

Brown, T. (2020). What else do we know? Translingualism and the history of SRTOL as threshold concepts in our field. *College Composition and Communication, 71*(4), 591–619.

Burke, L. (2021). "HSIs on the Rise." https://www.insidehighered.com/news/2021/04/07/hispanic-serving-institutions-growing-number

Chávez, K. R., Griffin, C. L., & Houston, M. (2012). *Standing in the intersection: Feminist voices, feminist practices in communication studies.* State University of New York Press. https://doi.org/10.1353/book19031

Clifford, J., & Marcus, G. E. (Eds.). (1986). *Writing culture: The poetics and politics of ethnography; A School of American Research advanced seminar.* University of California Press.

Collins, P. H. (2000). *Black feminist thought: Knowledge, consciousness, and the politics of empowerment.* (Rev. 10th anniversary ed.). Routledge.

Condon, F. (2012). *I hope I join the band: Narrative, affiliation, and antiracist rhetoric.* Utah State University Press.

Cooper, B. (2016). Intersectionality. In L. J. Disch & M. E. Hawkesworth (Eds.), *The Oxford handbook of feminist theory.* Oxford University Press.

Crenshaw, K. (1989). Demarginalizing the intersection of race and sex: A black feminist critique of antidiscrimination doctrine, feminist theory, and antiracist politics. *University of Chicago Legal Forum, 1989*(1), article 8.

Cruz, C. (2012, August 3). Making curriculum from scratch: Testimonio in an urban classroom. *Equity & Excellence in Education, 45*(3), 460–471.

Daniel, J. R. (2016). Crisis at the HBCU. *Composition Studies, 44*(2), 158–161. https://www.jstor.org/stable/24859535

Delgado, R., & Stefancic, J. (2001). *Critical race theory: An introduction*. New York University Press. http://www.jstor.org/stable/j.ctt9qg26k

Delgado Bernal, D. (1998). Using a Chicana feminist epistemology in educational research. *Harvard Educational Review*, 68(4), 555–583.

Delgado Bernal, D., Burciaga, R., & Flores Carmona, J. (2012). Chicana/Latina testimonios: Mapping the methodological, pedagogical, and political. *Equity & Excellence in Education*, 45(3), 363–372.

de Nooijer, R., & Sol Cueva, L. (2022). Feminist storytellers imagining new stories to tell. In W. Harcourt, K. van den Berg, C. Dupuis, & J. Gaybor (Eds.), *Feminist methodologies: Gender, development and social change* (pp. 237–255). Palgrave Macmillan. https://doi.org/10.1007/978-3-030-82654-3_11

DePalma, M.-J., & Alexander, K. P. (2015). A bag full of snakes: Negotiating the challenges of multimodal composition. *Computers and Composition*, 37, 182–200. https://doi.org/10.1016/j.compcom.2015.06.008

Dewey, J. (1933). *How we think: A restatement of the relation of reflective thinking to the educative process*. D. C. Heath & Co Publishers.

Driscoll, D., & Powell, R. (2016). States, traits, and dispositions: The impact of emotion on writing development and writing transfer across college courses and beyond. *Composition Forum*, 34.

Dupuis, C., Harcourt, W., Gaybor, J., & van den Berg, K. (2022). Introduction: Feminism as method—navigating theory and practice. In W. Harcourt, K. van den Berg, C. Dupuis, & J. Gaybor (Eds.), *Feminist methodologies: Gender, development and social change*. Palgrave Macmillan. https://doi.org/10.1007/978-3-030-82654-3_1

Elbow, P. (1993, February). Ranking, evaluating, and liking: Sorting out three forms of judgment. *College English*, 55(2), 187–206. https://doi.org/10.2307/378503

Emmons, K. (2003). Rethinking genres of reflection: Student portfolio cover letters and the narrative of progress. *Composition Studies*, 31(1), 43–62.

Endres, D., & Senda-Cook, S. (2011). Location matters: The rhetoric of place in protest. *Quarterly Journal of Speech*, 97(3), 257–282. https://doi.org/10.1080/00335630.2011.585167

Enoch, J. (2014). Feminist rhetorical studies—past, present, future: An interview with Cheryl Glenn [interview]. *Composition Forum* 29. https://compositionforum.com/issue/29/cheryl-glenn-interview.php

Enríquez-Loya, A., & Leon, K. (2017). Chicanx/Latinx rhetorics as methodology for writing program design at HSIs. *Composition Studies*, 45(2), 212–215. https://www.jstor.org/stable/26402792

Esposito, J., & Evans-Winters, V. (2022). *Introduction to intersectional qualitative research*. Sage.

Evans-Winters, V. E. (2019). *Black feminism in qualitative inquiry: A mosaic for writing our daughter's body*. Routledge.

Fiscus, J. (2017). Genre, reflection, and multimodality: Capturing uptake in the making. *Composition Forum*, 37.

Flash, P. (2016). From apprised to revised: Faculty in the disciplines change what they never knew they knew. In K. B. Yancey (Ed.), *A rhetoric of reflection* (pp. 227–249). Utah State University Press.

Flower, L. (2021, September). Hidden frames: Writing a path to change. *College Composition and Communication, 73*(1), 27–51.

Flower, L., & Hayes, J. R. (1981, December). A cognitive process theory of writing. *College Composition and Communication, 32*(4), 365–387. https://doi.org/10.2307/356600

Flynn, Elizabeth A. (1988). Composing as a woman. *College Composition and Communication, 39*(4), 423–435.

Gasman, M., Nguyen, T. H., & Conrad, C. F. (2015). Lives intertwined: A primer on the history and emergence of Minority Serving Institutions. *Journal of Diversity in Higher Education, 8*(2), 120–138.

Gilyard, K. (1999). African American contributions to composition studies. *College Composition and Communication, 50*(4), 626–644.

Glaser, B., & Strauss, A. (1967). *The discovery of grounded theory: Strategies for qualitative research*. Mill Valley, CA: Sociology Press.

Glenn, C. (2018). *Rhetorical feminism and this thing called hope*. Southern Illinois University Press.

Gonzales, L., & Kells, M. H. (2022). Introduction: Reflection, resistance, and resilience in Latina leadership. In L. Gonzales & M. H. Kells (Eds.), *Latina leadership: Language and literacy education across communities* (pp. 1–12). Syracuse University Press. https://doi.org/10.2307/j.ctv1c7zg20.6

Green, D. Jr. (2016). Expanding the dialogue on writing assessment at HBCUs: Foundational assessment concepts and legacies of historically Black colleges and universities. *College English, 79*(2), 152–173.

Guy-Sheftall, B. (1995). *Words of fire: An anthology of African-American feminist thought*. New Press.

Hamad, R. (2020). *White tears/brown scars: How white feminism betrays women of color*. Trapeze.

Hesford, W. S. (1990). Storytelling and the dynamics of feminist teaching. *Feminist Teacher, 5*(2), 20–24. http://www.jstor.org/stable/40545583

hooks, b. (1994). *Teaching to transgress*. Routledge.

hooks, b. (2009). *Teaching critical thinking: Practical wisdom*. Routledge.

hooks, b. (2013). *Teaching critical thinking: Practical wisdom* (1st ed.). Taylor and Francis.

hooks, b. (2015a). *Ain't I a woman: Black women and feminism*. Routledge.

hooks, b. (2015b). *Feminism is for everybody: Passionate politics*. Routledge.

Hsu, V. J. (2018). Reflection as relationality: Rhetorical alliances and teaching alternative rhetorics. *College Composition and Communication, 70*(2), 142–168. https://www.jstor.org/stable/26772558

Hull, Gloria T., Bell-Scott, P., & Smith, B. (2015). *All the women are white, all the Blacks are men, but some of us are brave: Black women's studies*. Feminist Press at the City University of New York. (Original work published 1982)

Hurtado, A. (2020). *Intersectional Chicana feminisms: Sitios y lenguas*. University of Arizona Press.

Ilmonen, K. (2020). Feminist storytelling and narratives of intersectionality. *Signs: Journal of Women in Culture and Society, 45*(2), 347–371. https://doi.org/10.1086/704989

Inoue, A. (2016). Afterword: Narratives that determine writers and social justice writing center work. *Praxis: A Writing Center Journal*, 14(1).
Inoue, A. (2019). 2019 CCCC chair's address: How do we language so people stop killing each other, or what do we do about white language supremacy? *College Composition and Communication*, 71(2), 352–369.
Inoue, A. B., & Richmond, T. (2016). Theorizing the reflection practices of female Hmong college students: Is reflection a racialized discourse? In K. B. Yancey (Ed.), *A rhetoric of reflection* (pp. 125–148). Utah State University Press.
Irvin, L. (2020). *Reflection between the drafts*. Peter Lang.
Jackson, B. (2020). *Teaching mindful writers*. Utah State University Press.
Jackson, H., & Jackson, K. K. (2016). We are family: I got all my (HBCU) sisters with me. *Composition Studies*, 44(2), 153–157.
Jackson, K. K., Jackson, H., & Tafari, D. N. H. (2019). We belong in the discussion: Including HBCUs in conversations about race and writing. *College Composition and Communication*, 71(2), 184–214. https://www.jstor.org/stable/26877929
Jankens, A. 2019. Learning how to ask writing questions with rhetorical reflections. *Composition Forum*, 41.
Jankens, A., & Latawiec, A. (2021). Revising reflection for results in teacher research. *Composition Forum*, 46.
Jarratt, S. (2001). Feminist Pedagogy. In G. Tate, A Rupiper, and K. Schick (Eds.), *A guide to composition pedagogies* (pp. 113–131). Oxford University Press.
Jordan, Z. (2012). Students' right, African American English, and writing assessment: Considering the HBCU. In A. Inoue and M. Poe (Eds.), *Race and writing assessment* (pp. 97–110). Peter Lang.
Kafer, A. (2013). *Feminist, queer, crip*. Indiana University Press.
Kells, M. H., Balester, V., & Villanueva, V. (Eds.). (2004). *Latino/a discourses: On language, identity, and literacy education*. Heinemann.
Kendall, M. (2020). *Hood feminism: Notes from the women that a movement forgot*. Viking.
Kirklighter, C. (2022). Foreword: Our personal academic literacy and language journeys. In L. Gonzales & M. H. Kells (Eds.), *Latina leadership: Language and literacy education across communities* (pp. xi–xviii). Syracuse University Press. https://doi.org/10.2307/j.ctv1c7zg20.4
Kirklighter, C., Cardenas, D., & Murphy, S. W. (Eds.). (2007). *Teaching writing with Latino/a students: Lessons learned at Hispanic serving institutions*. State University of New York Press.
Kirsch, G., & Sullivan, P. A. (1992). *Methods and methodology in composition research*. Southern Illinois University Press.
Kroll, B. (2008). Arguing with adversaries: Aikido, rhetoric, and the art of peace. *College Composition and Communication*, 59(3), 451–472.
Kynard, C. (2010). From candy girls to cyber sista-cipher: Narrating black females' color-consciousness and counterstories in and out of school. *Harvard Educational Review*, 80(1), 30–53. https://doi.org/10.17763/haer.80.1.4611255014427701
Kynard, C., & Eddy, R. (2009). Toward a new critical framework: Color-conscious political morality and pedagogy at historically Black and historically white colleges and universities. *College Composition and Communication*, 61(1), 24–44.

Lamos, S. (2012). Minority-serving institutions, race-conscious "dwelling," and possible futures for basic writing at predominantly white institutions. *Journal of Basic Writing*, 31(1), 4–35. http://www.jstor.org/stable/43741084

Latina Feminist Group. (2001). *Telling to live: Latina feminist testimonios*. Duke University Press.

Leaker, C., & Ostman, H. (2010). Composing knowledge: Writing, rhetoric, and reflection in prior learning assessment. *College Composition and Communication*, 61(4), 691–717. http://www.jstor.org/stable/27917869

Leavy, P., & Harris, A. M. (2019). *Contemporary feminist research from theory to practice*. Guilford Press.

Li, J. (2012). *Cultural foundations of learning: East and West*. Cambridge University Press.

Lindenman, H., Camper, M., Jacoby, L. D., & Enoch, J. (2018). Revision and reflection: A study of (dis)connections between writing knowledge and writing practice. *College Composition and Communication*, 69(4), 581–611.

Lockett, A., & Walker, S. (2016). Creative disruption and the potential of writing at HBCUs. *Composition Studies*, 44(2), 172–178.

Love, B. L. (2019). *We want to do more than survive: Abolitionist teaching and the pursuit of educational freedom*. Beacon Press.

Lu, M. (1991). Refining the legacy of Mina Shaughnessy: A critique of the politics of linguistic innocence. *Journal of Basic Writing*, 10(1), 26–40.

Lunsford, K. (2002). Contextualizing Toulmin's model in the writing classroom: A case study. *Written Communication*, 19(1), 109–174.

Martinez, A. (2014). Critical race theory: Its origins, history, and importance to the discourses and rhetorics of race. *Frame-Journal of Literacy Studies*, 27(2), 9–27. http://www.tijdschriftframe.nl/wp-content/uploads/2016/12/Frame-27_2-Critical-Race-Theory.pdf

Martinez, A. (2020). *Counterstory: The rhetoric and writing of critical race theory*. National Council on the Teaching of English.

McCann, C., Seung-kyung, K., & Ergun, E. (2021). *Feminist theory reader: Local and global perspectives* (5th ed.). Routledge.

McIntyre, A. (2016). Practicing mindfulness: A pedagogical tool for spotlighting whiteness. In T. M. Kennedy, J. I. Middleton & K. Ratcliffe (Eds.), *Rhetorics of whiteness: Postracial hauntings in popular culture, social media, and education*. Southern Illinois University Press.

McKee, H. A., & Porter, J. E. (2017). *Professional communication and network interaction: A rhetorical and ethical approach*. Routledge.

Menchú, R. (2010). *I, Rigoberta Menchú: An Indian woman in Guatemala*. Verso. (Original work published 1984)

Micciche, L. (2012). Feminist pedagogies. In G. Tate, A. Rupiper, & K. Schick (Eds.), *A guide to composition pedagogies* (2nd ed., pp. 128–145). Oxford University Press.

Miller, E. E., Mozafari, C., Lohr, J., & Enoch, J. (2023). Thinking about feeling: The roles of emotion in reflective writing. *College Composition and Communication*, 74(3), 485–521.

Miller, S. (1991). *Textual carnivals: The politics of composition*. Southern Illinois University Press.

Moss, B. J. (2021). Where would we be?: Legacies, roll calls, and the teaching of writing in HBCUs. *Composition Studies, 49*(1), 144–148, 206–207.

Nadar, S. (2014). "Stories are data with soul"—lessons from black feminist epistemology. *Agenda, 28*(1), 18–28. https://doi.org/10.1080/10130950.2014.871838

Nash, J. (2019). *Black feminism reimagined: After intersectionality*. Duke University Press.

Nash, R., & Virnay, S. (2013). *Our stories matter: Liberating the voices of marginalized students through scholarly personal narrative writing*. Peter Lang.

National Center for Education Statistics. (n.d.). *Characteristics of postsecondary faculty*. U.S. Department of Education, Institute of Education Sciences. Retrieved May 31, 2022, from https://nces.ed.gov/programs/coe/indicator/csc

National Council of Teachers of English. (2020). *This ain't another statement: This is a demand for Black linguistic justice!* Conference on College Composition and Communication. https://cccc.ncte.org/cccc/demand-for-black-linguistic-justice

NCTE. (1974). Students' right to their own language. *College Composition and Communication, 25*(Fall). https://cdn.ncte.org/nctefiles/groups/cccc/newsrtol.pdf.

Neal, M. (2016). The perils of standing alone: Reflective writing in relationship to other texts. In K. B. Yancey (Ed.), *A rhetoric of reflection* (pp. 64–83). University Press of Colorado. http://www.jstor.org/stable/j.ctt1djmhfg.7

Nowacek, R. (2011). *Agents of integration: Understanding transfer as a rhetorical act*. Southern Illinois University Press.

Paris, D., & Alim, H. S. (Eds.). (2017). *Culturally sustaining pedagogies: Teaching and learning for justice in a changing world*. Teachers College Press.

Paris, D., & Winn, M. (2013). *Humanizing research: Decolonizing qualitative inquiry with youth and communities*. Sage.

Penrose, A. (2012). Professional identity in a contingent labor profession: Expertise, autonomy, community in composition teaching. *WPA: Writing Program Administration, 35*(2), 108–126.

Perl, P. (1980). Understanding composing. *College Composition and Communication, 31*(4), 363–369.

Pianko, S. (1979). Reflection: A critical component of the composing process. *College Composition and Communication, 30*(3), 275–278. https://doi.org/10.2307/356394

Pink, S. (2015). *Doing sensory ethnography* (2nd ed.). Sage.

Plummer, M., & Young, L. E. (2010.) Grounded theory and feminist inquiry: Revitalizing links to the past. *Western Journal of Nursing Research, 32*(3), 305–321. doi:10.1177/0193945909351298

Pough, G. (2004). Personal narratives and rhetorics of Black womanhood in hip-hop. In K. Gilyard & V. Nunley (Eds.), *Race and ethnicity* (pp. 111–118). Heinemann.

Pratt, M. L. (1991). Arts of the contact zone. *Profession*, 33–40.

Prendergast, C. (2003). *Literacy and racial justice: The politics of learning after* Brown v. Board of Education. Southern Illinois University Press.

Raelin, J. (2001). Public reflection as the basis of learning. *Management Learning*, 32, 11–30.

Randolph, B. M., & Ross-Valliere, C. (1979). Consciousness raising groups. *The American Journal of Nursing*, 79(5), 922–924. https://doi.org/10.2307/3462300

Ratcliffe, K. (2005). *Rhetorical listening: Identification, gender, whiteness*. Southern Illinois University Press.

Ratcliffe, K., & Jensen, K. (2022). *Rhetorical listening: A concept-tactic approach*. Parlor Press.

Redd, T. (2003). "Tryin' to make a dolla outa fifteen cent": Teaching composition with the internet at an HBCU. *Computers and Composition*, 20(4), 359–373. https://doi.org/10.1016/j.compcom.2003.08.012

Relerford, J. (2012). Looking back in composition studies: What a narrative history of composition at HBCUs can contribute to the field today. *CLA Journal*, 56(2), 116–128. http://www.jstor.org/stable/44325818

Reyes, K., & Curry Rodríguez, J. (2012). Testimonio: Origins, terms, and resources. *Equity & Excellence in Education*, 45(3), 525–538. https://doi.org/10.1080/10665684.2012.698571

Ribero, A., & Arellano, S. (2022). Advocating cadrismo: A feminist mentoring approach for Latinas in rhetoric and composition. In L. Gonzales & M. Hall Kells (Eds.), *Latina leadership* (pp. 15–44). Syracuse University Press. https://doi.org/10.2307/J.Ctv1c7zg20.1

Ritchie, J., & Boardman, K. (1999). Feminism in composition: Inclusion, metonymy, and disruption. *College Composition and Communication*, 50(4), 585–606.

Rittel, H. W., & Webber, M. M. (1973). Dilemmas in a general theory of planning. *Policy Sciences*, 4(2), 155–169.

Rodgers, C. (2002). Defining reflection: Another look at John Dewey and reflective thinking. *Teachers College Record*, 104(4), 842–866. https://doi.org/10.1111/1467-9620.00181

Roozen, K. (2016). Reflective interviewing: Methodological moves for tracing tacit knowledge and challenging chronotopic representations. In K. B. Yancey (Ed.), *A rhetoric of reflection* (pp. 250–270). Utah State University Press.

Rothberg, S. (2020, October 19). *List of AANAPISIs*. College Recruiter. https://www.collegerecruiter.com/blog/2020/10/19/list-of-aanapisis

Royster, J. J. (1996). When the first voice you hear is not your own. *College Composition and Communication*, 47(1), 29–40. https://doi.org/10.2307/358272

Royster, J. J., & Kirsch, E. (2012). *Feminist rhetorical practices: New horizons for rhetoric, composition, and literacy studies*. Southern Illinois University Press.

Ruiz, I. D. (2016). *Reclaiming composition for Chicano/as and other ethnic minorities: A critical history and pedagogy*. Palgrave Macmillan.

Scharff, D. P., Mathews, K. J., Jackson, P., Hoffsuemmer, J., Martin, E., & Edwards, D. (2010). More than Tuskegee: Understanding mistrust about research participation. *Journal of Health Care for the Poor and Underserved*, 21(3), 879–897. https://doi.org/10.1353/hpu.0.0323

Schön, D. (1983). *The reflective practitioner*. Ashgate Publishing.

Schuller, K. (2021). *The trouble with white women: A counterhistory of feminism*. PublicAffairs.

Scott, T. (2005). Creating the subject of portfolios: Reflective writing and the conveyances of institutional prerogatives. *Written Communication*, 22(1), 3–35.

Selfe, C. L. (2009). The movement of air, the breath of meaning: Aurality and multimodal composing. *College Composition and Communication*, 60(4), 616–663.

Shipka, J. (2009). Negotiating rhetorical, material, methodological, and technological difference: Evaluating multimodal designs. *College Composition and Communication*, 61(1), 343–366.

Sias, R. E., & Moss, B. J. (2011). Rewriting a master narrative: HBCUs and community literacy partnerships. *Reflections*, 10(2), 1–16.

Siebler, K. (2008). *Composing feminism(s): How feminists have shaped composition theories and practices*. Hampton Press.

Smith, B. (1980). Racism and women's studies. *Frontiers: A Journal of Women Studies*, 5(1), 48–49. https://doi.org/10.2307/3346304

Smitherman, G. (1999). "Students' right to their own language": A retrospective. *The English Journal*, 84(1), 21–27.

Smitherman, G. (2006). *Word from the mother: Language and African Americans*. Routledge.

Sommers, J. (1988). Behind the paper: Using the student-teacher memo. *College Composition and Communication*, 39(1), 77–80.

Spencer-Maor, F., & Randolph, R. E. (2016). Shifting the talk: Writing studies, rhetoric, and feminism at HBCUs. *Composition Studies*, 44(2), 179–182. https://www.jstor.org/stable/24859539

Spigelman, C. (2001). Argument and evidence in the case of the personal. *College English*, 64(1), 63–87.

Stenberg, S. (2015). *Repurposing composition: Feminist interventions for a neoliberal age*. Utah State University Press.

Sullivan, P. A. (1992). Feminism and methodology in composition studies. In G. Kirsch & P. A. Sullivan (Eds.), *Methods and methodology in composition research*. Southern Illinois University Press.

Taczak, K. (2016). Reflection is critical for writers' development. In L. Adler-Kassner & E. Wardle (Eds.), *Naming what we know* (pp. 78–83). Utah State University Press.

Taczak, K., & Robertson, L. (2017). Metacognition and the reflective writing practitioner: An integrated knowledge approach. In P. Portanova, J. M. Rifenburg, & D. Roen (Eds.), *Contemporary perspectives on cognition and writing* (pp. 211–230). WAC Clearinghouse.

Thompson, B. (2018). *Teaching with tenderness: Toward an embodied practice*. University of Illinois Press.

Thompson, K. D., Singletary, Z. T., Morse, T. A., & Morris, A. L. (2022). Boundaries, self-care, and empathy: Building an empathic teaching survival kit. *Composition Studies*, 50(2), 34–52.

Thomsen, J. (2021). *Alternative cartographies: Reflection(s) for the complexities of writing and sustainability* [Doctoral dissertation, Florida State University, 28546565]. ProQuest Dissertations Publishing.

Torrez, J. Estrella. (2015). Translating Chicana testimonios into pedagogy for a white midwestern classroom. *Chicana/Latina Studies*, 14(2), 101–130.

U.S. Department of Education. (n.d.). Hispanic-Serving Institutions (HSIs). *White House Initiative on Educational Excellence for Hispanics*. Retrieved on October 10, 2022, from https://sites.ed.gov/hispanic-initiative/hispanicserving-institutions-hsis/

Wenger, C. (2015). *Yoga minds, writing bodies: Contemplative writing pedagogy*. WAC Clearinghouse.

Yancey, K. (1996). The electronic portfolio: Shifting paradigms. *Computers and Composition*, 13, 259–262. https://doi.org/10.1016/S8755-4615(96)90014-6

Yancey, K. (1998). *Reflection in the writing classroom*. Utah State University Press.

Yancey, K. (2004). Made not only in words: Composition in a new key. *College Composition and Communication*, 56(2), 297–328. https://doi.org/10.2307/4140651

Yancey, K. (2016). *A rhetoric of reflection*. Utah State University Press.

Yancey, K. (2018). 2018 CCCC exemplar award acceptance speech. Believing in the cause: Composing's past, present, and future. *College Composition and Communication*, 71(1), 159–163.

Yancey, K., Robertson, L., & Taczak, K. (2014). *Writing across contexts: Transfer, composition, and sites of writing*. Utah State University Press.

Ybarra, M. G. (2022). Testimoniando: Chicana/Latina feminist reflections on embodied knowledge, literacies, and narrating the self. In L. Gonzales & M. Hall Kells (Eds.), *Latina Leadership* (pp. 250–267). Syracuse University Press. https://doi.org/10.2307/J.Ctv1c7zg20.1

Zakaria, R. (2021). *Against white feminism: Notes on disruption*. W. W. Norton.

Index

Page numbers followed by t indicate tables.

AANAPISIs (Asian American and Native American Pacific Islander Serving Institutions), 6, 34, 35, 41, 46, 47, 53. *See also* Urban State U
ableism, white feminism, 64
abstractness of reflection, 138
academia, white supremacist values, 97
academic literacy, 47, 59
academic writing, 106
accessibility of research participants, 38
accredited institutions, 46
action-present in the writing process, 20
active listening space in the classroom, 170, 175–80
activism in feminist research, 38, 59, 64
adaptability of pedagogy, 114, 118–19, 149–50
Adobe Illustrator, 109
affect theory pedagogy, 77, 101, 102
African intellectualism, 58–59
agency, reflection, 21, 201–2
Ahmed, Sara, 23–24, 38–39
Ain't I a Woman: Black Women and Feminism, 48
allyship of white researchers, 50, 57
alphabetic communication, 117
analytical thinking, 113

anti-oppression pedagogical practices, 11–12, 67–68
antiracism in academia, 16, 40, 50, 67–68, 72, 87, 95, 96, 97
Anzaldúa, Gloria, 15, 62, 63
approachability of researchers, 55
argumentation style, 14
Aristotle, 14
artist statements, 108, 117
Asian American and Native American Pacific Islander Serving Institutions. *See* AANAPISIs; Urban State U
assessments, writing assignments, 103
assignments, scaffolding, 89
Audacity, 109, 158
audial data collection, 42–44
audio notes, reflective activity, 197
autoethnographic reflective writing, 13, 57
Avery College, 110
awareness, 78, 80; cultural diversity, 110; identity, 145; metacognition, 102, 146; reflection-for-awareness, 140t; reflection-for-learning, 145; reflective activity, 18, 193, 201; rhetorical effects, 189; whole-group discussions, 154–55

Baker-Bell, April, 57, 66
baking, 55
Baldwin, James, 148, 178, 196–97
Banks, Adam, 58–59
Banks, David, 114
Beal, Frances, 62
Beck, Koa, 63
beliefs, exploration of, 150
benefits for research participants, 36
Berg, Karijn van den, 56
Berila, Beth, 12, 67–68, 201, 202
best practices, research methods, 41
BIPOC students. *See* students of color
birth control, 64
Black English, 111
Black Feminism in Qualitative Inquiry, 40
Black feminist research, 24–25; contextual understanding, 40; ethical research, 61–62; feminist theory (BFT), 15, 62; lived experience, 67; mosaic mixed-method approach, 6, 41, 40–48; scholars, 62, 63; storytelling, 57, 58, 59; white researchers, 63–66
Black intellectualism, 58–59
Black literacy practices, 15, 50, 113–14
Black literature, 148–49, 174, 196–97
Black Women in White America: A Documentary History, 48
Blankenship, Lisa, 27
borderlands theory, 63
boundaries in student-teacher relationships, 195
brainstorming, 8, 9, 103, 138, 153, 154, 157, 197, 199
breakthroughs in reflective practices, 199
Brown, Tessa, 20
Burke, Kenneth, 138
But Some of Us Are Brave, 15, 62

Canvas, 44–45, 83–84
capitalism, 16
CFSHRC (Coalition of Feminist Scholars in the History of Rhetoric and Composition), 61
Cheyney University, 110
Chicanx students, 31, 47, 48, 51, 52*t*, 53, 59, 63, 82, 86, 89. *See also* Hispanic students; Latinx students
choice articulation, 101, 102, 146, 147
civic engagement, 124
Civil War, American, 110
class observations, 41
classroom environment: active listening space, 170, 175–80; community-building, 80*t*, 88, 90–91, 113–14, 154, 158, 168–74; critical reflection, 175–80; disengagement, 129, 194–95; layout, 29, 89; online communication, 188; outside contexts, 101; peer review, 188; personal narrative, 170, 175–80; public-facing reflection, 190–91; reflective activity, 25, 75, 108, 129–33, 138, 152, 156, 192–93; reflective pedagogy, 109, 159; research methods, 29; rhetorical activity, 187–88; safe space, 96, 111, 113, 116, 126, 136, 158; strategy goals, 12; technology, 109; trust, 190–91, 195–98; whole-group discussion, 168–74, 188, 195; Zoom classes, 87–88
cleaning, 55
Coalition of Feminist Scholars in the History of Rhetoric and Composition (CFSHRC), 61
code-switching, 111
collaborative reflective communication, 157
College Composition and Communication Conference, 61
College Composition and Communication, 47
Collins, Patricia Hill, 65
Combahee River Collective Statement (1977), 62, 64
community colleges. *See* HSIs; Rural CC
community-building in the classroom, 80*t*, 88, 90–91, 113–18, 154, 157, 158, 168–74
Composing Feminism(s): How Feminists Have Shaped Composition Theories and Practices, 12
Composition Studies, 47
composition theories, 12
computer-integrated classrooms, 105–9
Condon, Frankie, 50, 57, 68, 196, 202
Conference on College Composition and Communication 16
conferences, 139
confidence-building, 73
constructive reflection, 18–19, 132, 133, 161, 162–63*t*, 164
Contemporary Feminist Research from Theory to Practice, 38
contextual factors in reflective activity, 40, 77, 97, 99, 120, 121, 134–36, 153, 156
Cooper, Anna, 62
Cooper, Brittany, 15
counterstory, 13, 56, 57, 190
Counterstory: The Rhetoric and Writing of Critical Race Theory, 57
course assignments, 79*t*, 80*t*, 108, 153, 161, 162–63*t*, 189, 191–92, 197–98
Covid-19, effect on education, 30, 33, 44, 75–76, 90–91, 94, 97
Crenshaw, Kimberlé, 61–63
critical race theory, 57, 58, 67, 203

critical reflection, 95, 175–80
critical thinking skills, 12, 26, 67, 111
cross-cultural communication, 13
cue for transfer, 90, 126, 129, 136, 139, 154, 155t. *See also* knowledge transfer
cultural awareness in pedagogy, 50, 58, 72, 87, 97–98, 109–14, 116

data collection/data analysis, 6, 11, 13–14, 17, 23t, 24–25, 30, 40–43, 46, 56–57, 59, 67, 98–99
Davis, Angela, 15
deadlines for project assignments, 84
decision-making, 80, 93
definition of reflection. *See* reflective activity; reflective writing
Delgado, Richard, 57
demographics: AANAPISIs, 48, 99; HBCUs, 48; HSIs, 48, 81–82, 99; primary white institutions (PWIs), 99; research participants, 51, 52–53t, 54, 109–10
Descartes, René, 14
Dewey, John, 19, 20, 22
Digital Griots: African American Rhetoric in a Multimedia Age, 58
disability theory, 67
disclosure, 84
discourse conventions, 26, 199
discussion boards, 77, 79t, 90, 115, 138, 153, 154
disengagement of students, 129, 170, 194–95
diversity, 7, 27, 67, 111
Dobbs v. Jackson, 197
dominant narrative in academia, 56, 97–98
doodling, 138, 153
drafting process, 84, 103, 120, 154, 156, 197
dropout rates, 88
Dupuis, Constance, 56

Eddy, Robert, 6
embodied processing, 161, 162–63t
Emig, Janet, 60
emotion factor, 77
emotional labor, 190, 195
end-of-class ePortfolio, 132
engagement of students, 170, 194–95
Enoch, Jennifer, 65
Enríquez-Loya, Aydé, 47, 81–82
Esposito, Jennifer, 7, 67
ethical research practices, 24–25, 32, 37, 38, 48, 50, 61–66
ethnographic methods, 23t, 38–39, 42, 44, 56–57
Evans-Winters, Venus E., 6, 7, 24–25, 40, 41, 67

exemplary moments of reflection, 140–44t
exercise, 54
exploration of beliefs/ideologies, 150
external/internal processing, 92, 139, 161, 162–63t, 164, 185, 186, 188
extracurricular activity: journaling, 145, 153–54; meditation, 151; moments for reflection, 145; perspective shift, 150–51; poetry, 145, 154; reflective activity, 138, 161, 162–63t, 164; scrapbooking, 145, 151; writing, 131, 134, 135, 139, 188

faculty meetings, 11
faculty of color, 7, 53
failures/successes, 147
familismo, HSIs, 72, 87
feedback activities, 85, 117, 118, 139, 154, 155t, 161, 162–63t
feminist activism, 40, 60, 62, 197
feminist composition pedagogy, 12, 13, 16, 61
feminist listening, 23–24, 36, 39, 43–44
Feminist Methodologies: Experiments, Collaborations and Reflections, 56
feminist pedagogy, 13, 60–63, 67–68, 201
feminist research methodologies, 6–7, 13, 24–25, 56–60, 62, 65, 67
feminist research methods, 7, 38–40
first-generation college students, 33, 54, 88–89, 97, 111, 171, 173
first-year writing courses: AANAPISIs, 99; HBCUs, 111; HSIs, 88–89; multimodality, 99, 123–24; outcomes, 100; pedagogy, 10, 26–27, 117; programmatic goals, 146; reflective writing, 3, 33, 106–7, 118, 120; research participants, 122–25
Flash, Pamela, 11
flexibility of reflective pedagogy, 112, 149–50, 165, 190, 193
focal students. *See* student research participants
"For Loretta: A Black Woman Literacy Scholar's Journey to Prioritizing Self-Preservation and Black-Feminist-Womanist Storytelling," 57
foundational experience, 81, 139, 140–44t, 165
frameworks, white bias, 16
freewriting, 79f, 106, 108, 117, 127–28, 131–36, 147, 153–56, 158, 188
Freire, Paulo, 12, 16, 50
frequency of observations, 77
From the Suffragettes to Influencers and Who They Leave Behind, 63–64
funding for scholars of color, 49, 50

Gay, Roxane, 15
Gaybor, Jacqueline, 56
gender studies departments, 60
generations of reflection research, 9–10
genre analysis, 23*t*, 160
gestural reflection, 67
Gilyard, Keith, 114
Glenn, Cheryl, 24, 65
global majority, 5, 57
Gonzales, Laura, 72
González Ybarra, Mónica, 59
Google Driver products, 108–9
Google Slides, 107
GoPro, 43
graduate student instructors (GSIs), 3, 99
Great Black Awakening, 110
griots, 58–59
grounded theory, 17, 25, 78, 153–54
group work, 79*t*, 100, 107–9, 117, 126, 138, 139, 153–54, 155*t*, 161, 162–63*t*

habitual reflections, 75
habitual reflective activity, 193
Hall Kells, Michelle, 72
Hamad, Ruby, 63
Harcourt, Wendy, 56
Harris, Danielle, 38
HBCUs (Historically Black Colleges and Universities), 5, 6; accredited institutions, 46; critical creativity, 111; history of, 110; intersectional research methodologies, 6–7; pedagogy, 109, 110; research participants, 66, 110–11, 138, 167; scholarship, 49, 50; teacher-scholars, 49. *See also* Southern HBCU
hero essays, 157
higher order transfer, 100
Hispanic students, 5, 15, 33, 44, 52*t*, 53, 81, 82, 110. *See also* Chicanx students; Latinx students
Hispanic Serving Institutions. *See* HSIs; Rural CC
Historically Black Colleges and Universities. *See* HBCUs; Southern HBCU
Hmong research participants, 14
hobbies, 54, 55
Hood Feminism: Notes from the Women That a Movement Forgot, 64
hooks, bell, 12, 15, 16, 25, 48, 58, 60, 62, 192
Horner, Winifred Bryan, 61
HSIs (Hispanic Serving Institutions), 5, 6, 32, 34, 41, 46, 48, 72, 81, 82, 87. *See also* Rural CC

Hsu, V. Jo, 17
Hurtado, Aída, 63
hush space, 57

I Hope I Join the Band, 50, 68
ideation assignments, 154
identification of reflection, 8, 33, 37–39, 68, 121, 137, 193, 201
identity factor, 42, 58, 77
Ilmonen, Kaisa, 57
in-class participation, 106, 127–28, 130, 132–33
inclusive pedagogy, 12–13, 38, 47–48, 72, 87, 95, 96, 97
in-person observations, 30, 45–56
individual practice, 192
individualization, 102, 103
initiate, respond, evaluate (IRE) speech pattern, 104
Inoue, Asao, 14, 16, 64–65, 202
instructor feedback, 154
Integrating Mindfulness into Anti-Oppression Pedagogy: Social Justice in Higher Education, 12, 67
intellectual rigor, 130
intentional introspection, 119
interactive reflection, 104
internal processing, 18, 79*t*, 80*t*, 92, 139, 152
International Research Bureau (IRB), 41
international students, 151–52
intersectional research methods, 6–7, 24, 38, 40, 62, 63–66, 67–68
interview research method, 23*t*, 38–39, 42, 43, 69–70, 112–16, 122–25
Introduction to Intersectional Qualitative Research, 7
introspection, 55, 78, 116, 119, 141–42*t*, 150–51, 165, 189
iPhone notes, 205
IRE speech pattern. *See* initiate, respond, evaluate (IRE) speech pattern
Irvin, Lennie, 11, 19, 20

Jackson, Hope, 49, 50
Jackson, Karen Keaton, 49, 50, 110
Jarrat, Susan, 13
Jensen, Kyle, 23–24, 39
Johnson, Nan, 61
Jordan, June, 62
journaling, 25, 55, 125, 134, 139, 145, 150, 153–54, 159, 200, 206–7

Kairos, 47
Kendall, Mikki, 64
Kincaid, Jamaica, 196
King, Deborah, 62

Kirklighter, Christina, 59
Kirsch, Gesa, 37, 65
knowledge and knowing, 40
knowledge transfer, 8, 14, 15, 18–22, 26, 94, 100–101, 118, 139, 146, 161, 162–63t, 188. *See also* cue for transfer
Kroll, Barry, 11
Kynard, Carmen, 6

Language as Symbolic Action, 138
Latina Leadership: Language and Literacy Education across Communities, 59
Latinx students, 15, 33, 47, 48, 59, 81, 98, 99. *See also* Chicanx students; Hispanic students
Laymon, Kiese, 149, 174, 197
learning, 165
learning as reflective activity, 78, 81, 107, 145, 165, 189
Leavy, Patricia, 38
Leon, Kendall, 47, 81–82
Lerner, Gerda, 48–49
letter writing, 116, 148–49, 151, 175–80, 181–87, 192
LGBTQ+ research participants, 54
life choices, 147
Lincoln University, 110
linguistic diversity, 26, 111
literature-themed course, 13–14, 99
lived experience: Black feminist research methods, 67; cultural background, 94; data collection, 67; foundational memories, 165; non-Western students, 202; reflection, 8, 14, 75, 134, 138–39, 147, 188–89, 201, 208; scholars of color, 49; students of color, 26, 160, 194; writing composition, 12
Living a Feminist Life, 39
logic and argument, 14
Lorde, Audre, 15, 62
Lu, Min-Zhan, 94

mainstream feminism, 62–63
mandated course outcomes, 100
marginalized students, 26
martial arts, 11
Martinez, Aja, 13, 57
master narratives, 57
materials factor, 77
McKee, Heidi A., 24
meaning of language, 138
meditation, 55, 138, 151, 152, 153, 159, 208
mental health, 44–45, 147–48
mentor/mentee relationships, 3, 25, 190
meritocracy, 16

meta-awareness, 105
meta-moment, 105, 108
metabolizing thoughts, 154
metacognition, 15; awareness, 94, 102; choices, 101, 102; coursework, 108; pedagogy, 105; process of reflection, 81; programmatic context, 109; reading processes, 92–93; reflective writing, 16, 196, 199; rhetorical rationales, 145–47; self-awareness, 105; transfer of knowledge, 146
methodologies. *See* research methodologies
methods. *See* research methods
Micciche, Laura, 13
midterm essays, 75
mindfulness, 11, 78, 143–44t, 151–52, 165, 189
mind mapping, 200
Miner Institute, 110
Minority Serving Institutions (MSIs). *See* AANAPISIs (Asian American and Native American Pacific Islander Serving Institutions); HBCUs (Historically Black Colleges and Universities); HSIs (Hispanic Serving Institutions)
mixed-method research, 6, 40–48
mixtape assignments, 75, 76–77, 89, 90–91, 157–58
modalities. *See* multimodal reflective activity
moments for reflection, 129–33, 145
mosaic research method, 6, 23, 40–48
MSIs (Minority Serving Institutions). *See* AANAPISIs (Asian American and Native American Pacific Islander Serving Institutions); HBCUs (Historically Black Colleges and Universities); HSIs (Hispanic Serving Institutions)
multidialectal/multilingual speakers, 54, 81–82, 97, 99, 111, 139
multimodal reflective activity, 67, 98, 99, 109, 123–24, 153, 154, 158, 193, 197–98, 200
music, 54, 55, 115, 138, 153

Nadar, Sarojini, 58
naming reflection, 33, 37–38, 121
Naming What We Know, 20
narrative writing, 58
Nash, Robert, 58
National Women's Studies Association Convention, 62
Native American students, 5–6, 48, 99
naturally reflective identity, 75
NCTE (National Council of Teachers of English), 60, 111
Neal, Michael, 67

nomo, 114
nontraditional reflective activity, 23–25, 33, 89–91
non-Western students, 202
Nooijer, Rosa de, 56
notetaking, 42–44, 46

objectivity, 24
observation research method, 42–46, 77, 106
online classes, 30–34, 44–45, 96–98, 153–54, 155*t*, 161, 162–63*t*, 197–98
open-ended prompts, 103
openness in pedagogy, 11, 12, 68, 103, 137, 165
oral tradition. *See* storytelling
Our Stories Matter, 58

Paint, 109
paper medium, 136
parenthood, 206–8
Paris, Django, 113
participant-centered methodologies, 60
past experience. *See* lived experience
pedagogy: adaptability, 118–19, 149–50; antiracism, 11, 38, 47, 68, 72, 87, 95, 96, 97; classroom context, 97, 109, 126, 136, 159, 168–74; Covid-19, 75–76, 90–91, 94; cultural awareness, 50, 72, 87, 109–10, 111–16; feminism, 12–13, 17, 61, 67, 201; inclusivity, 47–48, 72, 87, 95, 96, 97; individualization, 102; intersectionality, 67–68; metacognition, 105; openness, 103, 137; physical practice, 11; predominantly white institutions (PWIs), 110; processing time, 103, 104; programmatic context, 95, 108, 109; public-facing, 196; "punk," 73, 87, 90; reflection, 10, 12, 16, 24, 26, 55, 76, 78, 80*t*, 89, 108–9, 117–21, 168–74, 200; skills-based lessons, 107; storytelling, 25; technology, 45; white bias, 7; writing studies, 81, 91–98, 103
peer review, 85, 108, 117–20, 138, 148, 152–54, 160, 188
Peitho, 47, 61
perception, 94, 134
performative nature of reflection, 130
personal narrative, 25, 56, 57, 70–71, 116, 148–49, 153, 154, 170, 196–97, 203. *See also* lived experience; storytelling
"Personal Narratives and Rhetorics of Black Womanhood in Hip-Hop," 59
personal reflection, 139, 152–53, 156–59, 165, 175–80
perspective/perspective shift, 19, 39, 78, 95, 134, 135, 144*t*, 150, 151, 154–55, 165, 189

physical reflection, 11
Pianko, Sharon, 124
Pink, Sarah, 42
place, 8, 9, 204–6
Plato, 14
podcasts, 126–28, 158
poetry, 145, 150, 154, 159
Porter, James E., 24
portfolio cover letter, 11, 13, 15, 117, 118, 135, 188
positionality, 24, 38–39, 62, 63, 64–65, 190, 193–96, 198
potential moments for reflection: asynchronous classes, 157; classroom contexts, 156; extracurricular activity, 145; patterns, 153–59; reflective activity, 155*t*, 160–61, 162–63*t*; rhetorical context, 137; student rejection, 129–33
Pough, Gwendelyn, 59
power dynamics, 12
PowerPoint, 109, 158
Pratt, Mary Louise, 13
prayer as reflection, 54, 55, 138, 153
pre-writing, 90, 113, 117–18, 134–35, 140*t*, 148, 153–54, 158–59
predominantly white institutions (PWIs), 7, 36, 49, 99, 110, 115
preemptive reflection, 19
presentation, 88–89
process memos, 115
process reading notes, 75
processing time, 74, 81, 92, 97, 103, 104, 139, 152, 154, 155*t*, 161, 162–63*t*
professional development, 49
programmatic pedagogical context, 95, 108, 109, 146
project assignments, 84, 85, 86
prompted writings, 90, 127–28, 133
public-facing reflection, 170–74, 190–91, 196–98, 203
publications, scholarly, 47
"punk" pedagogy, 73, 87, 90

qualitative research methods, 17, 23–25, 30, 38–39
queer theory, 58, 67

racial diversity, 7
racism, 47, 62–64, 115
Randolph, Robert, 48
Ratcliffe, Krista, 23–24, 39
rational reflection, 14
re-drafting, 154

reading and writing pedagogy, 47, 112–14
reading processes, 92–93
reciprocal reflective writing, 197–98
Reclaiming Composition for Chicano/as and Other Ethnic Minorities: A Critical History and Pedagogy, 47
Reconstruction period, 110
reflection assignments, 25, 79*t*, 80*t*, 90
Reflection Between the Drafts, 11, 20
Reflection in the Writing Classroom, 10, 18
reflection-for-awareness, 18, 25, 78, 79*t*, 80*t*, 140*t*, 147, 150, 154
reflection-for-introspection, 18, 25, 78, 80*t*, 116, 141–42*t*, 203
reflection-for-learning, 18, 25, 78, 79*t*, 81, 107, 145, 150
reflection-for-mindfulness, 18, 25, 78, 143–44*t*
reflection-for-perspective, 18, 25, 78, 95, 97, 203
reflection-in-action, 11, 18, 20, 84, 88, 132, 133, 161, 162–63*t*, 164, 190–91
reflection-in-motion, 5, 6, 21, 22, 23, 27, 41
reflection-in-presentation, 18, 19, 84, 88–89, 132, 133, 161, 162–63*t*, 164
reflection: anti-oppression, 11–12; definition of, 17, 74, 119–20, 149–52, 161; diversity, 27; failures/successes, 147; feminist pedagogy, 201; foundational experiences, 139; identification, 8, 33, 37–38, 68, 121, 137; lived experience, 8, 75, 134, 138, 188–89, 202, 20; metacognition, 145–46; multimodal, 67; performative, 130; perspective shift, 19, 95, 134, 135, 144*t*, 150, 151; processing, 92; religious, 124–25; representation, 13; resistance to, 54–55; rhetorical awareness, 22, 97, 117–18, 165, 187–88; self-prompted, 155–56, 159; social media, 207–8; teacher expectations, 78, 79–80*t*, 81, 134, 137; transfer of knowledge, 20, 26, 118; Western theories, 6; writing process, 6, 16, 19, 20, 21, 31, 204–6
Reflections, 47
reflective activity, 12, 38, 40; awareness, 140*t*, 143–45, 151–52, 165; brainstorming, 103, 199; decision-making, 93; discussion boards, 79*t*; extracurricular activity, 161, 164, 188; feedback, 161; group work, 79*t*, 108, 161; introspection, 55, 79*t*, 80*t*, 116, 141–42*t*, 150–51, 165; lived experience, 14, 94, 134, 136, 138, 201, 208; mixtapes, 75–77, 89, 90–91; multimodality, 98, 109, 200; online communication, 157, 197–98; parenthood, 206–8; podcasts, 126–28; potential moment patterns, 137, 153–54, 155*t*, 156–59, 160–61, 162–63*t*; processing, 80*t*, 164, 185, 186, 188; public-facing, 196, 197; research, 13–14, 201; rhetorical effects, 10, 94, 189; self-care, 147–48, 205; storytelling, 13, 15, 25; student-teacher relationships, 135, 147, 152, 158, 160, 164, 165, 188, 198–200; technology, 105–9; transfer of knowledge, 13–14, 161, 188; trust, 195–98; whole-group discussion, 79*t*, 80*t*, 104, 115, 116, 161, 192–94
reflective pedagogy. *See* pedagogy
reflective spaces, 139
reflective tools, thing power, 135
reflective writing: argumentation style, 14; artist statements, 108, 117; autoethnographic, 13; Black literature, 148–49, 196–97; course assignments, 79*t*, 80*t*, 90, 161, 162–63*t*, 189, 191–92; drafting process, 84, 103; first-year writing, 106–7; freewriting, 79*t*, 106, 108, 117, 127–28, 131–33, 136, 137, 147, 158, 188; journaling, 4, 8, 125, 134, 150, 153, 159, 206–7; letter writing, 116, 148–49, 151, 181–87; metacognitive writing, 196; midterm essays, 75; paper medium, 136; peer review, 108, 148, 152, 160; personal narrative, 116, 148–49; poetry, 150; portfolio cover letters, 11, 117, 118, 135, 188; pre-writing, 90, 148, 117, 118, 158; process memos, 115; reading notes, 75; revisions, 10, 103, 148, 158, 161, 162–63*t*; rhetorical rationales, 101, 119–20, 159, 161, 162–63*t*, 164; scrapbooking, 150, 199; self-assessments, 75; short stories, 116; translingual, 193; writer choices, 100; writer's memos, 11, 117, 118, 130, 135, 160, 188; written responses, 197
rejection of potential moments of reflection, 129–33
relationships factor, 77
relationships with research participants, 38–39, 66
Relerford, Jimesha, 46–47
religious reflection, 124–25
reluctance of student research participants, 45, 51
representation, research participants, 13, 38
research location, contextual factors, 40
research methodologies, 6–7, 24–25, 36, 64–65
research methods: classroom observation, 29, 41–43; critical race theory, 57, 67; data collection, 6, 11; disability theory, 67; ethical practices, 24–25, 32, 37, 38; ethnography, 42, 56–57; feminist theory, 39, 67; generations of, 9–10; intersectionality, 24, 38;

interviews, 15, 42, 77; mainstream definition, 22–23; mosaic, 6, 40; openness, 68; place, 8, 9; positionality, 24; predominantly white institutions (PWIs), 7; queer theory, 67; reflective activity, 11, 13–14; reflexive practices, 38, 40; reshaping, 208; rhetorical power, 8, 9, 10, 68; self-awareness, 16; surveys, 41–42, 44, 77; textual analysis, 42; white epistemologies, 38; wicked problems, 68; writing process, 10; Zoom, 30–33
research participants, 6–7, 24, 27, 34, 36, 47–49. *See also* student research participants; teacher research participants
researchers: approachability, 55: ethical practices, 66; mental health, 44–45; positionality, 38–39; scholars of color, 46–47; self-reflexivity, 38; teaching practices, 205–6; transparency, 65–66
reshaping reflection research, 208
resistance to reflection, 54–55
respect, student-teacher reflective relationship, 168–74, 190
retroactive reflection, 19
revision process, 155t; drafts, 154; reflective activity, 158, 161, 162–63t; reflective writing, 148; revisions, 103, 139; rhetorical reflection, 10; writing process, 9, 117, 197
rhetoric and composition: activity, 22, 187–88, analysis, 126–28; awareness, 10, 96–97, 101, 117–18, 165, 199, 200; Black English, 111; context, 27, 137, 152, 153; counterstory, 57; effects, 189, 145, 201; feminist pedagogy, 6–7, 60–63; linguistic diversity, 111; reflective practice, 26, 27; traditions, 58–59, 65
A Rhetoric of Reflection, 9–10, 14
Rhetorical Feminism and This Thing Called Hope, 61, 65
Rhetorical Listening as a Concept-Tactic Approach, 39
rhetorical listening, 23–24, 36, 40, 68, 81, 94
Rhetorical Listening: Identification, Gender, Whiteness, 39
rhetorical power of reflection, 8–10
rhetorical rationales, 77: drafts, 103; first-year writing courses, 118, 120; metacognitive activity, 146–57; reflective activity, 161, 162–63t, 164; reflective assignments, 85, 86, 139t, 153, 154, 155t, 201; revision processes, 10; self-assessments, 96–97; writing process, 75, 110–20, 159
Richmond, Tyler, 14, 202
risk mitigation for research participants, 36–38, 66

Rittel, Horst, 68
Robertson, Liane, 13–14
roles of identity, 42
Roozen, Kevin, 11, 43
roundtable discussions, 109, 126
Royster, Jacqueline Jones, 13, 23–24, 43–44, 65
Ruiz, Iris, 47
running, 145, 159
Rural CC: course assignments, 83–86; demographics, 48, 81–83, 99, 109–10; first-year writing courses, 88–89; pedagogy, 110; reflection-for-awareness, 80t, 140t; reflection-for-mindfulness, 144t; student research participants, 34, 51, 52t, 138, 155t; teacher research participants, 70, 79–80t; traditional college writing pedagogy, 91–98; Zoom research, 30–33, 87. *See also* HSIs

safe space in classrooms, 8, 96, 111, 113, 116, 158, 193, 194, 195
Sanger, Margaret, 64
scaffolding, 153; assignments, 32, 75, 89, 90, 148–49, 158; explanations, 138; first-year writing, 107; metacognitive rhetorical rationales, 146–47; reflection, 10, 86, 104, 116; rhetorical rationales, 83; student-teacher reflective relationship, 192–93; supplemental technology tools, 104
Schön, Donald, 19, 20, 22
scholars of color, 46–47, 49, 50, 64
Schuller, Kyla, 64
Scott, Tony, 14
scrapbooking, 25, 145, 150, 151, 152, 199
screencast videos, 154
self-addressed letters, 148–49, 151
self-assessments, students, 75, 96–97, 119
self-awareness, 16, 105, 146
self-care, 170, 171, 205
self-prompted writing, 131, 133, 134, 135, 155–56, 159
self-reflection, 67–68, 81, 181–87, 201
semi-structure interview method, 43
sensory ethnography, 42
sensory reactions factor, 77
service-learning course, 99
sexism, 62, 115
Shaughnessy, Mina, 94
short stories, 116
Siebler, Kay, 12, 13
silence and listening, 65
skills-based lessons pedagogy, 107
Smith, Barbara, 62

Smitherman, Geneva, 111, 114
social identity theory, 63
social justice initiatives, 12, 13, 125, 196, 197
social media, 25, 115, 117, 139, 154, 157, 190, 195, 207–8
Sol Cueva, Lillian, 56
Southern HBCU: demographics, 48; potential moments for reflection, 155t, 156–58; reflection-for-awareness, 140t; reflection-for-introspection, 141–42t; reflection-for-mindfulness, 143–44t; reflective activity, 112–16, 150–51; student research participants, 33–37, 52–53t, 66, 110–11, 138, 148–49, 167, 180–83; teacher research participants, 33–38, 79–80t, 81, 189–92, 194–95. *See also* HBCUs
space between thinking and doing, 81, 107, 108
space for reflection, 4, 5, 8, 9, 26, 27, 89, 108, 139
Spark, 47
spatial reflection, 67
speech genres, 25
Spencer-Maor, Faye, 48
Spotify playlists, 154, 159
Stanton, Elizabeth, Cady, 64
"Stories are Data with Soul-Lessons from Black Feminist Epistemology," 58
storytelling: Black feminist-womanist, 57, 58; Black literature, 196–97; counterstory, 13, 56, 57; critical race theory, 203; dominant narratives, 56; feminist methodology, 6–7, 59–60; hush space, 57; oral tradition, 113–14; personal narrative, 25; public-facing reflection, 203; reflection research, 15; research method, 42; students of color, 56–58; testimonio, 13, 15, 59
stress factors, students, 170–74
structured pedagogy, 107
student research participants: burnout, 129; confidence-building, 73; demographics, 51, 52–53t, 109–10; first-generation, 54, 88–89; focal students, 31–32; goals, 123; group presentations, 100–102; incentives, 45; interviews, 3–5, 11, 23t, 77, 122–25; letter writing, 180–83; MSIs, 7, 27, 34, 36, 48; needs of, 12; non-Western students, 202; personal narrative, 71, 123–25, 134–37, 165; potential moments of reflection, 129–33; reflection, resistance to, 54–55; reflective activity, 8–9, 25–27, 137, 140–44t, 145–47, 161, 162–63t, 164, 165; reluctance, 51; researcher relations, 38–40, 205–6; risk mitigation, 36–38, 66; self-assessments, 75; storytelling, 15; students of color, 33–38, 40, 48, 53, 65–66; writing process, 20, 21, 139; *See also* Rural CC; Southern HBCU; Urban State U
student-teacher relationships: community-building, 168–74, 192–93; conferences, 79t, 117–19, 132, 135, 138, 147, 152, 158, 160, 161, 162–63t, 164, 188, 199–200; disclosure, 84; emotional labor, 190, 195; engagement/disengagement, 129, 170, 194–95; flexibility, 190, 193; positionality, 190, 195–96, 198; public-facing reflection, 170–74; reflection-in-action, 190–91; relationships, 90–91, 199; respect, 190; safe space, 192, 193, 194, 195; self-care, 170, 171; social media connections, 190, 195; trust, 88, 113, 190, 191, 194–96, 197–98; whole-group discussion, 191; Zoom meetings, 71–72
students of color: academic literacy, 47; Covid-19, 45; lived experience, 160, 194; MSIs, 47; predominantly white institutions (PWIs), 49, 115; research participants, 7, 33–38, 40, 48, 65–66; STEM fields, 110–11; storytelling, 56–57; white bias, 14; writing studies, 47
Students' Right to Their Own Language, 111
subjectivity, 21
Sullivan, Patricia, 37
surveys, 23t, 41–42, 44, 77
Swearingen, C. Jan, 61
synchronous in-person class, 155t

Taczak, Kara, 13–14, 20
Tafari, Dawn N.H., 49
tape-recording, 44, 46
Tate, Gary, 13
TCUs (Tribal Colleges and Universities), 5–6
teacher research participants: classroom observation, 28–30, 44, 45, 100–104, 126–28, 155t; cultural awareness, 58; definitions of reflection, 78, 79–80t, 81, 88–91; demographics, 51, 52–53t, 54; equity, 38; faculty of color, 53; goals, 123; HSIs, 34, 89; intersectionality, 62; interview method, 23t, 43, 70–77, 122–25; literature-themed class, 13–14; MSIs, 7, 27, 34, 36, 48; non-Western students, 202; personal narrative, 71; perspectives, 39; predominantly white institutions (PWIs), 36; reflective practice, 25, 26, 27, 137; researcher relations, 38–40, 205–6; space, 8, 9; student-teacher conferences, 8–9, 117; students of color, 33–38, 40, 48, 53, 65–66; teaching-for-transfer class, 13–14; writing instructors, 112–16; Zoom

meetings, 30–33, 87. *See also* Rural CC; Southern HBCU; Urban State U
teacher reflexivity, 12
teacher-student relationships. *See* student-teacher relationships
teacherly expectations, 6, 85, 129–33, 134, 137, 138
teaching for transfer (TFT), 13, 14
teaching methods, 11, 12, 13, 205–6
Teaching to Transgress, 192
teaching-for-transfer class, 13–14
technology in the classroom, 77, 104–9, 117, 138, 153, 158, 200
terministic screens, 138
Terrell, Mary Church, 62
testimonios, 13, 15, 59
textual analysis research method, 42
thing power, 42, 135
thinking and doing, space between, 107, 108
This Bridge Called My Back, 15, 63
Thompson, Becky, 11
Thomsen, Jessica, 14
thought process, 19, 154
time factor, 22, 77
Toulmin's model, 14
traditional data collection, 23–25
traditional pedagogical practices, 90–91, 98
transfer of knowledge. *See* cue for transfer; knowledge transfer
translingual reflective writing, 193
transnational feminist movement, 60
transparency, 24, 65–66
trauma, 203
Tribal Colleges and Universities (TCUs), 5–6
trust-building, 8, 88, 113, 190–91, 194–98
Truth, Sojourner, 62

unconscious bias, 6–7, 14
underrepresented voices in reflection research, 6, 47
Urban State U, 44; classroom observation, 28–30, 44, 100–104, 126–28, 155*t*; demographics, 48, 51, 52*t*, 99; metacognition, 145–46; multimodal projects, 158–61, 164, 200; overview, 98–99; reflection-for-introspection, 141–42*t*; reflection-for-mindfulness, 143–44*t*; roundtable discussions, 126; student research participants, 3–5, 99–102, 122–25, 138, 152, 160*t*, 162*t*; teacher research participants, 8–9, 79*t*, 105–10, 117, 162*t*. *See also* AANAPISIs (Asian American and Native American Pacific Islander Serving Institutions)

verbal processing, 80*t*, 97
verbal/vocality. *See* storytelling
videos, 197
Villanueva, Victor, 13
Viray, Sydnee, 58
visual data collection, 42–44
visual reflection, 67
voice memos, 205

Walker, Alice, 62, 148, 196
walking, 55, 138, 153
Webber, Melvin, 68
Welch, Kathleen Ethel, 61
Wenger, Christy, 11
Westernized institutionalized spaces, 202
Western theories, 6, 22
WhatsApp, 154
"When the First Voice You Hear is Not Your Own," 43–44
white bias, 14, 16
white epistemologies, 38
white feminism, 48–49, 62, 63–64
White Mainstream English, 97–98, 199
white privilege, 7, 12, 13, 63–64
white racial habitus, 65–65
white researchers: allyship, 50, 57; antiracist research methods, 40; ethical research, 48, 63–66; MSIs, 24; personal narrative, 70–71; positionality, 64–65; self-reflexivity, 57
white supremacist values, 12, 38, 97
White Tears/Black Scars: How White Feminism Betrays Women of Color, 63
whiteness, 47
whitewashing feminism, 64–65
whole-group discussion, 79*t*, 80*t*, 139, 154, 155*t*; Black literature, 174; brainstorming, 158; classroom community, 115, 168–74, 188, 195; interactive reflection, 104; IRE (initiate, respond, evaluate) speech pattern, 104; processing, 97; reflective activity, 115, 116, 161, 162–63*t*; reflective pedagogy, 117, 118; roundtable, 126; scaffolding, 113; student-teacher relationships, 191; Wilberforce University, 110
withdrawal rates, 88
women's studies departments, 60
Woods, Marjorie Curry, 61
Words of Fire, 15
writer memos, 11, 13, 117, 118, 130, 132, 135, 160, 188
writerly choices, 100, 117–18
Writing Across Contexts, 14
writing across the curriculum course, 99

Writing Across the Drafts, 19
writing classroom, 6, 16, 25, 31
writing in the disciplines course, 99
writing instructors, 14, 99, 111–16
writing practice, 204–6
writing process: assignments, 14; brainstorming, 8, 9, 197; composing, 9; multimodal projects, 197, 200; reflection research, 10; reflection-in-action, 88; reflective process, 18, 19, 20, 21; rhetorical awareness, 199; rhetorical rationales, 75; self-assessments, 119
writing studies: antiracism, 50; assessments, 103; asynchronous online courses, 30; code-switching, 111; coursework, 113; discrimination, 60; mandated course outcomes, 100; scholarship, 49; students of color, 47; traditional pedagogy, 91–98; white privilege, 13
written genres, 25

Yancey, Kathleen, 9–10, 12, 14, 16, 18, 19, 20, 84, 161, 164
Yellow Dig, 115, 154, 157
yoga, 11, 55, 138, 153, 159, 208

Zoom meetings, 30–33, 45, 69–72, 83–84, 87–88

About the Author

Jaclyn Fiscus-Cannaday is assistant professor at the University of Minnesota, Twin Cities. She specializes in critical composition theories and pedagogies—including feminist, accessible, antiracist, queer, and linguistically informed strategies for teaching writing. Her research explores how teaching writing works, how people think teaching writing should work, and how we might learn from classrooms, communities, and writing programs that support and welcome all writers.

www.ingramcontent.com/pod-product-compliance
Lightning Source LLC
Chambersburg PA
CBHW060556080526
44585CB00013B/587